Cities by Design

For NAH

Cities by Design

The Social Life of Urban Form

Fran Tonkiss

polity

First published in 2013 by Polity Press

Polity Press
65 Bridge Street
Cambridge CB2 1UR, UK

Polity Press
350 Main Street
Malden, MA 02148, USA

ISBN-13: 978-0-7456-4897-2
ISBN-13: 978-0-7456-4898-9 (pb)

A catalogue record for this book is available from the British Library.

Typeset in 10.5 on 12 pt Plantin by
Servis Filmsetting Ltd, Stockport, Cheshire
Printed and bound in Great Britain by T.J. International Ltd, Padstow, Cornwall

The publisher has used its best endeavours to ensure that the URLs for external websites referred to in this book are correct and active at the time of going to press. However, the publisher has no responsibility for the websites and can make no guarantee that a site will remain live or that the content is or will remain appropriate.

Every effort has been made to trace all copyright holders, but if any have been inadvertently overlooked the publisher will be pleased to include any necessary credits in any subsequent reprint or edition.

For further information on Polity, visit our website: www.politybooks.com

Contents

Acknowledgements

My thinking about cities, space and issues of design has been deeply informed in recent years by the experience of working as a sociologist among architects, urban designers, planners and others in the London School of Economics' Cities Programme. I would like to express my thanks to Juliet Davis, Suzanne Hall, Philipp Rode, Savvas Verdis and Ricky Burdett for their collegiality, support and generosity. At Polity, Emma Longstaff commissioned the manuscript and Jonathan Skerrett saw it through to publication, and I'm grateful to both for their encouragement, patience and professionalism.

The discussion in Chapter 4 originated in an earlier essay, 'Informality and its discontents', in M. Angélil and R. Hehl (eds) *Informalize! Essays on the Political Economy of Urban Form*, Berlin: Ruby Press, 2012, 55–70. Parts of the Afterword draw on 'Austerity urbanism and the makeshift city', *City* 17/3 (2013): 312–24.

All photographs by Claire Mookerjee.

North Kolkata, 2010.

1

Introduction: Cities by Design

The architect, the planner, the sociologist, the economist, the philoso-
pher or the politician cannot out of nothingness create new forms and
relations. More precisely, the architect is no more a miracle-worker
than the sociologist. Neither can create social relations . . . .
(Lefebvre 1996 [1968]: 151)

City-making is a social process. This book examines the relationship between the social and physical shaping of cities, between how
people use, create and live in space, and the material production of
urban environments. It treats the 'design' of cities as a social, economic and political problem – not simply or primarily a technical or
aesthetic challenge; and even less the specialist domain of any single
expert as 'miracle-worker', as Henri Lefebvre so eloquently avers.
Contemporary city design is a matter not only of iconic architecture, flagship projects or ambitious masterplans, but also of formal
and informal practices that shape urban environments, produce and
address urban problems, organize people as well as ordering space.
If viable responses are to be developed to issues of environmental
damage and energy use, economy inequality and social injustice, then
cities will be crucial contexts for such solutions; but current processes
of urbanization and practices of city-making too often intensify environmental problems and compound social and economic inequities.

With cities taking a majority and a growing share of the global
population, and with rapidly increasing urban populations in developing contexts in particular, urban forms and urban experience are
central to the study of human settlements and social arrangements.
Focusing on the interplay between the social and the physical shaping
of contemporary cities makes it possible to see how the material

organization of urban space is crucial to the production and reproduction of social and economic arrangements, divisions and inequalities. The discussions that follow explore these issues in relation to
critical aspects of contemporary urbanization: urban growth, density
and sustainability; inequality, segregation and diversity; informality, urban environments and infrastructure. These are elements of
urban form that mediate the physical and spatial with the social and
economic. This is to define 'urban form' in a multi-dimensional
way, composed of material structures and physical spaces, but also
and perhaps more fundamentally by social, economic, legal and
political modes of organization and interaction. The design of cities
emerges from the complex interaction of socio-economic with spatio-
technical processes and practice. The forms in which cities take
shape are deeply determined by economic arrangements, social relations and divisions, legal constructions and political systems; in turn,
the material forms of cities provide the conditions in which key social
and economic processes are produced.

Thinking about the design of cities in this extended way is relevant to cities in developed and developing economies. It would be
a mistake to differentiate cities in high- and low-income contexts
around a distinction between the 'planned' and 'unplanned', or
'designed' and 'organic' urban forms – even if such a distinction has
been conventional in many accounts. The text focuses on processes
and effects of urbanization in developed and developing cities, not
so as to do away with the distinctions between them – much less to
suggest that their urban experiences are somehow equivalent – but
to explore how issues of population growth and decline, densification and sprawl, segregation and division, formality and informality,
play out in different urban contexts and under very different socio-
economic conditions. This in part responds to the challenge of what
Ananya Roy has called 'provincializing global urbanism', taking
seriously the character and the contexts of urbanization in different
settings without unthinking recourse to categories minted in or for
the cities of the global north. But it also seems important to insist on
points of commonality in the conceptual repertoire of urban analysis:
to underline the fact, for instance, that 'informality' is not a property
of cities in developing economies, but a way of doing urban life pretty
much everywhere; or that many poor- as well as rich-world cities are
increasingly divided around the spatial secessions of affluent elites.
It follows that my interest is in the connections between quite different and often distant cities – between the consumption economies of
rich-world cities, for example, and the environmental vulnerabilities

of the urban poor – as well as the marked divergences between them. This seeks to avoid the twin errors of subsuming various cities under a common logic of urban development, at one extreme, and, at the other, of over-stating the radical particularity of cities in ways that make broader urban theory and comparative analysis virtually pointless (see Beauregard 2010).

The challenges posed to urban thinking by the diverse conditions of urban life globally are compounded by the loose disciplinary fit of urban studies, broadly conceived. Cities and urban processes are objects of analysis for a number of social science disciplines, as well as for architecture, urban design and planning, engineering and environmental sciences. The disciplinary lens through which urban forms are viewed is an important basis for how 'the city' comes to be defined. The discussion that follows in this chapter takes up that problem in more detail, but throughout this text the aim is to explore key issues in current debates that cut across urban disciplines, and which mediate the social and economic with the physical designs that shape contemporary cities. This implies a critical understanding of design in terms of both 'formal' processes and informal (or less formal) practices, involving a range of actors from makers of law and policy, developers, planners, engineers, architects and designers, producers and consumers, and the everyday inhabitants of the city. Such a range of actors raises questions about differential rights to make decisions about and interventions in urban environments, and variable claims to use, make and inhabit city spaces. The design of cities appears less in terms of a planning model in which technical experts 'predict and provide', and more as a provisory field in which many different, and often conflicting, interests must 'debate and decide' (see Kenworthy 2006). Core themes in urban design, more conventionally understood – connectivity, permeability, accessibility, integration – are as much social objectives as they are spatial conditions, having to do with how people live together, or apart, in urban environments. Similarly, the physical forms of the city – distributions and densities of population; housing stock, public buildings and places of work and consumption; the design of transport systems and other services; the balance between public and private space; the relation of the city to its environment – are products of social, economic and political designs for the city before they become products of architects or engineers.

Questions of definition: cities by design

It may be a conventional critical move to put the basic terms of any discussion into question, but the key concepts in play here do bear some closer examination. The very notion of the city is a slippery one, considering the many guises it assumes as a territorial, legal, political or economic entity. Setting urban limits under any of these definitions can be hard, given the difficulty of spatializing cities within clear urban boundaries or coherent urban hierarchies. The mismatch between economic, political and everyday urban geographies means that cities cannot easily be secured in place: whether as objects of government, as economic systems, as units of analysis or as imaginative entities. Such an assertion is now well established in urban studies. Not only does it require urbanists to cast their nets more widely, working within an expanded spatial boundary given by the functional urban economy or extended metro-region; it also means working with a finer mesh that might catch at the complex interactions and trans-local networks – of people, capital, goods, ideas and images – through which urban lives and things are reproduced below and across the space of any single city. This may be to give up the notion of the boundary altogether. Whether understood as a site within a larger urbanized region, or as a series of points within a drawn-out space economy, it may be difficult to maintain that cities (or parts of cities) are anything more than nominal nodes within extended urban networks.

And yet. Most people, I would suggest, think they live or work in or visit specific cities, not some more or less functional cog in a regional metroplex, or more or less arbitrary way-station in an urban assemblage. To think about cities in general – and any city in particular – as distinctive, identifiable, irreducible, is not simply a matter of redundancy, nostalgia or a slightly embarrassing category error. Of course this partly has to do with all the work done by law, government and Google maps to stabilize urban boundaries and fix urban places. It is also partly about the notion of the city as conventional and, indeed, sentimental. And insofar as this understanding of being 'in' a city is existential or phenomenal, it is rather hard to talk about in an analytical way. Adelaide and Abidjan are both cities; Bath is a city, and so is Beijing, Dubuque as well as Dhaka, Helsinki as much as Harare. In this book I adopt a fairly nominalist approach to the concept of the city (a concept, it must be said, I happen to like, in theory as well as on the ground). The category of the 'city' is a useful one insofar as it gives us a handle on the organization of urban processes in space; a basis for making claims to systems of urban power; and some socio-spatial match between the concepts we reflect on as critics and those we tend not to reflect on too closely as ordinary urban denizens. The challenge is to hold together an understanding of urban intercon-nectedness, the poor definition of 'the city' as a discrete spatial or functional form, the extreme variety of actually existing cities, and a more ordinary understanding of how cities are imagined and lived as real places. Eugene McCann and Kevin Ward (2010) argue for a nuanced approach to dynamics of *relationality* and *territoriality* in thinking about cities in themselves and 'in the world': placing the focus on how things move across splintered space-economies but also the ways they break the surface within specific urban contexts, and underlining the need to account for both flows and fixities in analys-ing contemporary processes of city-making.

The second term in the equation – that of design – is also open to question. If my approach to the concept of the city is a pragmatic one, however, my approach to the matter of design is more purpose-ful and less conventional. I take 'design' to refer to social practices and processes that shape spatial forms, relationships and outcomes in intentional as well as in less intended ways. It includes physical designs, but also legal and policy design, the design of organizations and processes, economic strategies and various 'designs for living' in the complex social environment of the city. While this definition goes beyond disciplinary conventions of urban design, it is one I take from the city planner Kevin Lynch. As a process that emerges from the 'interrelations between urban forms and human objectives' (Lynch and Rodwin 1958: 201), city design captures a range of activities and interventions that shape urban environments, construct and respond to urban problems, and integrate social, spatial and material forms in the city. This is in part a technical sphere, in which planners, sur-veyors, engineers, architects and urban designers purposively organ-ize urban space and make urban forms. But the design of cities and urban life takes place within a much broader domain, involving legal divisions, entitlements and decisions, economic relations and distri-butions, political infrastructures and deliberations, social institutions and interactions, organizational forms and policy processes. These often less visible 'designs' create the conditions under which anything gets built, occupied and inhabited in the city. Indeed, the nominal 'designer' may have least of all to do with the ways in which urban spaces come to be produced, as any frustrated architect might aver.

This approach to city design engages critically with a number of concepts with which the practice is more usually associated:

formality, expertise, coordination and intentionality. An emphasis on
formality, as noted earlier, doesn't capture the majority of practices
of contemporary city-making, most of which occur off the plan, off
the books or under the radar of official designs and development.
In a material sense, moreover, urban form is not confined to fixed
elements of morphology – what Lynch (1981: 47) described as 'the
spatial pattern of the large, inert, permanent physical objects in a city'.
An understanding of urban form must also take in more dynamic and
provisional features of city environments: patterns of mobility; inward
and outward flows of people and things, whether daily, seasonally or
over longer time-frames; events and interactions; interim structures
and temporary patterns of settlement or occupation – such elements
may be highly formative for cities even if they are neither fixed nor
permanent. A concept of expertise, secondly, trains too narrow a lens
on the range of actors involved in the design of urban spaces and city
life. It both places too much emphasis on agents (planners, engineers,
architects or designers) who may have relatively little power over how
urban spaces ultimately are produced, and renders invisible other
kinds of agency implicated in the making of cities (from financialized property schemes, pension funds and asset managers, to banks
and international organizations, politicians, entrepreneurs and crime
bosses, or stubborn and resourceful local populations). While coordination, thirdly, remains an important category for thinking about the
design of cities, the instrument of coordination is not only the planning department, the architectural practice, the engineering office or
the municipal government. What happens in a city happens as the
result of innumerable more or less conscious designs and plans on the
part of urban inhabitants: improvised or long-game, intentional or
incidental, temporary or more permanent. The instruments of coordination at work in these settings may be social networks (personal
and impersonal, local or distributed), neighbourhood organizations
(formal or informal), families or households, or more simply that
principle of urban order which is the 'manifestation of the freedom of
countless numbers of people to make and carry out countless plans',
as Jane Jacobs (1961: 391) so memorably expressed it.

  The notion of intentionality or *conscious* urban design, fourthly,
raises a number of issues of its own. Much of what occurs in real
urban environments can be understood in terms of the unintended
consequences of design. This is true in a very basic sense – the
map, or the plan, is never the same as the territory – but it is also
true in a more extended way. Modernist designs on the city, for
rational, socially beneficial, clean environments, too often produced

their opposites in alienating housing environments or dysfunctional, deteriorated and disconnected zonings (see Scott 1998). As Lewis Mumford (1938: 235) grumpily noted, the signal effect of intentional designs to ease congestion in the modern city has generally *increased* congestion – as in the contrary equation that more roads equals more cars, not less congestion. Furthermore, the work of time, even over the short term, means that urban forms tend to outgrow their designers' intentions. There is an emphasis in contemporary urban studies on the growth of new cities, but many urbanites still live in old cities: driving cars or motor-cycles down streets made for foot traffic; living in housing designed for fewer or more inhabitants; running electrical wiring and plumbing through pre-modern buildings; working at computers in buildings designed for looms; setting up market stalls or rugs on pavements meant for movement or on dual-lane carriageways; living middle-class lives in housing built for those on low incomes, and vice versa. The intentions of those who designed industrial mills, subway interchanges and brutalist tower blocks can help us understand something of their times and their cities, but less about the way in which these forms work or fail to work now. There is, after all, no end-user for any urban design; there are only users over time. Just as in the long run we are all dead, all urban occupations are temporary. And urban contexts are given to change more quickly than urban forms. In the United States, Australia and elsewhere, suburbs are still being laid out in the face of peak oil, sub-prime and family breakdown. Intentional designs and the resulting built forms are subject to numerous subversions, not just over the *longue durée* but over more everyday time scales: re-tooling and derailing are also practices of design, however unfaithful these may be to original intentions. Finally, a great deal of urban form is made not on the basis of conscious design objectives, but out of our intentions to do *other* things: to make a living, find a space to sleep, get from A to B and on to Z according to routes and along desire paths unanticipated by the transport planners.

While it is crucial to stress the many 'ordinary' or minor actors who participate in the design and re-design of cities, it is equally critical to stress – against an emphasis on *conscious* design – the impersonal effects of human agency as this is sedimented in economic and political structures. For those interested in city-making as a social process, it is important to take seriously the figure of the middle-class gentrifier, the rural migrant, the electricity pirate or the street trader, but also to understand their agencies in the context of larger and more impersonal processes: of post-industrial restructuring, environmental crisis, urban immigration and legal exclusions. These latter processes – economic, environmental, political and legal – may appear abstract, but are not less *social* for being harder to individualize.

It follows, therefore, that the notion of urban form deployed in this text is necessarily a broad one. A building can be taken as the tip of the design iceberg; not least in the sense that it can help us read the larger (socio-economic, political and legal) conditions that underlie it. Architecture and urban design are 'expressive' in this socio-economic sense at least as much as they are expressive in a more aesthetic sense. What is formative of urban space is not only that which takes on physical shape. Cities are composed of physical structures, but also by the patterning of urban life by social actors as this reproduces the city in built and unbuilt forms, and in more or less stable morphologies. Some of this is purposeful, much of it is routine, unintentional, even accidental. The design of cities is legible in terms of programmatic, purposive or planned outcomes but equally in the making and re-making of spaces as conditions for, and effects of, doing something else: seeking shelter or solidarity, making a livelihood (or a fortune), marking out social distinction, moving from one place to another. It raises the question of what becomes visible as design in the city, and which processes – in spite of their powers of city-making – remain hiding in plain sight: property rights and economic power, social hierarchies and solidarities, informal ties and organizations, unequal shares of vulnerability and risk, mundane practices of urban life.

Ordinary urbanism

This tension between an expert language of city planning and the demotics of everyday design is caught in Rem Koolhaas' (1995) engaging lament for urbanism from the mid-1990s. He writes of the twentieth century's 'losing battle with quantity': modernist planning and design had sought to transform quantity – mass urbanization – into urban and architectural quality, but by the end of the century the expert stood among the wreckage of design's best efforts and intentions, overwhelmed by the unruly magnitudes of the ever-expanding city. There was a peculiar pathos in the observation that 'urbanism, as a profession, has disappeared, at the moment when urbanization [is] everywhere' (Koolhaas 1995: 961). The failure was not only one of urbanism as a profession or project, but also one of urbanism as a quality of socio-material environments. Koolhaas (1995: 961) pointed to the 'disconcerting and (for architects) humiliating' fact

Little Italy, New York City, 2012.

of 'the city's defiant persistence and apparent vigor, in spite of the collective failure of all the agencies that act on it or try to influence it – creatively, logistically, politically'. Compelling as such an account might be, this was to overlook the primary 'agencies' that act on the city: the everyday inhabitants who make and re-make their cities, although not always, it might be said, under circumstances of their own choosing. Persistent and vigorous, like the city itself, these actors engage creatively in the logistics and politics of urban life in ways that go beyond the masterplan, the design commission and the competition entry, and which confuse any easy distinction between the expert and the ordinary, the technical and the amateur, the formal and the informal.

There is now a large critical literature on the 'ordinary city' or 'everyday urbanism' (see, *inter alia*, Amin and Graham 1997; Chase et al. 1999; Hall 2012; Legg and McFarlane 2008; Murray 2013; Pieterse 2011; Robinson 2002, 2006). Three important points arise from these perspectives that are particularly relevant here: the critique of prevailing conventions within urban theory; a concern with the distinctiveness of different cities; and an emphasis on the range of actors engaged in processes of city-making. Such approaches, firstly, offer an important corrective to some of the blind-spots of globalizing urban theory, and the homogenizing effects of dominant categories of urban analysis. Few cities sit neatly in boxes marked either 'world city' or 'Third World city', or nest cleanly in hierarchies of global primacy; only a tiny number are included in the category of 'mega-city'. The big narratives of contemporary urban theory – whether the 'global' pedigrees given to certain financial centres (Robinson 2002), or the 'disastrous tendency' often attributed to African urbanism (Pieterse 2011) – rarely capture the diverse realities of urban form and process. These large categories have the effect of simplifying the cities that do come under their lens, while consigning the great majority of actual cities to analytic invisibility or marginality.

Secondly, theorists of ordinary urbanism aim to think against very powerful conceptions of cities today as over-determined by processes of economic and spatial development which tend to render them *indistinct*. Such accounts stress the particularities of different urban formations as well as their internal variety. This is not to deny the salience of development logics that can make it difficult to distinguish (certainly visually, but also analytically) between different cities and even between different parts of cities. A primary argument for growing urban indistinctiveness is the way in which city governments pursue growth strategies through standard repertoires of development and delivery, of architectural gesture and building technologies, of social pacification, clearance and upgrading. This new international style draws on a managerial and a visual language of urban development that works against differentiation; it is in large part about making urban spaces that are recognizable to, safe for and accommodating of transnational investment flows and that class of economic actors who attempt to ride them. It's often been noted, but is worth noting again here, that urban attempts to create forms of spatial distinction – to embed and reproduce power in space, to secure and mobilize various forms of capital – are frequently expressed through the creation of *indistinct* spaces: new financial centres and waterfront developments; post-industrial arts quarters or high-rise apartments for identikit urban lifestyles; gated residential developments or mall-ed shopping experiences. Against these logics of increasing homogenization, however, it can seem important to highlight the ordinary distinctiveness of different cities in their more everyday realities. As Ash Amin and Stephen Graham (1997: 411) put it, 'contemporary urban life is founded on the heterogeneity of economic, social, cultural and institutional assets' that are spatialized in different ways in different cities.

Thirdly, the concept of ordinary urbanism requires us to think more broadly about the forms of agency entailed in processes of city-making. The range of actors involved – 'creatively, logistically, politically', as Koolhaas would have it – in the design and development of cities goes well beyond the experts, the technicians and the power-brokers. It is not limited to those most obviously engaged in practices of spatial planning, physical design and construction. If city life is composed around a 'heterogeneity of economic, social, cultural and institutional assets', then the work of city-making is undertaken by the diverse and often anonymous crew who create, build and exchange those assets: producers and traders, consumers and lenders; organizers, go-betweens and foot-soldiers; blow-ins and die-hards; householders and workers; children and old heads. 'Mongrel cities', in Leonie Sandercock's (2003) wonderful phrase, are made and re-made by these motley crews of minor actors. Moreover, the production and reproduction of urban life by diverse human actors is augmented, constrained and distributed through an extended array of material devices, legal constructions, policy measures, conventions of practice, social norms and rules of engagement. The everyday tasks of making, stabilizing and running the city are worked out in multiple sites of interaction, production, calculation and regulation;

in this sense, all designs on the city 'are "collaborative" designs –
even if in some cases the "collaborators" are not visible, welcomed,
or willing' (Latour 2008: 6; see also Latour and Hermant 1998).

Un-disciplining design

This enlarged conception of what constitutes the design of cities puts
into question a disciplinary division of labour between 'qualified'
urbanists and those outside the field. I have argued that the design
and development of cities must be seen not simply as a technical,
environmental or aesthetic project, but also as a socio-economic,
legal and political problem. However, planning theory in particular is
littered with warnings against planners and designers over-reaching
their remit in an attempt to solve social and economic issues through
spatial interventions. Kevin Lynch and Lloyd Rodwin (1958: 203)
decry the 'integrated, comprehensive incompetence that results from
planners' attempts to plan for economic, social or psychological
outcomes – the planner takes the spatial environment as the focus of
his work, and does not pretend to be a sociologist, an economist, an
administrator, or some megalomaniacal supercombination of these.'
From the other side of the disciplinary divide, the urban sociologist
Ruth Glass (1989: 18) cautions against planners developing their
own 'home-made brew of sociology' in seeking physical solutions to
social problems. The spectre of social engineering through spatial
planning may create anxieties, but it would be wrong-headed to
assume that it is possible to make space without producing economic,
social or psychological outcomes.

One is reminded in this moment of Henri Lefebvre's conviction
that the 'urban phenomenon, taken as a whole, cannot be grasped
by any specialized science'; the nature of urban 'complexity makes
interdisciplinary cooperation essential' (Lefebvre 2003 [1970]: 53).
He argues, however, that while 'the urban phenomenon, as a global
reality, is in urgent need of people who can pool fragmentary bits of
knowledge', the answer is not to be found in efforts to 'bring spe-
cialists (in the fragmentary sciences) around a table'. The problem
is often one of language: these experts rarely 'agree on the words
and terms they use, and even less rarely on the underlying concepts'
(Lefebvre 2003 [1970]: 75, 53). In the field of design, there are
further problems of translation between visual, textual and numerical languages. As Mike Biddulph (2012: 10) notes, 'The principal
language of urban design – the drawing of (urban) forms in space

– is also at odds with the written and numerical languages employed extensively within the social sciences.'

These divergent expert languages, however, may be necessary for making sense of the 'wicked problems' (Biddulph 2012: 11) that the design of cities entails: these are always contextual and often conflictual, framed by complex interdependencies within extended social and environmental systems, marked by powerful political and economic constraints, and subject to frequent change or stubborn inertia. The complexity of these problems means that urban design is necessarily a 'multi-disciplinary activity of shaping and managing urban environments . . . at all scales of the socio-spatial continuum' (Madanipour 1997: 381). For Lefebvre (2003 [1970]: 75), however, the gathering of the fragmentary sciences around a table is pointless so long as the urban is considered an object of analysis, rather than configured in terms of an urban strategy for social change. His argument for engaged urban practice is echoed by Bruno Latour's later assertion of the inevitable politics of any act of design:

> [I]f you begin to redesign cities, landscapes, natural parks, societies, as well as genes, brains and chips, no designer will be allowed to hide behind the old protection of matters of facts. . . . By expanding design so it is relevant everywhere, designers take up the mantle of morality as well. . . . [T]his normative dimension that is intrinsic to design offers a good handle from which to extend the question of design to politics. (Latour 2008: 5–6)

It would appear, too, that Kevin Lynch's position shifted over time, such that his later conceptualization of the 'immature arts of city design' (Lynch 1984) assumes that this practice must be framed in terms of politics, economics and sociology. This intriguing text bears closer reading, as it works through an understanding of city design that goes beyond an expert sub-discipline to include the collective and everyday work of making the city. Lynch (1984: 10) takes issue with the fallacy of thinking about city design simply as a 'branch of architecture'. The design of cities is concerned, rather, with

> things and activities that are connected over extensive spans of space and time, and that are formed and managed by numbers of actors. It operates through intervening abstractions: policies, programs, guidelines, specifications, reviews, incentives, institutions, prototypes, regulations, spatial allotments, and the like. Through all this clutter, it seeks to influence the daily experience of a bewildering variety of people.

This, in the end, is what a city is: a complex of things and activities connected over space and time, formed and managed by many different actors. Lynch departs from a conventional, and limited, understanding of city design as dealing in 'big new parts' of the city's fabric, the conservation of existing forms, or 'preliminary programming' of urban spaces (Lynch 1984: 13). He proposes six alternative possibilities for what city design might entail. In this expanded account, design practice is also concerned, firstly, with the *perceived structure* of urban space – the connections of centres, landmarks and districts to each other in both physical and visual terms. Such points of connection become 'crossings of social meaning' as well as physical relationships: they require a 'mode of design [that] fixes essentials and leaves openings; it is loose and tight at the same time' (Lynch 1984: 14, 13). City design, secondly, might be concerned with the design of urban journeys or *sequence design*; while street layouts and transport planning are part of the conventional repertoire of urban logistics, they are less often treated as 'sequential experiences: as comings out and goings in, as arrivals, glimpses, risings, fallings, a winging around, a sudden view – as approaches, progressions or foretellings' (Lynch 1984: 16). Beyond the logistics of mass mobility, movement through the city should not be seen only as matter of routine or instrumental transit; it is a crucial part of urban experience, but too often experienced as bland, blighted or arduous. A third mode of city design is that of *renewal*, considered in terms not just of refurbishment, but also of 'tinkering' with the balance of old and new in a place – acts, that is, of 'creative design, not just preservation' (Lynch 1984: 16). Lynch is less concerned with historical correctness than with the capacity for such urban tinkering to reaffirm the history and function of often disregarded urban places. His arguments for the value of creating 'a disruptive pattern', which, like 'a tattooed face[,] can blow the mind' (Lynch 1984: 17), seem to anticipate the *favela* painting projects in neighbourhoods such as Santa Marta and Vila Cruzeiro in Rio – and their successor, 'Philly Painting', in neighbourhoods in North Philadelphia – or the painting programme during the 2000s that inked the faces of Communist-era apartment blocks in Tirana. Such a mode of city design, of course, can easily be criticized for the alleged errors of façadism or beautification (depending, it would seem, on just how the balance of power and paint between local residents, foreign artists and ambitious mayors is perceived by critics), but these are design interventions in the ordinary environments of the city that go beyond the narrow precepts of 'big architecture', fine art or historical preservation.

In a similar vein, Lynch argues for the design of *events* as a fourth element in the practice of city design. Lynch is alert to the deadening potential of the 'deliberate "animation" of a city street' that turns people into 'passive viewers' or 'manipulated participants', but a focus on events as objects of design negates the idea that this should be concerned solely with physical and permanent interventions in space. Such interventions should be concerned not 'to compel the actions of its audience, but to give them opportunities for action' (Lynch 1984: 17). Insofar as city design *is* concerned with the physical and the fixed, this includes the routine design of 'those small repeating pieces of which the city is composed' (Lynch 1984: 17): outdoor lighting and seating, trashcans and kerb-sides, fences and steps, paving, signs and shelters. Engaging with these elements involves, fifthly, a *system design* of the 'constellations of things' that often go unnoticed in the city but which structure everyday urban experience in unobtrusive ways; an exemplary form of ordinary urbanism (see Carter et al. 2011; Molotch 2011). Finally, city design extends to more propositional engagements: interventions which do not come under the remit of any existing agency, whether public or private, and which go beyond official understandings of present needs and demands. It deals in *prototypes* of neglected or unexplored designs; and in such a way makes it possible that 'design services are brought to those who would not normally use them or could not afford them' (Lynch 1984: 19). These may include designs for self-build housing, shopfronts and street-vendors' stalls, community gardens and workshops.

Structuring urban connections; journeys or sequence design; creative gestures of renewal; the design of events; routine design of mundane repeating pieces; prototypes of neglected forms – this is a version of city design as consisting in minor practices and 'uncertain acts' (Lynch 1984: 19). Such practices only partly come under the purview of existing public or private agencies, they tend to imply decentralized actors and audiences, and in many cases can only be effective given some redistribution of urban power. And yet Lynch (1984: 21) makes a compelling case for this kind of ordinary urbanism: these small acts 'deal with the large environment in daily use; they are comfortable with continuous change, partial control, pluralism and participation; and they are creative arts, eliciting an aesthetic response.' This emerges as a mode of design that is fit for the kind of problem a city is. Moreover, it mediates between the agency of the expert and that of the amateur, between the intentional and the improvised, the permanent and the temporary.

These modest proposals, however, do not claim to address some of the larger issues that urban environments entail. In their more ambitious 'urban design manifesto', written at this same moment of disciplinary self-examination, Allan Jacobs and Donald Appleyard (1987) set out a series of 'problems for modern urban design' that are socio-economic as much as they are spatial. These include: increasingly *poor living environments*, in which collective urban conditions become more 'dangerous, polluted, noisy, anonymous' even as private housing conditions may improve; *giantism and loss of control* in relation to over-scaled cities that are 'increasingly in the hands of large-scale developers and public agencies'; *privatization and the loss of public life*, characterized by defended private spaces and abandoned or threatening public environments; *centrifugal fragmentation* around 'homogeneous social enclaves' and 'extensive monocultures'; *destruction of valued places* in the pursuit of 'profit and prestige'; conditions of *placelessness* in which people rarely know where 'materials and products come from, who owns what, who is behind what, and what was intended' in 'cities where things happen without warning and without our participation'; patterns of urban *injustice* where 'the discrepancy between the environments of the rich and the environments of poor' produce cities as 'symbols of inequality'; and finally a *rootless professionalism* that sees too many urbanists 'design for places and people we do not know and grant them very little power of acknowledgment' (Jacobs and Appleyard 1987: 114–15). This baleful roll-call is drawn from the authors' US experience, but it speaks to a broader set of urban conditions that are recognizable in different cities – there is no particular American exceptionalism, I would suggest, in respect of urban fragmentation, privatization, giantism or loss of control, even if these factors take on particular force and shape in specific urban contexts. The lesson to be taken from these problematizations of the modern city is that 'problems for design' – even as these are manifest in physical arrangements – are rooted in social, economic and political processes. The *social life of urban form* in this way refers to how cities are structured as spatial environments around and through social relations, practices and divisions. It moves from large to small scales: from problems of placelessness in which urban citizens do not know where things come from, who owns them or who has authority; through the connections and sequences that structure actors' perceptions of urban space; on to the sortings of rich and poor into very different urban environments; down to the mundane furnishings that ease or obstruct everyday public life, and events that transform space in transitory time.

The social life of urban form

The chapters that follow address different aspects of the 'social life of urban form' through a set of conjunctions between social and spatial processes in the city. The design of cities is understood throughout in terms of critical 'interrelations between urban forms and human objectives' (Lynch and Rodwin 1958: 201), as these are played out through more or less official, more or less explicit, and more or less informal means. In the last part of the present discussion, I outline the key elements of socio-spatial form with which the following chapters are concerned.

The growth of the city: scale, size and shape

In one of the founding texts of urban sociology, Louis Wirth (1938: 2) wrote: 'The growth of cities and the urbanization of the world is one of the most impressive facts of modern times.' In this and other statements, Wirth made it clear that the Chicago School's central concern was with the 'urbanization of the Western world'; inspired by the 'throbbing life of the exuberantly growing metropolis' (Wirth 1940: 744–5), 'occidental' social science was now necessarily urban in its orientations. However, what was true for the 'West' in the early to mid-twentieth century was true for the world by the early twenty-first. Wirth and his colleagues were writing in the context of a rapidly urbanizing American population; patterns of urbanization over the next century would be concentrated and distributed in different ways – with significant trends of urban growth in Latin America, parts of East Asia and Southeast Asia, and in Eastern Europe over the middle and latter decades of the twentieth century. Current patterns of accelerated urban growth also have a particular spatial distribution. By the first decades of the twenty-first century, the most significant rates of urbanization were taking place in South Asia, in China and in sub-Saharan Africa. Today, the urbanization of the world is no longer an 'occidental' preoccupation, as the 'final buildout of humanity' (Davis 2006: 2) takes shape around new metropolitan geographies.

These ongoing patterns of urbanization are visible at the level of cities' physical forms and material environments in terms of dual logics of densification and sprawl; the consumption of peri-urban land under conditions of urban growth as well as the intensification of inhabitations within existing cities. However, the physical reach of urbanizing processes is not defined by any distinguishable city limits, as urban economies and forms stretch across extended geographies of interaction and interdependence. This is also not new. At the same time that Louis Wirth was writing of the 'throbbing life of the exuberantly growing metropolis', Lewis Mumford (1938: 255) was regretting its expanded reach: 'Though the physical radius of the metropolis may be only twenty or thirty miles, its effective radius is much greater: its blight is carried in the air, like spores of mold. The outcome is a world whose immense potential variety . . . has been sacrificed to a low metropolitan standardization.' The shape-shifting character of the contemporary city – definite but indistinct, both there and always somewhere else – makes scale a critical category for thinking about urban conditions, connections and constraints, and in two ways. One of these has to do with size – both the growth of urban populations and the spatial take of cities' physical footprint. The complexities of organizing social life at this human and territorial range is a problem for which relatively few urban governments have adequate capacity, such that the coordination of economic activity, the provision of infrastructure and urban services, the distribution of land and resources, is for many cities handled below the level of the state or outside formal institutions of government. That a major-ity share of the global population now lives in cities is either a very profound or a very banal proposition, but the even greater majority live in economies that are linked into urban networks, and within a day's travelling distance of an urban centre. The scale problem is one that is *internal* to cities: from the individual problem of bearing the proximity of that many others, to the collective problems of housing, employing, feeding, educating, policing, moving and sanitizing very large populations. Problems of scale also pertain to cities' 'external relations': how cities sit within a nested spatiality of political and eco-nomic power, exchange and control.

Neil Brenner (2000: 373) has argued, in this second respect, that 'the urban question is today increasingly assuming the form of a scale question.' His argument is premised on a broader re-scaling of eco-nomic and political processes both above and below the nation-state: the hollowing-out, that is, of social, economic and political processes to the supra- and infra-national scales. For Brenner, as for other criti-cal urban theorists, the urban is a crucial mediating scale in analysing processes of capitalist accumulation that operate through complex and sometimes contradictory effects of globalization, fragmenta-tion, de- and re-territorialization (see also Brenner 2013). Such an argument is found in a simplified way in Henri Lefebvre's concep-tualization of the urban as a mediating level between 'global' forces of state, economy and power, and the 'private' level of experience, inhabitation and everyday life. A central critical task in Lefebvre's work in *The Urban Revolution* (2003 [1970]) was to move from a concept of the city as a definite place, to the urban or 'urban society' as a dimension of social practice, one that mediates the lived experience of everyday inhabitation and the 'global' social processes and institutions of state and economy. His formulation of the urban was as a field of encounter, information and exchange, which came to ground in particular spaces, built and unbuilt.

These arguments can seem rather removed from everyday urban contexts, but there is an experiential bite in thinking about cities as sites both in which 'global' or impersonal forces are reproduced, and in which meaningful private lives are lived. Social actors, adroit as they are, live in cities as both these spaces at the same time. It is this mediation between different scales of social process and social practice – more, perhaps, than the crude size of population and territory – that shapes cities as socio-spatial forms. Thinking scale in relation to cities involves analysis of the networks and territories mapped out by the economic exchanges, political rationalities, social relations and imaginary attachments that produce and reproduce the city. Thinking scale also means, of course, working at a level below the often abstracted plane of the city. At the same time, this concern with mediating scales, suggested by Lefebvre and developed by Brenner and others, is useful for thinking about cities not only as modes of social practice but also as physical forms. At a 'global' scale, the material size of the city – whether this is measured in terms of land use or in terms of population figures – is fundamental to its environmental and its social 'carrying capacity', as well as its relationship to its near and more distant locality. At the scale of the everyday, the territorial imagination of the city as a physical place is basic to how individuals think about where it is they live, how they position themselves in space and in relation to others, how they negotiate the textured surfaces of the everyday city. The capacity to work across and between scales is a necessary one for urban analysis, just as it is for urban life.

Inequality and informality

Jacobs and Appleyard (1987: 115) saw modern cities as 'symbols of inequality'. The central chapters that follow – on unequal cities and urban informalities – consider how conditions of inequality, informality and insecurity are designed into contemporary cities as spatial relations, physical divisions and social striations. The '*structures of*

privilege and spatial advantage based on differential wealth and power'
(Soja 2010: 48; italics in original) that embed injustice in space scale
up from temporary and low-level displays of power and social distinction, to urban geographies of income disparity, and again to severe
economic inequalities at the inter-urban scale. Current patterns of
urbanization involve processes of acute 'unequalization', producing
stark geographies of inequality and polarization within cities as well
as between cities and regions. Conventionally, cities have been seen
as sites of inequality owing to their tendency to concentrate large
low-income populations. This remains the case, but current trends in
inequality in numerous cities reveal a 'pulling apart' of the wealthiest segments of the population, especially those whose incomes are
derived from capital rather than from labour, but also on account of
increasing returns to those working in advanced sectors in finance,
information and communications technologies. Such patterns are as
relevant to explaining deepening inequalities in US cities as they are
to understanding relatively new systems of inequality in Chinese or
Indian cities. Cities are sites of innovation, creativity and knowledge
production, but the economic returns to these assets and resources
appear increasingly skewed around polarizing urban labour markets.
Moreover, 'older' roots of inequality have not gone away: race, eth-
nicity and gender remain key markers of urban inequality in cities
across the global income distribution; as do patterns of informality
in housing and economic life, and legality in respect of citizenship
rights. In these ways, 'old' and 'new' relations of inequality reproduce cities as segmented socio-economic spaces. A global geography
of urban centrality and economic marginality is configured not just
around the disparities between high- and low-income cities and
regions, but *inside* cities, and often within quite fine-grained urban
localities.

Such disparities are more or less visible at the level of urban form.
Inequalities – of income, consumption, opportunities for mobility,
degrees of security or overall life chances – are rendered especially
durable in their spatial expression as patterns of segregation, inequities in physical access, disparate urban environments, differential
patterns of mobility and fixity. 'Durable inequalities' become so
tenacious in part because of the ways that they are compounded,
reinforced and shaped by the production of uneven urban forms (see
Tilly 1999). An especially important basis for urban inequality is
grounded in the differentiation between formal and informal urban
economies and settlements. The largest share of current patterns of
urban growth is in these informal sectors, in low-income cities which

lack the government capacity or will to secure urban housing; to plan for population growth, service provision, and infrastructure needs; or to regulate economic activities. Urban informality is a complex and multi-dimensional phenomenon. The informal sector can provide access to housing and economic opportunities at low or no entry costs; allow small-scale entrepreneurs to develop businesses while avoiding red tape and prohibitive start-up and operating costs; afford space and materials for shelter for low-income households; mobilize credit; and offer forms of mutual support and self-help among low-income urban populations. It can also involve high entry costs and even higher barriers to exit for sub-contractors in informal networks; exploit entailed and often indentured workers at low rates of pay, through debt bondage, and in the absence of any kind of employment protection; leave householders vulnerable to both slum landlords and state evictions; encourage cronyism, racketeering and stand-over tactics by housing, employment and protection mafia; and redouble all these forms of vulnerability by leaving individuals and house-holds without recourse to protection by the law or the police – or, indeed, in danger *from* them. The opportunities for self-provisioning, mutual aid, petty entrepreneurialism and urban innovation are par-alleled by conditions of abandonment, insecurity, racketeering and immiseration.

Moreover, it would be a mistake to think about practices and spaces of informality only in relation to the urban poor. Informality is a feature of urbanism at any point on the income scale: a great deal of middle-class housing across the urban world has rather shadowy status in respect of law and planning, while some of the most effec-tive and entrenched informal processes are pursued by the most privileged urban actors, who tend to be exemplary practitioners of 'self-help' and 'mutual aid'. Informality is not simply a hallmark of urbanization 'from below'; indeed, informal processes are often used most effectively by urban elites. The informality of the rich is a criti-cal factor shaping contemporary urban relations and outcome – in economic deals that take place off-shore, off-the-books or on the sly, in extra-legal real estate investments and development strategies, in appropriations and colonizations which operate through an elite version of 'eminent domain', in secessionary spaces of private gov-ernance and usurped legal title. The informality of urban processes, therefore, should not be seen simply as an index of abandonment or disempowerment; not only because informal urban practices are a productive sphere of operations for the urban poor, but because elective informality is frequently an index of power and privilege for urban economic and political elites. Thinking about urban informality in this extended way is part of a larger critical project to de-colonize an urban imagination that is given to see 'deregulation' for the rich and the 'informality' of the poor as unrelated conditions.

Urban environments and infrastructure

The final two chapters address the social life of urban form under-stood in terms of critical dimensions of cities' physical landscapes. The focus here is on the built and unbuilt environments that shape contemporary cities; both the 'natural' environment of urban ecolo-gies and the 'artificial' environment of urban infrastructure. This is not to draw a simple distinction between *social and economic* relations and practices – of density and diversity, inequality and informality – and *physical* forms – of environment and infrastructure. Rather, the concern here is to consider these explicitly physical forms as social, economic and political relations. As Ash Amin (2006: 1012) points out: 'The daily negotiation of the urban environment has become central in defining the privations, provisions, prejudices and prefer-ences of a very large section of humanity.' The urban environment is considered not simply as a biophysical problem but as a problem of *distribution* – of environmental goods and bads, advantages and vulnerabilities. These distributions, of course, are in part a set of bio-physical effects, but while it may yet be beyond the scope of human ingenuity to determine where rain falls in cities, the question of who gets wet is very much a social issue.

Urban environmental problems are structured around a number of very big narratives and innumerable more local spatial stories. The biggest story of all is that of climate and environmental change, and the role of cities and urban populations in either driving or amelio-rating these processes. Another large narrative is that of shelter dep-rivation, with more than one billion people reckoned to live in slum conditions globally. There are important connections between the two: first, because urban slum-dwellers are probably the least part of the problem of anthropogenic climate change; secondly, because those living in conditions of shelter deprivation tend to be most vul-nerable to its effects. There is in this sense a perverse distribution between the production of environmental harms and exposure to environmental risks. The geographies of risk are uneven, but there is a bleak logic that connects them. The environmental vulnerability of the urban poor in areas of pollution and contamination, toxic waste and radiation, deforestation, flood and fire risk – from low-income neighbourhoods under power-lines to New Orleans' deluged Lower 9th ward to waste-ground *favelas* – is a pattern seen time and again, and not falsified by the elective risk taken by some high-income residents in Malibu for the sake of an ocean view or brushwood privacy.

These links between poverty, shelter deprivation and environmental vulnerability are visible across different urban contexts, in definite sites of disadvantage, damage and distress. Those between affluence, over-consumption and environmental harm can be harder to trace, given the extended geographies of demand, production and distribution across which emissions and toxicities are produced. A conventional series of distinctions distinguishes the environmental problems variously associated with poverty, production and consumption economies in terms of 'brown', 'grey' and 'green' environmental agendas. 'Brown' politics have to do with basic issues of urban water and waste, sanitation and sewerage; 'grey' issues are related to air pollution, water and surface contaminations caused by productive and extractive industries; and the 'green' agenda has to do with issues of bio-diversity and consumption choices. To a degree, these different environmental politics can be connected to poverty environments, to industrializing economies and to advanced consumer economies. However, these different agenda are related in critical ways. A large part of the problem of urban waste, for instance, is created by wealthier populations, but recycled and re-used by the poor – in their immediate living environments or in outsourced (and especially toxic) waste facilities. Factory pollution is an increasing problem for emerging industrial economies, but might be sourced to the demand for goods by high-income consumers at a distance. The geographies of environmental overflow both extend across transnational spaces of production, distribution, consumption and disposal, and are localized within divided cities where the polluting and the polluted live in relations of proximity and often tension.

Cities in this sense represent complex environments of biophysical, social and spatial interactions. These interactions are materialized through urban infrastructures that organize flows of energy, resources, materials, goods, information, waste and people. The design of urban infrastructures is in part a technical project, but is, moreover, a social and political project that integrates the city as a space of collective provision, or segments it into uneven patterns of infrastructural access and exclusion. Transport systems, urban utilities, networks of waste and disposal, make the city 'a machine for the manufacturing and maintenance of distributional inequalities' (Soja 2010: 49). While modern systems of infrastructure can be understood in terms of the shaping of a 'body social' as a practical expression of the larger 'body politic' (see Isin 2007), contemporary urban infrastructures more often support a splintering of urban citizenship along lines of privatization, preferential access, secession and exclusion. At the same time, state and corporate actors do not monopolize the field of urban infrastructure. The ordinary infrastructures of the contemporary city are embodied by many social actors, integrated (if sometimes patchily) through everyday networks of exchange and enacted through the often arduous human labour of collecting, storing, transporting and distributing fuel, food, resources, goods, information and people. From the pizza delivery boy to the human billboard, the rickshaw wallah and the drug-runner, to the water-carrier and the waste-picker, the infrastructures of everyday life are composed out of embodied labour, mundane materials and quotidian connections.

Conclusion

'It is clear', write Asef Bayat and Kees Biekart (2009: 823),

> that modern cities are not merely by-products of the operation of capital, nor simply products of the benign imagination of urban planners. Cities are the sites of intense struggles between disparate interests and multiple stakeholders, whose ideas, influences and actions together ultimately shape today's urban realities. The foreign capital, local businesses, the poor, the young, environmentalists, politicians and planners all imagine their cities in their own distinct ways.

Moreover, these different actors all *make* the city in their own distinct ways, through purposive and unconscious practices of human design that are more or less effective, more or less durable and more or less visible. The argument throughout this book is that thinking critically about the 'design' of cities goes beyond seeing this as the task of architects, planners and engineers; it is equally the work of politicians and developers, landlords and householders, buyers and sellers, comers and go-ers. An integrated approach to urbanism sets issues of design within the social, economic and spatial contexts in which they emerge, and on which they go to work. The relationship works both ways: just as such an approach seeks to socialize our understanding of city design, so a concern with urban form might help us grasp the materiality of social, economic and legal processes.

This is not to abandon more disciplinary theories of urban design and planning altogether. But it *is* to read these theories as accounts of social action and social form. Kevin Lynch and Lloyd Rodwin's construction of design in terms of the 'interrelations between urban forms and human objectives' is in fact a deeply sociological one, and it informs all of the discussions that follow. The production and use of space is a social as much as it is a technical problem. City-making is about making spaces of collectivity and segregation, of inequality and illegality, of mobility and materiality. These designs are scored into the city in built and unbuilt patterns. Urban form therefore is not simply about buildings and the spaces between them, street layouts and open spaces, skylines and city boundaries – although it is about all of those things. Urban form is also about densities and distributions of people, spatial relations between social groups, the spatial markings of legal boundaries and entitlements, urban environments and the submerged or social infrastructures that shape and segment them. Those who seek to understand the city, as much as those 'agencies that act on it or try to influence it – creatively, logistically, politically' (Koolhaas 1995: 961), need to think about the human clay as well as about the concrete.

2

The Social Life of Urban Form: Size, Density, Diversity

What is the link between the physical organization of the city and its social forms? This chapter focuses on the most basic elements of urban form – size, scale and mix – and considers how these shape cities in social, economic and environmental terms. In doing so, it reworks the categories set out in a classic text (perhaps *the* classic text) in urban studies: Louis Wirth's essay 'Urbanism as a Way of Life' (1938). In this piece, Wirth contends that cities are distinct from other forms of human settlement by virtue of their size, their density and their heterogeneity. This treatment of the urban in terms of raw physical and social facts may be redolent of older and more positivist ways of thinking about cities, but such a concern with matters of size and shape is paralleled today in research and debate tracking the rapid growth of cities, a planetary transition from rural to urban modes of existence, and concerns over the limits, the impacts and the sustainability of urbanism as a way of life.

It is against this backdrop of widespread and rapid urbanization, and of related debates over urban sustainability, that the following discussion takes up Wirth's earlier framework for understanding the 'spatial order of urban life'. It begins by considering debates over the contemporary growth of cities, and in particular the terms of a global urban shift in which populations are expanding most markedly in developing cities. How do these processes sit within longer histories of urbanization across different regions, and what might their implications be for the shape of the emerging urban world? What are the advantages and disadvantages of growing city size, and to what extent does a focus on size tell us the story of contemporary urbanization? The chapter goes on to consider the second distinctive character of cities as forms of human settlement. Density represents a critical point at which spatial categories become social arguments; in recent urban debates, it has been promoted as a key principle for producing more sustainable, compact and manageable cities. This chapter examines the claims to be made for and against densification, considering – as Kevin Lynch (1962) put it – the 'tricks' that can be played with density in the context of major debates about the sustainability of urban environments. If sustainability is to be taken as a social and economic problem, as well as an environmental challenge, what are the physical strategies that follow? And can these strategies apply in very different urban contexts: at local and metropolitan scales, in large and small cities, in developing and rich urban economies (see Jenks and Burgess 2000)?

Kevin Lynch (1981: 47) provided a minimalist definition of urban form as 'the spatial pattern of the large, inert, permanent physical objects in a city'. How these are organized, however, takes on quite variable forms and varying degrees of complexity in particular urban contexts. Spatial patternings around city size, density, grain and shape are configured by the basic elements of street patterns and urban blocks, and at a larger scale around different urban morphologies – circle or ribbon developments, linear cities or urban corridors, in star shapes or finger plans, around a constellation of satellite or regional cities. Lynch at one time argued for a rigorous separation in the work of the planner between the pattern of physical forms and the patterns of activity in the city (see Lynch and Rodwin 1958), but this is an impossible separation. The orthodoxies of urban design – legibility, permeability, density, grain, use, connectivity, diversity – are all principles of relationship: principles, moreover, that overlap the 'relation of people to things' and the 'relation of people to each other' (Lynch 1995c [1975]: 789). Similarly Gordon Cullen (1961: 10), the British originator of the Townscape movement, saw urban design as an 'art of relationship'; while Ali Madanipour (2010: 352) more recently argued for an understanding of planning as a 'connective activity' concerned with relating events, functions and institutions across time and space. Lynch's criteria for assessing good urban form – accessibility, adequacy, diversity, adaptability, comfort – are not simply about the arrangements of spaces, but precisely about the pattern and integration of activities across them.

This concern with relationships between things and people opens onto the third term in Wirth's triad: urban diversity. Cities integrate a mix of different functions, and often struggle to integrate a mix of different people. While compelling cases can be made for the value of functional diversity in economic and environmental terms, it can be harder to make a sustained case for the urban pay-offs from social diversity. Arguments for social diversity are often politically fraught, and social diversity is 'produced' in contemporary cities through processes – histories of colonialism and indenture, labour and economic migration, as well as class differentiations – which continue to structure urban diversity in unequal and often unjust spatial patterns. However, social mix in cities, if its benefits can be hard to measure in empirical terms, is perhaps the most powerful feature of urbanism as a way of life; the register in which the shape of the city is lived as a social condition. Urban form is not confined to 'large, inert, permanent physical objects', as Lynch would have it – if it was, urban design, planning and management might be much easier tasks – but equally is composed by patterns of difference, connection and disconnection, mobilities and interactions that make urban diversity an urban social fact and a contested urban value.

A focus on questions of size and shape can seem a rather plodding, even out-dated, way of representing the city. Thinking about cities in terms of physical form, as those concerned with their design are obliged to do, jars somewhat with a recent critical concern in other disciplines to understand the urban in terms of networks, connections and mobilities. 'As geographical entities,' Ash Amin (2006: 1011) has written, 'cities are hardly discernible places with distinct identities. They have become an endless inhabited sprawl without clear boundaries and they have become sites of extraordinary circulation and translocal connectivity, linked to processes of spatial stretching and interdependence associated with globalization.' Whether the city is conceived in terms of territory, however, or as networks of connection, the spatial and the physical organization of the urban is critical to its social experience and its future prospects. The discussion that follows explores different ways of thinking about the relationship between the physical organization of cities, their modes of social organization, and their economic and environmental performance. It considers in turn the constitution of city form in terms of size and growth; densities and intensities; and diversity and connection. It concludes with the issue of how these spatial patterns play out over time, in the temporal life of urban form.

The city as a spatial form

Thinking about cities as spatial entities is a conventional, but not entirely fashionable, way of understanding the urban. It underpins historical conceptions of the city, in part because of the walls that once enclosed many towns and cities, and was also foundational for twentieth-century urban sociology. Louis Wirth (1940: 748) drew a broad distinction between urban and rural modes of life as the difference between 'societies based upon kinship as distinguished from those based upon territory'. This is a crude definition, but it is provocative in compelling us to think about forms of human society understood primarily in terms of group relations (defined around family, ethnos, caste, tribe, etc.) in contrast to a kind of human settlement defined primarily in spatial terms. That Wirth's distinction between kinship and territory as bases for understanding human social life can seem so outmoded may say less about his antiquated thinking than about the assumptions of our own urban imagination. And while Wirth's thinking is steeped in nineteenth-century attitudes concerning the transition from traditional to modern social forms, his own framework for understanding the difference between the rural and the urban is not so much temporal development as spatial transition. (It might be remembered that Wirth emigrated to the United States in 1911 from a German village of 900 inhabitants; one hundred years later it still had only around 1,200 residents. Then and now, it surely would seem a bit different from Chicago.) Wirth (1940: 748) goes on to suggest that 'recognition of the significance of this difference has led to a preoccupation with the spatial order of urban life arising from the dense concentration of large masses of people into a compact territory, and with the manner in which men and institutions arrange themselves under these conditions.' Such a preoccupation was the basis for a new discipline – that of human ecology – concerned with 'the physical structure and the ecological processes of concentration, dispersion, segregation, and succession of men, institutions, and cultural characteristics' (Wirth 1940: 748). Few urbanists would think of themselves as human ecologists now – even if they are happy to take another concept from biology, that of morphology, to describe their analysis of urban form – but Wirth's premise still holds in respect of a concern for how the 'physical framework of the urban world' shapes social, institutional and cultural processes in the city. These are processes, that is, which are not assumed to be organized according to some prior set of precepts based on kinship ties, group norms or shared cultures, but which are co-produced with the physical forms of the city.

Whatever else contemporary urbanists might want to reject in Wirth's thinking and that of other early urban sociologists, this original concern with 'the spatial order of urban life' is not one of them.

Wirth (1940: 748) outlines the basic condition of this spatial order as the 'dense concentration of large masses of people in a compact territory'. Questions of size and scale remain crucial to understanding the modern urban condition. Thinking about raw size may seem an unsubtle kind of urban analysis, but what was a major concern for urban economists and ecologists in the past is of renewed interest given current patterns of urbanization and the projected growth of 'mega-cities' with populations of ten million or more. Recent arguments about the prospects and problems of large and rapidly growing cities recall an earlier set of debates about the merits of city size. In particular, urban economists in the 1970s argued the case for the advantages of big cities, tracking the relation between higher wage and output levels and larger city sizes, apparent in a number of developing as well as developed economies (see Gilbert 1976; Hoch 1972). Superior rates of productivity in big cities were evidence of the value of urban agglomeration (Mera 1973; Segal 1976; Sveikauskas 1975). Arguments for city size, and counter-arguments concerning the problems of large cities and the need for urban decentralization and rural development, took place against the backdrop of rapid urbanization in parts of the developing world, and especially in Latin America (see Gilbert 1976; Richardson 1972, 1976; see also Henderson 2003; Jones and Corbridge 2010; United Nations 2012: 11, Table 6). While certain critics argued for the economic benefits of larger city size, others voiced concerns over the urban inefficiencies resulting from diseconomies of scale, relations of uneven development and dependency between urban and rural settlements, the inequitable distribution of urban growth, and the fact that the social costs of living in big cities – overcrowding, congestion, pollution – tended to be borne most heavily by the urban poor. At the same time, low-income and immigrant groups demonstrably were drawn to big urban centres: in the US context, for instance, it was argued that any policy efforts to contain urban population growth were less likely to impact on largely white suburbs than on black American populations moving to cities away from rural conditions of poverty and discrimination (Mills 1972).

The fact that these debates were in part prompted by processes of industrialization and urbanization in developing economies has its parallel today in the new urban contours emerging around cities in the global south. The regional focus, however, has largely shifted from Latin American to Asian or African cities. Moreover, these arguments from the 1970s were dealing in smaller numbers than we are used to today. In earlier analyses of city size and productivity, 'big' was anything much over two million, while the debate around the disadvantages of large cities centred on populations of five million and above. By the early decades of the twenty-first century, the rhetorical focus had shifted to so-called 'mega-cities'. There are now more than twenty cities with populations of ten million or more, and at least five cities over twenty million, with UN agencies projecting this count to rise over the coming decade or two. Earlier critics were writing in what was still a minority urban world, but their worries regarding the future of rural settlements, land and livelihoods – as well as the prospects for rapidly growing cities internationally – were prescient. By the end of the first decade of the twenty-first century, the majority of the global population was reckoned to live in urban areas, with UN projections that more than two-thirds of the global population would be urban by the middle of this 'century of the city' (UN-Habitat 2008: 11). The debate is no longer around the relative advantages of a New York over a Detroit; cities in the developing world accounted for nearly all urban growth and three-quarters of the global urban population by 2011, with Asian cities expected to take more than a half-share and Africa around 20 per cent by 2050 (United Nations 2012: 11). The apocalyptic overtones of some of this discourse can be misleading: in a majority urban world, it makes straightforward sense that the most populous nations and regions will also take the greater share of urban population. Some of the most striking current rates of urbanization, in parts of Asia and Africa, are occurring in the least urbanized regions of the world where the majority of the population is still rural. Rhetoric of an urban 'explosion' in the developing world and the growth of mega-cities in sub-Saharan Africa belies the fact that up to 60 per cent of urban Africans live in small cities under half a million, and fewer than 10 per cent in cities of more than five million; while in contrast the modest or negative rates of urbanization expected in Europe, North America or Latin America reflect the fact that these regions are already super-urbanized (see Cohen 2006; Montgomery 2008; Satterthwaite 2007; United Nations 2012; United Nations Population Division 2008).

Even so, the twenty-first century 'global shift' in economic power towards low- and middle-income countries, and Asian economies in particular (see Dicken 2007), has been inseparable from a marked shift in urban population patterns. Current trends of urban growth have a particular spatial distribution: the urban population of China is now as large as the urban population in Europe as a whole, while India's urban populace is larger than North America's. It is worth noting that – as in the case of relative economic power – the growth of urban Asia into the twenty-first century may represent the reversal of a quite brief historical 'blip' rather than any unprecedented new development. Historically, the Asian powers of China and India have been urban as well as economic giants. Together they accounted for nearly 50 per cent of world economic output in 1820; by the 1970s this share had fallen to less than 10 per cent, but by the early 2000s had recovered to around 20 per cent, with some way – presumably – to go (see Frank 1998; Maddison 2001). Similarly, in 1800 sixty-four of the world's one hundred largest cities were in Asia; in 2000 the region had forty-nine, the majority of these in South and East Asia (Satterthwaite 2007: vi). In parallel with the movement of economic weight and power from the established 'triad' of the United States, Western Europe and Japan, the global urban league is changing with accelerated growth of cities in South and East Asia and – to a lesser degree – in sub-Saharan Africa, and with low or no growth projected for the largest cities in Europe and the United States. These patterns of urban development vary, from the state-led urbanization of the Chinese boom (which has seen the development of some fifty new cities over one million since the 1990s) to different patterns of 'unplanned' urbanization driven by both positive 'pull' factors (including economic growth and liberalization, improving urban infrastructure and provision) and negative 'push' factors (such as civil and military conflict, or environmental crisis).

A common factor across these different urban contexts is significant patterns of in-migration into cities – both internal (most notably in China) and transnational (as seen in a number of sub-Saharan African cities). Rural-to-urban migration is a key factor in current processes of urbanization, but this also varies by nation and region. Cities grow in three ways: through natural population growth (net birth rates); inward migration; and spatial expansion and consolidation incorporating peri-urban or rural populations. To take the three countries that currently host the world's largest urban populations: internal migration and urban consolidation is almost wholly responsible for current and predicted urban growth rates in China; two-thirds of India's urban growth in the first half of the twenty-first century is projected to result from urban migration and expansion, with one-third coming from natural population increase; and in the already highly urbanized United States, urban growth will largely come from an overall increase in population numbers, likely to be driven by non-white and Hispanic groups (United Nations 2012: 14). Where urban populations are stagnating or declining – as in much of urban Europe

– low birth rates and certain trends for outward migration from cities each take a causal share.

Recent patterns of urban growth have occurred sometimes in succession to, and sometimes in spite of, long-standing government efforts to restrict the expansion of cities in both developed and developing economies, through such measures as policies for rural and regional development, tax-breaks and subsidies for suburbanization and decentralization, investment in new towns, and the more repressive systems of household registration, housing allocation, movement restrictions and pass laws variously associated with Communist and colonial governments (see Beall and Fox 2009; Satterthwaite 2007). While crisis-driven urbanization – population movements to escape conflict, environmental risk and disaster, or economic devastation – plays no small part in these shifts, the major factor driving the growth of cities is economic opportunity. If de-industrialization in western economies was accompanied during the 1970s and 1980s by urban decline (temporary in some cases, more permanent in others), the shift of manufacturing to low-wage economies in the global 'periphery' since then has seen the growth of both new and old cities. Export-processing zones have generated new cities (Shenzhen) and augmented older ones (Guangzhou); new industry has intensified second-tier cities (Bangalore or Hyderabad); while established centres of political and economic power (Beijing and Delhi), finance and trade (Mumbai and Shanghai) have also seen significant economic and population growth under this changing global settlement. The shifting balance of global power in turn has generated a kind of 'second-generation' urbanization, as Chinese and Russian investment has driven growth in African cities such as Accra, Addis Ababa, Lagos, Lilongwe, Luanda, Lusaka and Nairobi, characterized both by infrastructure and other development in these cities and by an emerging trend for elite satellite developments outside existing urban centres.

Older concerns about 'over-urbanization' (or 'premature urbanization') where urban population increase outruns rates of economic growth – particularly in African cities – have given way in the last decade to a more complex picture, with rising levels of foreign investment and local enterprise, expanding middle classes and accelerated economic output occurring alongside persistent poverty and shelter deprivation, and infrastructure and governance failure (Kessides 2006). Historically, higher levels of urbanization have been the marker of the world's richest economies, but most of the world's urban population now lives in low- and middle-income countries.

The close linkage of economic growth and urbanization is hardly unprecedented: North America and parts of Western Europe saw rates of urbanization in the late nineteenth century similar to that of the fastest growers today; so, too, did the early East Asian industrializers (Japan, South Korea and Taiwan) in the mid-twentieth century, and the Latin American region in the latter decades of that century (Satterthwaite 2007: 43–4). To put it crudely: '[D]eveloping countries are sailing in waters charted by developed nations, which experienced a similar rush to towns and cities. The speed is similar, and the routes are the same' (World Bank 2009: 49). What is distinctive is not so much the rate or direction of change, but the scale of the numbers involved. This is somewhat confounding for critics who have been used to question simple models of economic convergence, unilinear models of development or any easy notion of 'catch-up' urbanization. David Satterthwaite (2007), analysing UN data over time, notes that the period since 1950 shows a general and positive correlation between faster urbanization and more rapid economic growth (see also UN-Habitat 2010). He notes, too, that the world's biggest cities are mostly situated in the world's largest economies, given China and India's entry into the top rank.

Still, certain risks associated with hyper-urbanization remain salient. These include: the loss of rural and peri-urban land; pressures on infrastructure and on natural resources, including clean water; pollution and congestion; overcrowding and sub-standard housing; rising crime rates and public disorder; welfare inequalities; and the real diseconomies of scale that can dog the government of large and rapidly growing cities. The numbers game can be diverting, and the rhetoric of urban explosion distracting, but the more immediate question is not really how fast or how big, but how *well*? Lewis Mumford (1938: 233) decried the 'shapeless giantism' of the modern city. 'What is called the "growth" of the metropolis', he argued,

> is in fact the constant recruitment of a proletariat, capable of accommodating itself to an environment without adequate natural or cultural resources: people who do without pure air, who do without sound sleep, who do without a cheerful garden or playing space, who do without the very sight of the sky and the sunlight, who do without free motion, spontaneous play, or a robust sexual life. (Mumford 1938: 249)

Does the sheer weight of numbers involved mean that newly urbanizing cities, regions and nations are condemned not only to repeat but also to redouble the inequities, the enclosures and the environmental ills that attended the growth of the nineteenth- and early

twentieth-century city? Robert Cervero (2001: 1654) argues that a
'big is bad' school tends to take a particularly malign view of very
large cities in the developing world: 'Mega-cities like Jakarta, Cairo
and São Paulo are often criticised for being too expansive and too
expensive to manage and govern efficiently. The world's giant cities,
critics contend, suffer woefully from the ill effects of agglomeration.
Overcrowding is manifested in the form of traffic paralysis, squatter
settlements, street crimes and foul air.'

But how big is too big? When it comes to cities, there *is* no one-
size fits all formula, although there may be a 'best' fit for different
size economies and levels of economic development (see Henderson
2003). The fact that the largest cities tend to be concentrated in the
world's largest economies suggests that a certain economic weight is
required to carry these leviathans without their constituting an untenable fiscal and resource drain on the rest of the nation. The experience of big cities (for the United Nations' purposes, with populations
between one and five million) and large cities (with five million
or more) varies considerably in respect of income and productivity growth, infrastructure and services, housing and environmental
standards, and quality of governance. The example of Tokyo, the
largest city in the world, would suggest that 'mega-cities' (indeed,
with over thirty-five million people in the wider metropolitan region,
it might need a new category of its own) are neither dysfunctional nor
ungovernable simply as a matter of definition. Meanwhile the experience of some fast-growing cities, such as Curitiba and Porto Alegre in
Brazil, suggest that rapid urban growth can be managed both effectively and more equitably (see Satterthwaite 2007: 62). Moreover,
growth rates in the decade up to 2000 – other than in China, where
large cities grew fastest – were highest for small cities of fewer than
500,000 people (UN-Habitat 2008). The 'urbanization of the world'
(Wirth 1938; see also Soja and Kanai 2007) remains a fairly small-
town affair, with almost half of all urban growth in the period after
1975 accounted for at this level. The majority of the world's urbanites live in these small cities, with a further third in cities of up to five
million; fewer than one in five live in cities larger than that, and only
around one in ten in cities over ten million (United Nations 2012:
4–5). After all, and the recent achievements of Chinese urbanism
notwithstanding, it is rather easier to turn a rural settlement into
a small *urb* than it is to throw up a new mega-city between census
periods.

Size, which mattered for Wirth, becomes a difficult category to
think through given the great elasticity in what we term 'city'. This

is due not only to the fact that different cities vary widely in terms of their size and scale, but because urban settlement forms are increasingly complex, given patterns of peri-urban development, the growth of inter-urban networks and urban corridors, and the spread of urban functions across extended city-regions and 'mega-regions' (see Cohen 2006; UN-Habitat 2010). We should bear in mind, too, that population prediction is a highly uncertain science – indeed, the increase in the world's urban population so much discussed in the first decade of the twenty-first century came rather later, and was somewhat lower, than previous predictions had foreseen – but nonetheless it seems fair to say that the experience of a significant minority of the world's urbanites is or will soon be lived out at the very big urban scale, most of them in middle- or low-income econo- mies. In 1900 there were some seventeen 'million-cities'; in 2000 there was the same number of 'mega-cities' of ten million or more (Satterthwaite 2007: 16). At the same time, it remains the case that the majority of the world's urban population lives in cities of 500,000 people or fewer. Duluth is a city; so is Delhi, albeit their populations vary by a factor of more than 250. Mega-cities make for better images in dispatches from the urban frontline, but a randomly chosen urban- ite today would be more likely to live in a city like Ahmednagar, with a population of fewer than 500,000, than a city like Mumbai, 250 kil- ometres away and with more than eighteen million inhabitants. Size in raw terms does not appear as a particularly meaningful category for thinking about the city as a concept, although it might (more finely graded) be useful in analysing differences between individual cities. Neither is size – as a key characteristic of the urban mode of life – in itself a *social* category. The weight of numbers becomes socialized in its spatial organization.

As Robert Cervero (2001: 1651) has argued: 'In the developing world, the debate over urban form and economic performance has less to do with the shape of cities and more to do with their size. Giant cities are often considered dysfunctional – too congested, unserviceable, fiscal drains on national treasuries and unmanageable from a governance standpoint.' He goes on to postulate, however, that, 'all else being equal, large cities that are compact and that enjoy good accessibility matched by efficient transport infrastructure (i.e. good mobility) are among the most productive of all urban settle- ments' (Cervero 2001: 1652). This proposition is based on analysis in the US context, such that the assumption of 'all else being equal' becomes an extremely difficult one to make; moreover, the question of 'good' urbanism is not only about whether or not a city is highly productive in an economic sense. But Cervero's larger point is persuasive: the brute fact of numbers – as well as the physical size of cities – needs to be cut through by consideration of how urban areas are structured spatially, how they sit within a wider space economy and geography, and how far their spatial organization is fit for a range of economic and social objectives.

Density by design

Lewis Mumford (1938: 234) saw 'sprawl and shapelessness as an inevitable by-product of [the] physical immensity' of the modern city, but there are different things that cities can do with the numbers of people they pack into them. Wirth's second key element, density, makes the size of cities a relational matter. As the point at which the social and spatial come together, density is a critical means for thinking about the social life of urban form. How are people, things and activities distributed in relation to each other? What effects do different modes of density have on urban environments, on social interaction and cohesion, on public order, on economic vitality, on individual well-being and quality of life? These questions are always contextual, and lack firm answers, but they underline the role of urban form in organizing the social life of cities. Density, moreover, cannot simply be read off from city size: some of the world's biggest cities can also be seen as 'compact' in functional terms (e.g. Tokyo, with its high density levels and high public transport usage), while many smaller cities, for example in North America and Australia, sprawl and over-rely on private transport.

Urban densities have been a concern for policy-makers and urban reformers, engineers, planners and designers since the rapid growth of industrializing cities in nineteenth-century Europe and North America: overcrowding could be seen as a source of a variety of urban ills, from contagion and pollution, to criminality and promiscuity, to disorder, rabble-rousing and insurrection. The standard discourse of urban density by the end of the twentieth century in these same contexts was quite different: higher urban densities in post-industrial cities were seen as conducive to environmental sustainability, economic innovation, cultural vitality, social diversity and public safety. Cities such as London, Paris or New York have changed a great deal over the course of a century or more, but the inversion of the language of density is striking: from a social and environmental evil to a positive social and environmental good. Meanwhile, in cities of more

Turf Club, Kolkata, 2010.

recent and rapid population growth and industrial development, the problem of density sits in an uncertain place in-between: the point at which density becomes overcrowding, especially in slum settings, is never quite clear. One could almost conclude that density is bad for poor people; except that it is poverty that is bad for poor people, and 'bad' densities tend to follow from that.

'Good' density, in a contemporary context, has a privileged relationship to ideas of urban sustainability, given its positive contributions along the three axes of the economic, the environmental, and the social. Urban densities are conducive, firstly, to economic sustainability in producing thicker labour and consumer markets; lowering transport costs for workers and goods; increasing productivity and wage levels; supporting innovation, skills, creativity and other spillovers from investments in human capital; and making public service provision more cost-efficient (Andersson et al. 2007; Carlino et al. 2007; Carruthers and Ulfarsson 2003; Ciccone and Hall 1996; Florida 2002; Florida et al. 2012; Glaeser 1994, 2011; Glaeser and Gottlieb 2009; Glaeser and Resseger 2010; Glaeser, et al. 1992; Knudsen, et al. 2008; Rauch 1993; Storper and Venables 2004). Denser market concentration in cities promotes efficiency, competition and diversification. This last relationship, between density and economic diversity, is critical – highlighting the benefits not only of economic clustering *per se*, but also of the agglomeration of diversity. The positive spatial returns to economic diversity are nicely captured in the notion of 'Jacobs externalities' to describe the circulation of knowledge, innovation and market opportunities generated by the proximity of different industries and skills in a dense urban economy (see Jacobs 1969).

Higher urban densities, secondly, represent environmental goods in their capacity to reduce resource use, energy consumption and emissions: denser and more compact cities consume less land for building and roads; reduce energy use and emissions by decreasing the demand for motorized transport, especially private cars; create environmental economies of scale in respect of combined and alternative power sources; and support collective provision of open and green space, transport and other infrastructure, energy and recycling. Given that buildings and motorized transport account for cities' major share of resource consumption and emissions, producing fewer of these per capita (lower overall volumes of building, fewer private cars, less extensive road and rail networks), and simply using less land per person, represents a fairly basic environmental equation. It's hardly rocket science, and if there remains debate over the benefits of urban compactness, it cannot be based on an argument that extensive highway systems, large single-family houses, private swimming pools and plenty of hard-landscaped car-parking represent environmental positives rather than individual – and developer – preferences (see, among very many others, Banister 2011; Cervero 2003; Forsyth et al. 2007; Frey 1999; Glaeser and Kahn 2010; Jabareen 2006; Jenks and Dempsey 2005; Jenks et al. 1996; Newman and Kenworthy 1989, 1999, 2000, 2006; Newton 2000; Williams et al. 2000; Woodcock, et al. 2007; for a good counter-blast see Bruegmann 2005).

The social benefits of density appear less conclusive, but urban compaction has been linked to social sustainability in a number of ways: by facilitating spatial access to public transport, urban services and amenities; decreasing economic segregation and spatial inequality; offering greater possibilities for social interaction; enhancing community safety via the informal policing offered by well-used streets and overlooking; and increasing the range of social, cultural and consumer choices for different urban residents, especially minority and marginal groups (Bramley and Power 2009; Burton 2000; Dave 2011; Dempsey et al. 2011, 2012; Glaeser 2004; Jacobs 1961; Ng 2010; Wheeler 2004, 2006). While increasing density at the overall city scale is generally linked to greater income inequality (and, in the United States, can be linked to greater racial segregation at neighbourhood scale – see Glaeser 2004), intra-city density can also be seen to provide access to urban resources, employment opportunities, services and choice that can ameliorate certain effects of inequality. Again, the relationship between density and diversity is key to the claims around social sustainability, as these 'thicker' social spaces create geographies of opportunity that serve the needs and the preferences of a range of users.

In sum, in terms of productivity and efficiency, transport and energy infrastructure, land use and accessibility – and potentially for social diversity, equity and vitality – denser and more compact urban development is linked to greater economic, environmental and social sustainability. The benefits of compactness are taken to lie not only in land use, efficiency, energy and emissions, but also in the density of social interaction. For all of these claims, however, context is all. As in respect of city size, the sheer fact of higher density or greater compaction is not in itself a guarantor of any particular benefits. Whatever benefits might derive from urban density will depend both on its spatial organization – patterns of land use and location, the design and integration of built form, networks of transport access – and on the ways in which density is *lived* socially – the patterns of behaviour that operate in more or less dense urban contexts, whether environmental (transport behaviour and resource use), economic (employment activity and enterprise development) or more strictly 'social' (levels of interaction, attitudes to others, the management of urban proximity).

Debates over the relationship between built form and patterns of social life in cities are especially fraught in respect of the links between urban density and transport behaviour. The question of how far the design of cities can or should shape individual and collective behaviour is redoubled by current concerns with finding more sustainable models for urban settlements and the way we live in them. But a number of critics have questioned any simple equation between built form, density, sprawl and travel patterns (see, e.g., Boarnet and Crane 2001; Breheny 1995; Ewing and Cervero 2010; Gordon 2008; Gordon and Richardson 1997; Williams 2000; Wright 2008). Taking density as a single explanatory variable – much less as a single planning tool – is problematic, given that land use patterns and issues of transport access are also critical for understanding transport behaviour (Ewing 1997). High-density residential developments will do relatively little to reduce car use, transport congestion and emissions if they are zoned in mono-functional parcels at a distance from employment and services, and without reasonable access to public transport networks. This kind of functional sprawl, even in higher-density settings, may prove just as car-needy as the more 'classic' model of low-density, spatial sprawl.

An exemplary case comes from debates over density in the United States, which have tended to centre on the cities of New York, San Francisco and Los Angeles: the former two provide evidence for the link between urban density and higher public transit use and walking (as do cities such as Boston, Chicago, Philadelphia and Washington, DC), while the latter queers the figures, with high urban densities but low levels of public transit usage and walking. The confounding factor here is, in part, urban form. Los Angeles has a quite even density distribution within its physically defined boundaries, and lacks a higher density downtown that acts as a major employment centre. New York and San Francisco, in contrast, have much steeper density gradients, with far greater densities towards the centre and lower-density suburban fringes. Its version of dense sprawl (or 'dysfunctional density', as Eidlin 2010: 4 puts it) makes Los Angeles a rather exceptional case. Reid Ewing (1997) cautions that urban compactness is not simply an effect of high densities; the benefits of urban compaction derive, rather, from degrees of concentration, clustering and urban mix. Similarly, 'sprawl' is not simply equivalent to 'suburban' or low-density urban forms, but definable in terms of poor accessibility, weak functional integration and volumes of redundant or under-used open space. It is not merely distributions of residential density, moreover, that produce or limit sprawl, or sustain public transport alternatives; the distribution of employment densities is also key. Erick Guerra and Robert Cervero (2012) calculate for the US case that densities of around forty-five persons per gross acre within a half-mile radius of transit stops is the threshold for providing new heavy rail cost-effectively; light rail requires densities around thirty persons per acre. Their figures are based on an analysis of performance (capital and running costs by passenger miles travelled) for a sample of fifty-four rail investments undertaken across the United States between 1970 and 2006 (analysts in the UK case have argued that somewhat higher densities are needed to ensure transit viability – see LSE London 2006; Whitehead 2008). Given that only New York sustains these kinds of average residential densities around stations, and in face of general resistance to intensifying residential densities, Guerra and Cervero argue that promoting greater employment density – more jobs – around transit nodes has to be central to making public transport economically viable at a reasonable level of performance. The kinds of transit leverage to be gained from these patterns of 'tent-pole density' around transport hubs are based as much on the density of jobs as of residents.

These numbers games are always as controversial as they are uncertain – even if planners need thresholds and targets in order to do their job – partly because real-time changes (demographic shifts, employment and economic cycles, technological innovations, environmental blind-siders) tend to out-run or confound the best-laid plans. Peter Gordon and Harry Richardson (1997) argue quite plausibly against the case for compact cities, but note that they are writing in the context of 'a global energy glut', which the authors take to be a return to normal after the 1970s oil crisis. Normal looked rather different less than a decade on. But urban policy-making is not simply a question of crunching the numbers and hoping for the best; it determines the shape of cities in more decisive ways. The difference between San Francisco and Los Angeles is not just their size and density distributions, but policies towards highway construction and investment in public transit. People can only ride public transport if it exists; they will only choose to ride it if it is reasonably efficient, physically accessible and economically affordable.

Even if all of these criteria are met, however, preferences and practices around public transit will vary. Beyond the relevant physical and policy factors, *cultures* of density vary across different contexts. 'Outside of Manhattan, Chicago's Loop, and a few other urban pockets,' Guerra and Cervero (2012: 2) write, 'most Americans dislike density.' Cultural norms and consumer preferences may be 'softer', but they are critical factors in shaping attitudes towards density, transport behaviour and the management of proximity. In the US context, high-density living may well be either a matter of 'boutique appeal' (Gordon and Richardson 1997: 97) or an indicator of relative deprivation, but the relatively low densities at which people live in – and around – many American cities looks like another instance of American (or maybe Anglo) exceptionalism (see also Breheny 1997). English-speakers don't seem to like walking or cycling much either – only in the United Kingdom, amongst the Anglo-economies, does the share of trips by these low-cost, no-emissions modes take more than a 20 per cent share of all journeys (Buehler and Puecher 2012). There is more than a degree of irony in the fact that so much debate in this area is over the capacity for sustainable transport development in rapidly urbanizing low-income economies, when it appears that cities such as Las Vegas or Phoenix – amongst the fastest-growing internationally in recent decades, and in that one to five million sweet-spot in which much future urban growth is predicted to be concentrated – are being given up as lost causes. While cities such as these have the wealth, technology and capacity to innovate in transport systems (even if they are not blessed with high density), there is little evidence of political will or public willingness, and so almost nine out of ten journeys are made by car. Low-density living may be the expressed preference of most residents of the United States, and of the United Kingdom and Australia for that matter – who knows, it *could* be nearly everyone's preference, if they had both the consumer power and the spatial capacity to choose – but the urban reality is that for most people in cities in the developing world, high-density living is the norm (Dave 2010; Ng 2010). The debates over density and sprawl become not only sterile or semantic, but also increasingly irrelevant, for the majority urban experience. This assuredly is one instance in which the rest of the urban world cannot learn from Las Vegas.

While it is simply the case that people in higher-income cities live at relatively lower densities, it is not the case that density is little more than an indicator of deprivation, as the experience of inner London or Manhattan, Singapore or Hong Kong mid-levels, central Paris, Ginza or West Side Tokyo only too clearly attests. It does, however, need to be managed. While the urban rich can afford to trade off space for position, amenity and comfort, the management of density is not necessarily dependent on levels of income to secure a live-able standard of space, privacy and security. Seema Dave notes that acceptable levels of density vary across all cities, not only between high- and low-income settings. Her research in India suggests 'that high density in itself is not a problem in cities like Mumbai and positive impacts can be achieved within an area or a neighbourhood, if links between built form, layout, design, minimum standard of living space and culturally acceptable amount of mix of uses are established'(Dave 2010: 25). Climate is an important factor promoting higher-density living in Mumbai (as denser urban fabric reduces the cost of cooling, offers better shading, etc.), but it doesn't have the same effect in Phoenix, where residents spend more (in both income and emissions) to cool their houses – and their cars.

The design and management of density scales down from the level of the city to the level of the individual, and between these limits, is mediated by the design of open spaces, neighbourhood forms, street layouts, housing and other built typologies. Density may be 'the defining characteristic of urban settlements' (World Bank 2009: 49), but different cities, and different groups and individuals, *do* density differently. Moreover, density – as a defining characteristic of urbanism – is itself defined in a number of different ways. Kevin Lynch (1962) held that there were various tricks that could be played with density standards. The physical measurement of urban densities can be taken at the level of the individual plot – whether measured in terms of floor area ratio (FAR), site ratio, plot ratio or lot coverage, height and space standards; or at the area or city level – in measures of persons per hectare (pph), dwellings per hectare (dph), population/km^2, and as gross and net densities that respectively include or exclude road layouts, natural features and open spaces. At the city scale, a raw measure of population by area gives only a limited understanding of how densities are produced across space. Understanding the shape of the city in density terms means looking at the 'density distribution' or 'density gradient' – the way in which densities are organized across space. The classic model of the modern city with higher residential densities towards the core around a commercial downtown, and lower densities towards the periphery, which works for Shanghai or New York, works less well for cities with high densities overall but more evenly spread – such as Mexico City or Los Angeles – or cities that sustain high densities at the edge, such as São Paolo.

These distributions are important for thinking about *perceived* density: that is, how urban density is experienced on the ground (Churchman 1999). The notion of perceived density can be analysed quantitatively by weighting the raw density measure by the proportion of the urban population living at different levels of density as the gradient slopes away (see Eidlin 2010). So, in the context of debates over relative densities in New York and Los Angeles, the LA urban area has higher gross density at the overall city scale, but the majority of New York's residents live at significantly higher densities, with a very low-density hinterland. Perceived density is higher in New York in the sense that most people who live there are living at high densities. Average density is a bit like average income – the numbers give us a notion of how dense or how rich a city is overall, but don't tell us how the densities or dollars are distributed. A key question for the distribution of densities (as well as of dollars) is 'who is getting how much of it?', and whereabouts (to paraphrase Lynch 1981: 118). The measure of perceived density gives us a means of scaling down from the gross city level to district and neighbourhood scales, and also points to how residents live in different density contexts even at quite a micro-level. These are shaped not only by neighbourhood patterns and built forms, but also by household environments, socio-economic conditions and subjective responses. In qualitative terms, Amos Rapoport (1975) uses the concept of 'affective density' to refer to the subjective perception of density. Very simply, he suggests, the urban experience of overcrowding represents excessively high affective density, and that of isolation excessively low affective density. In between these extremes, perceptions will vary not only culturally and contextually but also individually, just as we know is true of personal space.

Like different individuals, different cities *do* density differently, both in terms of how it is lived and how it is spatially organized. These local ways of producing density in London, New York or Shanghai are embedded in distinctive urban morphologies: the material forms in which cities are shaped and reproduced. In terms of how density is lived, moreover, the question of layout is important not just at the level of the neighbourhood, street, block or building, but also at the level of the individual dwelling (see Lindsay et al. 2010; Raman 2010). The place of private living space in the production of urban densities is only underlined by changing household forms. There is a consistent link across different urban contexts between economic growth and decreasing family size; households on average have fewer children, and in the richest cities, people living alone represent a significant share of all households. In such settings, as Katie Williams (2009) points out, higher densities may be unable to offset decreasing household sizes, such that people actually end up consuming more living space. In tracing these physical patterns in the city, a number of factors are in play: the organization of streets, the relationship of

Density by design: London (Notting Hill)
(*Source:* LSE Cities).

Density by design: New York (East Village)
(*Source:* LSE Cities).

Density by design: Shanghai (Hongkou)
(*Source:* LSE Cities).

open space to built form, the layout of urban blocks, density of plot coverage, the grain of individual buildings, and the relation of big to small. Such different urban morphologies underline the fact that there is no standard way to produce density in the city. Moving from the morphology of urban space to the typology of buildings, again we see the various 'tricks' that can be played with density. The well-known visual from the 1999 report of the United Kingdom's Urban Task Force shows the way in which the same level of density can be achieved through quite different built forms on the same site. As noted earlier, relatively low-rise cities such as Mexico City or Los Angeles sustain levels of urban density commensurate with those with greater concentrations of high-rise.

These debates are generally based on measures of residential density. As noted earlier in respect of economic vitality and transport viability, however, commercial or employment densities are crucial for thinking about how cities work. Day- and night-time densities can vary considerably for different urban areas – the City of London, the square mile that marks the capital's finance centre, has one of the thickest economic densities in the world given its office-hour productivity, but fewer than 10,000 residents (a third of whom,

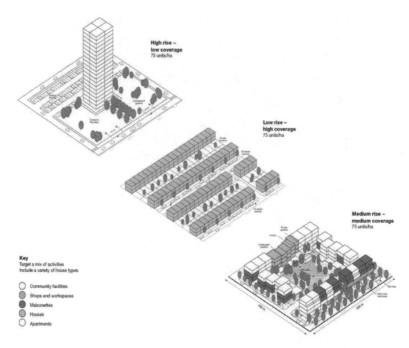

The 'tricks' that can be played with density standards: the relationship between density and typology

(*Source:* Rogers Stirk Harbour + Partners).

unsurprisingly, walk to work) and therefore one of the lowest population densities in the wider city and easily the lowest near the centre. Day-time densities based on working or commercial populations can also be crucial for individuals' sense of affective density. You might find the density of your inner-city neighbourhood liveable and even attractive when you go out in the evening, but the daily commute to work on packed trains, buses and pavements intolerable, uncomfortable and exhausting. Affective density levels, that is, are likely to shift even over the course of a day, as well as varying for different individuals and groups. What is experienced as urban 'buzz' at some times can feel like congestion at others. Crowds don't necessarily feel like particularly social contexts: living at greater urban densities can be linked to lower levels of social trust and social contact (see Lindsay et al. 2010), while Lewis Mumford (1938: 266) argued that the congested environment of the city gave 'positive encouragement to a-social or anti-social actions'. More affluent residents of gentrifying areas might deal with living at density in part by their extended mobility across and outside the city, while their lower-income neigh-bours put up with conditions of overcrowding and feelings of inva-sion (see Foord 2010). Young people in urban neighbourhoods can face the problem of having nothing to do as much as those living in suburbs – even if the former have more people not to do it *with*. Affective density, simply, is more complicated than anything that can be measured as a ratio of mass to area. 'It is impossible to get around, it is polluted, the rush-hour lasts from six in the morning to ten at night, it takes you forty-five minutes to buy anything in a shop,' one loyalist tells me, 'but Beijing is the most exciting city in the world.'

Expanding our understanding of urban density from living to working patterns still fails to capture the intensities of occupation, interaction and mobility that characterize the social life of urban form. Cities are defined in a more extended sense by 'their density as concentrations of people, things, institutions and architectural forms; the heterogeneity of life they juxtapose in close proximity; and their siting of various networks of communication and flow across and beyond the city' (Amin and Thrift 2002: 2). There are real limita-tions in confining our understanding of density simply to residential or employment densities. Where people live and where they work are of course basic features of the functioning and experience of cities, but if we want to think about this concept in a more textured and more spatially complicated way, then this requires an understanding of densities that includes mobility as well as dwelling; non-economic uses as well as patterns of employment; spaces we pass through in less purposeful ways, as well as points A to B on the daily journey to work. These densities – or rather *intensities* – of city life are harder to map. They don't show up in demographic or employment census data. But these many transitory or incidental ways of making space in the city have much to do with the pleasures and the pains of urban life. Density, to repeat, is where the social and spatial come together in the city. The kinds of physical and environmental strategies offered by both advocates and critics of urban density or compactness are at bottom concerned with *social* practices: they bear on norms of house-hold formation, patterns of living and working, consumption and travel behaviour, and attitudes towards the proximity of others. Some of these things can be measured and mapped, but there are certain normative dimensions that cannot be decided by recourse to statistical or behavioural facts. Emily Talen and Chris Ellis (2002: 42) put this very well:

[W]hether compact urban forms produce fewer car trips or impact social groups differently can be empirically treated. But there are aesthetic and ethical components to these theories that need to be debated on their own terms. They cannot be resolved by an appeal to data alone. Some principles are not provable in the conventional scientific sense, and indeed, the constant war of numbers engaging prosprawl and antisprawl debaters has not convinced anyone to change direction.

There is clearly no tipping point at which 'good' density becomes 'bad' density: this can change given context, over quite short spaces of time, and for different individuals. Moreover, density – so frequently associated with the dynamism and urban creativity of interaction and cross-pollination – at a certain level can become *static*, producing a rigidity in city form. Kevin Lynch (1995b [1968]: 776), for example, always an advocate for the lower end, argues that sufficiently low densities are required to ensure that there is scope for urban change – 'providing growth room or surplus capacity'. At a certain limit, urban land and fabric may become stitched so tightly as to become unbreathable, not easily allowing for re-use, adaptation or retro-fitting; let alone for breathing space.

City diversity

In planning and design terms, density is a device for achieving other objectives, rather than an end in itself. How you view ideal densities will depend on who you are and what you want: lower environmental costs or higher land, property and rent values; more housing supply or better space standards; collective life or greater privacy. Jane Jacobs suggested that the most important measure for urban density is its capacity to support a diversity of uses and of users. In this sense, urban density is the spatial key to a social and economic end. 'Densities are too low, or too high when they frustrate city diversity instead of abetting it,' she argued. 'Right amounts are right amounts because of how they perform' (Jacobs 1961: 209). Jacobs was interested in density as a means of promoting urban diversity, and it is this third aspect of Wirth's take on urbanism as a way of life that is definitively social, as much as it is physical. The point about cities, *pace* Wirth, is not simply that they contain a lot of people and that they tend to pack them in tightly, but that they support and intensify social, economic and cultural heterogeneity.

For Wirth, this was a matter of social scientific observation, and not in itself value-laden – even if the early urban ecologists were given to rather quick equations between heterogeneity and the potential for urban alienation and disorder. But much urban theory and critique has involved a more positive claim for the affinity of city life and difference. Ash Amin (2006: 1012) writes of the urban as 'the supremely visible manifestation of difference and heterogeneity put together'. And Henri Lefebvre (2003 [1970]: 96) put it this way: 'the urban can be defined as the place where differences know one another and, through their mutual recognition, test one another, and in this way are strengthened or weakened. Attacks against the urban coldly and lightheartedly anticipate the disappearance of differences.' The city is defined by and structured through difference. 'Difference is informing and informed,' Lefebvre (2003 [1970]: 133) continues: 'It produces form.' The physical differentiation of space does not simply reflect lines of economic and social diversity; these are co-produced in the production of urban space. Urban mix is conceived in functional as well as social terms, and it is unclear in which way the direction of causality runs. At the centre of Jane Jacobs' argument (1961: 14) was her insistence on the functional 'need of cities for a most intricate and close-grained diversity of uses that give each other constant mutual support, both economically and socially. The components of this diversity can differ enormously, but they must supplement each other in certain concrete ways.'

As is the case for urban density, diversity can also be seen to have a privileged relation to more sustainable urban forms; again along the three axes of the economic, the environmental and the social. Economic diversity, firstly – the mix of industries and employment sectors, of skills and income groups, of retail choice and different suppliers – is a basic condition for thinking about economic vitality. Socio-economic heterogeneity in the city can be said to support more dynamic labour and retail markets, tend to limit wage and price inflation, promote enterprise and market opportunity, and help avoid problems of spatial mismatch between housing and employment demand and long job-search and commuting journeys for lower-income and minority workers in particular. A recent current of research in urban economics has stressed the importance of social diversity for attracting highly skilled, and especially 'creative', workers to urban labour markets (see, *inter alia*, Florida 2002, 2003, 2004, 2005, 2008). At the larger, city scale, economic diversity is a structural condition for longer-term resilience. The crisis of industrial cities in the US rust-belt, in the north of England or in Germany's

Ruhr Valley during the 1970s and afterwards underlines the rigidity that can follow from over-specialized urban economies that are deeply embedded in existing physical forms, and slow to respond or adapt to economic change. A more recent case for the risks of economic over-specialization can be seen in the impact of the global financial and real estate crisis in Dubai, one of the world's fastest-growing cities in the previous two decades, but one over-dependent on the sectors that were hardest hit after 2008. Unfinished buildings, partly cleared development sites and abandoned residential properties became the twenty-first century analogue to the locked-down factories and idle cranes of the de-industrializing urban economies thirty years earlier.

In environmental terms, secondly, urban sustainability is linked to a well-integrated mix of land uses. The co-location of different urban functions – residential, commercial, industrial, leisure, civic and institutional – reduces routine travel distances, and makes non-motorized transport alternatives more viable. Access becomes not so much a matter of mobility as one of proximity. 'In dense, diversified city areas,' Jane Jacobs (1961: 230) averred, 'people still walk, an activity that is impractical in the suburbs and in most grey areas. The more intensely various and close-grained the diversity in an area, the more walking.' Mixed use enhances access and choice without the need for a private motor car, reducing emissions and traffic congestion while also supporting urban equity and efficiency. Indeed if there were anything like a sustainability 'magic bullet', this would be it: the contention that mixed land use offers efficiency gains in reducing travel time and cost and promoting economic interaction; provides environmental benefits in limiting transport emissions and resource consumption; and promotes social equity in de-linking access from affordability. Against the 'decontaminated sortings' of modernist urban zoning that Jacobs (1961: 35) so decried, we might counterpose the decongested and de-polluting benefits of urban mix.

Urban diversity, however, has a more complicated relationship to social sustainability, if by the latter we simply mean some version of social 'cohesion' or the minimization of conflict. Homogeneity may indeed be more conducive to the social peace, and to the observance and reproduction of shared social norms. Neither is this simply or necessarily a matter of preserving stable relations of social power: a long line of argument within urban studies holds that planning and policy efforts to promote social mix in the city can be read as liberal measures to pacify, disempower and dilute race and class solidarities in poorer neighbourhoods (Glass 1989; see Sarkissian 1976).

Broadway Market, London, 2012.

A limited understanding of social sustainability in terms of group capacity to reproduce a stable social order runs counter to arguments about the importance of diversity for social resilience. These begin with the low-level or everyday benefits of having a diversity of different users in space at different times, resulting in well-used streets, open spaces and public transit that enhance a sense of security in the common spaces of the city. It is one of the 'tricks' played with diversity that, in a context of routine difference, other people all become a bit more like you. It extends, too, to built forms, where a diversity of users – differentiated economically and demographically, in terms of culture, households and lifestyles – necessarily require different kinds of housing, work-spaces, public and cultural institutions, consumption and leisure spaces. Heterogeneity in terms of users and uses often is taken to be the enemy of monotony when it comes to built form. This may be to invoke, to borrow Talen and Ellis's (2002) phrase, 'aesthetic and ethical' criteria that are difficult to quantify, but the social value of urban diversity perhaps has more to do with the 'vitalizing challenge of dissonance' (Mumford 1938: 486) than it has with the security of sameness. Diversity as a defining character of urbanism is a reality that is lived both spatially and socially. Lefebvre (2003 [1970]: 37) writes of 'each place and each moment existing only within a whole, through contrasts and oppositions that connect it to, and distinguish it from, other places and moments.' Here diversity is defined through encounter; indeed, the urban can be understood in the form of the encounter, and by extension as circuits of communication, information and exchange: the pluses and minuses of 'urban concentration, with the attendant risks of saturation and disorder, and the opportunities for encounter, information, and convergence' (Lefebvre 2003 [1970]: 96).

Cities facilitate connection and interaction – certainly for those who want it, as well as for those who might not. The social experience of urban diversity is not only shaped by intentional designs for 'mixed' or shared urban spaces. 'Opportunities for encounter, information, and convergence' also happen in more unintended places. Saskia Sassen (2005b) reflects on the quality of what she calls 'cityness', based on urban intersections of difference that occur frequently, but in unobtrusive and often incidental ways. In coining this term she means to put into question a conventional notion of urbanity that has been too wedded to European conceptions of the city, including assumptions about the nature and role of urban public space. 'Cityness' happens in spaces that are not necessarily designed or demarcated for civic expression or convivial interaction. The encounters that Sassen has in mind happen in interstitial and unplanned spaces, across street-vendors' carts on the corporate pavements of midtown Manhattan, or under a Shanghai bus shelter in which a card-table is set up at night. One could instance others: the board games that take place on the porch of a tomb in Ahmedabad, or people eating lunch in IKEA display kitchens in Beijing. For Sassen, these kinds of encounter in these kinds of spaces express a quality of 'cityness' that is not reducible to western tropes of either ceremonial *or* cosmopolitan public space. They may be impossible, moreover, in urban contexts where difference is organized as extreme differentiation, in which 'certain inequalities and gaps might . . . keep the intersection of differences from happening, from being productive' (Sassen 2005b: 2). Spaces of decontaminated 'neutrality, precision, engineering', and spatial patterns of intense social segregation, can preclude this small change of urban encounter.

Such points of intersection, of connectivities and of disconnections, are at times legible in the built environment, at times below the level of easy visibility. The over-engineered city 'has provided the visual images and the programmatic narrative for a nearly universal narrative of growth', producing a 'hegemonic "global urbanism". . . of iconic architecture, gentrified residential districts, and more or less gated shopping areas' (Zukin 2009: 543, 544). Such landscapes of power may be highly differentiated visually from the downscale landscape of the ordinary city (see also Zukin 1991). The City of London and the new financial district around Canary Wharf regard each other as two clusters of corporate high-rise across a three-mile stretch of East London's increasingly variegated hinterland; the vertiginous skyline of Shanghai emerges from the densely packed low-rise of the older city. What is visible at this scale is the spatial proximity of quite different urban forms; what is not are the other intersections – the economic, social and micro-spatial connections and divisions – which link and de-link these markedly uneven urban morphologies. Sassen takes issue in particular with an assumption that the city can be understood as an urban aggregate where the whole is greater than, and resolves, the sum of its parts. Especially in contemporary contexts of skewed growth, she suggests, urban aggregates may not be greater than the sum of their parts; indeed may not *sum* in any legible way. So parts become important, not least in pushing against an understanding of the city in terms of the preferred representations of urban boosters, the architecture of advanced sectors or the spatial prerogatives of urban elites.

Alongside Sassen's 'productive' notion of cityness, it is just as important to attend to the points where these intersections of difference are corrosive, unjust or destructive. Cities make it easier for people and things to interact; they are excellent communication networks, with a great capacity to relay and to amplify what they circulate, whether this be information, germs, viruses or riots. Urban density and proximity, as Edward L. Glaeser (2004) has noted, is good for social interactions, both positive and negative. It's good for economic innovation and spill-over; it's also good for crime rates.

Conclusion: the temporal life of urban form

Louis Wirth's anatomy of the modern city in terms of size, density and heterogeneity can appear outmoded, but his terms take on new relevance in thinking about contemporary patterns of urban growth, and the links between city form and the conditions for urban sustainability. This discussion has been centrally concerned with these aspects of the city as a 'spatial order', based on the contention that the physical form of the city both shapes, and is shaped by, its patterns of social organization. Similarly, thinking about the city as primarily defined by territory can seem out of kilter with contemporary urban theory that is more disposed to understand cities in relational or network terms. It is not enough, of course, simply to think about the city as a spatial order: Michael Neuman's (2005) argument against the 'compact city fallacy' is an important one: cities – and their relationship to sustainability – need to be understood in terms of process rather than form. The point of the preceding discussion has been to underline how crucial urban form is for urban process. Form is, simply, *formative* for what goes on in urban settings, just as it is process and practice that create urban form.

An emphasis on process is an important corrective for any tendency to conceive urban form in static terms. Models of the compact city, or arguments for benign urban sprawl, cannot work only in three dimensions. The measure of urban form is in part a question of how it performs over time – whether by this we mean the working day, the change of seasons, the economic cycle, generational shifts or the *longue durée*. In this spirit, Kevin Lynch argued that a key 'performance characteristic' for urban form was its adaptability, its capacity to allow for the 'low cost of adaptation to new functions, and the ability to absorb sudden shocks'. Lynch's argument is strikingly contemporary in its tone, as he stresses the need for 'adaptability and resilience, a landscape easily changed by incremental effort and tolerant to experiment. The ability to change must itself be conserved, and that requires the avoidance of any dead-end, irreversible transformation' (Lynch 1995c [1975]: 789). In similar vein, Richard Sennett (2007) argues that the over-determination of urban form produces a 'brittle city', inadaptable, subject to decay, given to redundancy and obsolescence. An understanding of how cities work in time, such an approach suggests, is not only about a regard for urban histories but also about an openness to urban futures that allows space for change. Some building forms get lucky: the mass housing of many nineteenth-century cities has proved more pliable over time than the mass housing of the late twentieth century, while early twentieth-century industrial buildings have provided felicitous domestic spaces in post-industrial cities with a gentrifying service class. But some urban theorists are more exacting: 'Urbanists fail', Henri Lefebvre (2003 [1970]: 97–8) averred, 'when they propose temporary constructions that endure: a monotonous morphology' – a nice rebuke for any architect with an eye to his or her legacy.

This temporal dimension is central to the concept of sustainability, which deals in a version of the future that may be unknowable but is not entirely undecidable. Cities appear as both a problem and a resource in debates over sustainable development. They are, or might be, sites of environmental efficiency – with the capacity to create economies of scale and efficiencies of provision in respect of energy, resources, materials, waste, transport – even if too often they over-consume land and resources, and over-produce waste and emissions. They are sites of economic growth and innovation – urban densities are associated with higher per capita wealth and productivity rates – but also key production sites for economic inequalities. And cities are sites of social vitality – promoting social diversity, tolerance, collective learning and behavioural adaptations – except when they are crucibles of low trust, high crime, social conflict and tension. Debates over urban sustainability are so fraught not just because different sides can't get the numbers straight, but because they involve a set of social norms and political values that cannot be decided as matters of fact. 'Sustainability', as Peter Marcuse (1998) has put it, 'is not enough'; if by sustainability we mean the resilience of socio-spatial forms that may be durable in themselves – even environmentally sound – but inequitable, unjust or inhumane in social or economic terms. The World Commission on Environment and Development (1987) established the conventional definition of sustainability as being based on a relationship between 'present' and 'future generations'. Such an orientation to future generations is partly about the best guesses of population and environmental science, but is equally about projections of the future in terms not just of what is possible but of what might be seen as desirable. Marcuse (1998: 104) cautions against the language of sustainability as a 'camouflaged trap for the

well-meaning unwary'. It can also be an alibi for the cynical: however
aggressive its insertion in the surrounding fabric, however polarizing
its social impact or economic logic, an urban development can be
palmed off on the grounds of environmental innovation. Indeed, it
seems the more authoritarian the government that has commissioned
it, the more 'eco' the credentials of the 'starchitecture' which results.
But any passing engagement with the Brundtland Commission's
rhetoric of a 'common future' has to recognize that the first term –
what is held in common, and how it is shared – is at least as critical,
and just as problematic, as the second term is uncertain.

The question of good city form is, in the end, not a spatial one.
Those urban thinkers prepared to advance normative conceptions
of the city and urban life have advocated rather different city sizes
and densities – from the small is (more) beautiful school of Lewis
Mumford, Kevin Lynch and others, to confirmed metropolitans such
as Jane Jacobs or Richard Sennett. However the numbers might get
crunched around optimal size and densities, the positive and negative
effects of sprawl, the relationship between physical footprint, energy
use and emissions, ultimately these arguments over urban form rest
on normative grounds; sometimes even on personal preference. In
Good City Form (1981: 118), Kevin Lynch lays out a set of 'dimensions of performance' by which human settlements in general, and
urban form in particular, might be assessed: (i) vitality – support for
the well-being and capabilities of the group; (ii) sense – the clarity
with which the settlement is perceived by its inhabitants, and the
coherence between their physical, sensory and cultural understandings of place; (iii) fit – between physical spaces and patterns of social
behavior and functioning; (iv) access – both the quantity and diversity of things and people that can be reached; and (v) control – the
extent to which the management and modification of the environment is subject to the control of those who live in it. One could think
of counter-instances, too, along each of these dimensions: living
environments that are unhealthy, alienating, unfit for purpose, highly
fragmented or disempowering.

Lynch adds two 'meta-criteria' – of efficiency and justice – which
both depend on a certain consensus over values, and which pose
challenges for each of the five criteria of vitality, sense, fit, access and
control: '(1) What is the cost? and (2) Who is getting how much of
it?' The same city, as we know, can be healthy for certain groups –
providing sufficient space, clean water and air, clinics and hospitals
– and injurious to the health of others – in overcrowded, polluted and
unserviced settlements. An urban environment may cohere sensibly

for someone behind the wheel of a car, even without his or her GPS turned on, but make little sense to someone on foot who cannot find a route across the expressway or out of the car park. The design of city streets might function well for big retailers and corporate offices, but leave little room for small-scale trade or independent enterprise. An inner-city neighbourhood might provide all kinds of urban amenity in easy reach of the upscale incomer, and less and less that his or her older, low-income neighbour wants or can afford. Certain groups may have a significant voice in respect of what happens, or doesn't, in their backyard, while others are vulnerable to the decrees of public planning or the prerogatives of private capital when new roads, stadia or land-fill are being designed. There is a good case to be made that patterns such as these are inefficient in economic terms as well as being unjust, but all sorts of inequity can be productive or cost-effective at a city scale. The issue of 'who is getting how much of it?' is not simply a quantitative question, but a qualitative problem of the 'good' in good city form.

The discussion in this chapter ends where it began, with the idea of the city as an 'ecology', but now understood rather differently. The similarity in the language of a positivist urban social science and a normative conception of urban design is striking: Wirth and his colleagues' version of 'human ecology', we might recall, was concerned with 'the physical structure and the ecological processes of concentration, dispersion, segregation, and succession of men, institutions, and cultural characteristics'. Kevin Lynch (1981: 119) treats human settlements as a 'complex ecology' and his concern is with urban forms that allow for 'development, within continuity, via openness and connection'. It is very difficult to think about this set of objectives as being merely formal; it is a rubric for social development too, as Lynch himself recognizes. A statement about the physical and organizational qualities of urban form over time and in space – development, continuity, openness and connection – is part of a larger concern with social and individual good: 'So that settlement is good', Lynch (1981: 116–17) avers, 'which enhances the continuity of a culture and the survival of its people, increases a sense of connection in time and space, and permits or spurs individual growth: development, within continuity, via openness and connection.'

3

Unequal Cities, Segregated Spaces

Difference is incompatible with segregation, which caricatures it. When we speak of difference, we speak of relationships, and therefore proximity relations that are conceived and perceived, and inserted in a twofold space-time order: near and distant. Separation and segregation break this relationship. They constitute a totalitarian order, whose strategic goal is to break down concrete totality, to break the urban. Segregation complicates and destroys complexity.

Lefebvre 2003 [1970]: 133

Cities are machines for producing inequality. With their large and highly differentiated labour markets, their thick consumer markets and striated housing markets, cities routinely produce inequalities of both income and consumption. If inequality is a matter of urban fact, however, its spatial organization is a matter of urban design. Cities may be characterized by diversity, but they also involve a range of mechanisms (land and employment markets, legal divisions, cultural solidarities and differences) for 'sorting' diversity in spatial terms – mechanisms, that is, for converting social diversity into spatial division. Urban analysis has a core concern with the links between spatial segregation and social separation, what Jane Jacobs (1961) referred to as the mixing and 'unmixing' of cities. The discussion that follows considers how social and economic differentiation, division and distance are worked through urban fabric and form. It explores the conversions between spatial division and social difference in contemporary cities, examining the way segregation operates at both the 'low' and 'high' ends of residential patterns to reproduce not only impacted spaces of urban deprivation, but also wealthy and well-protected enclaves.

Andriyivskyy Descent, Kiev, 2011.

Setha Low (2011: 390–1) has argued that 'spatializing culture – that is, studying culture and political economy through the lens of space and place – provides a powerful tool for uncovering material and representational injustice and forms of social exclusion.' Cities sort by inequality. There is a double bind in play, here: cities are sites for both the production of inequality – through the spatial structuring of labour and property markets, the uneven impact of urban investment and location decisions – and its reproduction – the ways in which socio-economic disparities become embedded in place. Urban inequality is a common denominator in the world of cities – even more so than starchitecture and Starbucks – providing both an important and a problematic point of urban comparison. The first part of this chapter examines deepening profiles of income and consumption inequality across developed, transitional and developing cities. The discussion goes on to address current patterns of urban segregation, as these are variously organized around lines of racial and ethnic difference and class disparity. The focus is on persistent patterns of segregation, and emerging trends towards desegregation, in various US cities. The American experience represents an especially clear version of the diverse ways in which geographies of segregation are produced: including through legal coercions, economic constraints and cultural choices. In different contemporary cities, there is a grammar of segregation that structures urban inequalities around homologous (if never identical) spaces: the enclave or gated development; the secessionary suburb; the sink estate; the cardboard shelter; the waste-ground settlement; the refugee or migrant camp. Patterns of division, dispossession and displacement in the city are expressed in a kind of spatial Esperanto of exclusion.

A key trend in current patterns of segregation is 'the concentration of affluence' (Massey and Fischer 2003: 29) and the self-segregation of the rich, frequently secured by defensive architectures of walls and gates. Often associated with upscale urban developments in the United States, or fortified enclaves in Latin America, gated developments and security villages are now to be found in numerous urban settings, cutting across degrees of economic disparity or urban insecurity. This kind of bunker urbanism may be understood in terms of elite withdrawal and urban abandonment, but there is a counter-argument that the socio-spatial practice of gating is a way of keeping higher- and middle-income residents in unequal cities. Local or 'finer-grain' patterns of segregation might in this way be seen as a practical means of limiting the flight of more privileged groups out of urban centres, retaining a degree of urban 'mix' in contexts of often stark inequality.

The final part of the discussion turns to the question of 'diversity by design'. A range of policy programmes have been enacted in different urban contexts in the attempt to deconcentrate impacted spaces of poverty and promote socio-economic and functional mix. The mixing and unmixing of cities, however, takes shape through various means. I argue that it can be hard to differentiate 'market-driven' from 'state-led' processes in these contexts, and that patterns of gentrification in many cities have been at least as effective in diversifying urban areas as any policy design for creating mix. These logics of diversification – involving various degrees of displacement and dispossession – put into question any simple assumption that the pursuit of social diversity is an unalloyed urban good.

In thinking about how inequality is produced and organized in the

city, the focus generally has fallen on the ways in which cities concentrate large numbers of low-income residents. Similarly, analyses
of segregation have revolved around the spatial corralling of urban
minorities and the marginalized poor, while much research as well
as policy on socio-spatial mix has focused on the deconcentration
of lower-income groups. These dimensions of the unequal city have
not gone away. However, in this chapter I aim to stress the new
patterns of inequality that are emerging from the concentration of
wealth in many cities – income and consumption gaps, that is, are
being stretched at the top end of the scale. Moreover, spatial segregations are produced not only around the geographies of racial or
ethnic minority in the city, but also around those of a socio-economic
minority who can afford to sequester themselves from the 'do
without' parts of the city – even, at times, when they reside in areas of
proximity or conditions of apparent 'mix'.

Urban inequalities

These issues become particularly acute against the backdrop of
deepening inequality in the world's cities, markedly – although certainly not exclusively – in post-Communist and developing cities.
To a significant degree, contemporary processes of urbanization
are also processes of 'unequalization', with increasing disparity in
expanding as well as in established cities. Inequality is conventionally measured in terms of both income share and inequalities in
consumption. The latter are often less severe than income measures
would suggest, given that poor rural households may have access to
resources (food, water, building materials, fuel) at low or no cost
which their 'richer' urban counterparts do not, or in cases where
state subsidy and provision offer access to basic goods – as well as to
housing, education, health or transport – to those on low incomes.
At the national scale, rural–urban and regional disparities are the
most important factors in respect of both income and consumption
inequalities, but many big cities are more unequal than their wider
national economies. Intra-urban inequalities arise from a number of
causes: labour market segmentation and disparities; large informal
sectors; lack of social protections and services; inequalities of opportunity, especially for education; elite capture and state corruption;
racial, ethnic and gender discrimination – these factors combine in
various ways in different contexts to produce patterns of urban disparity. However, a common feature in recent trends is the impact of

economic liberalization in different national and urban contexts that has eroded incomes at the lower end and concentrated incomes at the top (see UN-Habitat 2008). Labour market liberalization has tended to increase insecurity, casualize employment and depress wages at the bottom end of the labour market, in high-income and transitional economies in particular; trade liberalization is linked to unemployment and downward wage pressures in sectors (particularly manufacturing) exposed to lower-wage competitors and import penetration; meanwhile financial liberalization, and the increasing integration of trade and financial markets, has seen the inflation of incomes at the upper end of financial and related service industries. Perhaps most significantly, widespread welfare retrenchment has both removed various social protections and weakened redistributive tax policies that seek to mitigate the effects of unequal market outcomes. This lock-step of economic with public policy has had the dual effect of rendering incomes increasingly unequal while cutting the state measures designed to offset the impact of these market inequalities.

Intensive urban growth in recent decades has been accompanied by deepening inequality at national levels, in large part owing to widening disparities between urban and rural incomes, and especially in rapidly growing economies such as China and India. The bleak global profile owes much to the fact that these two large economies, which have seen significant rates of both urbanization and economic growth, also started from relatively low rates of inequality. Inequality in India has deepened as its overall wealth and its urban population have grown, while China has seen grossly skewed growth, with average urban incomes reaching more than three times per capita rural incomes by the early twenty-first century (UN-Habitat 2008: 73). While there are established links between increasing inequality and both economic and urban growth, however, neither link is simply inevitable: Malaysian and Indonesian cities have experienced notable decreases in inequality and poverty in the context of strong economic growth since the 1990s (OECD 2011: 51; UN-Habitat 2008: 52, 54, 57), while highly urbanized Latin American economies, including Argentina and Brazil, have seen declining levels of inequality since the late 1990s – albeit from very high starting-points – in changing conditions of economic decline, recovery and growth (Lustig et al. 2011; OECD 2011). China has seen the steepest rise in income inequality among major emerging economies over recent decades; while the Chinese government has been reluctant to publish Gini co-efficients since 2000, when it was pegged at 0.41, inequality rose sharply in the preceding decade, and more recent estimates have been higher (see OECD 2011). Even so, Beijing remained the most equal city in a 2008 UN survey of cities in developed and emerging economies – with a Gini co-efficient of 0.22 in 2003, it stood out as a kind of Denmark of the urban world, and strikingly more equal than other Chinese cities, with Hong Kong (Gini of 0.53) and Shenzen (0.49) the least equal (UN-Habitat 2009: Table 27 – both figures 2004–5). National histories shape these urban profiles: South Africa has the world's highest levels of urban inequality by very stark margins, and the former Communist states of Eastern Europe among the lowest – although Russia itself sustains much greater levels of urban inequality than its neighbours: Moscow's Gini co-efficient in 2009 was calculated at 0.52 (Denisova 2012).

Urban inequality in some ways reproduces patterns of inequality at national and transnational scales: cities in southern Africa evince some of the most devastating indices of inequality. But in other ways patterns of urban inequality work against easy assumptions about a global urban order: Beijing remains for now one of the most economically equal cities in the world; US cities such as New York, Atlanta, New Orleans, Washington, DC or Miami support levels of urban inequality comparable to those of some of the world's poorest cities, which lack the legal protections, welfare measures or wider affluence that we find in the world's largest economy (UN-Habitat 2008: 65). Amongst high-income economies, the United States maintains inflated levels of urban inequality, and in these US contexts – as elsewhere – race is critical to the reproduction of inequality. If South Africa's apartheid history disfigures its landscapes of urban inequality today, enduring legacies of slavery and segregation continue to structure urban inequalities in the cities of the United States.

While patterns of contemporary inequality are embedded in these longer histories, there is also evidence that the contours of urban inequality are changing. The picture in the United States, notably, has altered over recent decades. In their study of 242 US metropolitan areas with populations over 50,000, and using Census data for 1980 and 2000, Edward Glaeser, Matt Resseger and Kristina Tobio (2008) found that inequality increased during that period in all metros in their sample except one (Ocala, Florida, as it happens). The chief factor explaining deepening income inequality in US cities over that time, the authors argue, was the unequal distribution of skill ('human capital') across urban populations, and the differential returns to skill in urban labour markets, particularly in terms of income premiums for higher-skilled workers in the growth sectors of finance and IT. Alongside the evidence of growing income inequality, the authors tracked a changing relationship between inequality and average incomes in a city. Conventionally, higher average incomes are associated with lower levels of income inequality – put simply, in 1980, 'almost all rich places were relatively equal, given the relative inequality of the United States' (Glaeser et al. 2008: 9). By 2000, however, this association was weakening, with higher average incomes far less strongly linked to greater equality. This suggests a re-shaping of urban inequality in the United States. Historically, cities are made more unequal by the presence of large numbers of poor people. The work of Glaeser and his colleagues suggests that significant income growth at the top is now shaping inequality in urban America in new ways: some of the nation's richest cities, such as San Francisco, have seen steep rises in inequality over recent decades, with New Haven–Stamford, 'with its combination of inner-city poverty and hedge-fund entrepreneurs' (Glaeser et al. 2008: 8), the most unequal metro in the sample for 2000. The blow-out of incomes at the top, especially for those working in finance and IT, has seen a pulling away of a wealthy elite – both on the graphs of income distribution, it might be said, and in social space.

The trends which Glaeser and his colleagues outline for the United States for the period after 1980 are relevant for other cities in both high-income and emerging economies. London is the richest region in Britain, and also the most unequal. London takes a disproportionate share of the nation's poorest households, as well as a highly skewed share of its richest earners. Around 12 per cent of British people live in London, but this includes around 25 per cent of the top 1 per cent of earners, and almost 40 per cent of the top 0.1 per cent; substantial numbers in the high-income groups also live in the wider southeast region around the capital (Brewer et al. 2008: 14). Highly skilled professionals (such as doctors and lawyers) are well represented in these groups, but high-income individuals are also significantly more likely to work in financial intermediation and real estate than are other British workers – taken together, 60 per cent of earners in the top 1–0.1 per cent work in finance, real estate, law and health, as compared to 30 per cent of the workforce as a whole (Brewer et al. 2008: 16). The single most distinctive feature, however, of Britain's highest earners is not where they live or what they do; it's the fact that they are men. Over 90 per cent of the top 0.1 per cent are male, as are around 75 per cent of the top 10 per cent. Gender persists as the most basic contour of economic disparity across very different social and spatial contexts. We might note that these figures refer only to those incomes declared for tax purposes; they take no account of the capital wealth stored off-shore in tax havens, or of property assets vested in London's inflated housing markets, or indeed of London's super-wealthy 'non-domiciled' foreign residents who pay only a nominal charge in lieu of UK taxation each year. But the income extremes in a city such as London are marked enough, even without including the hyper-rich, who rarely show up in socio-economic surveys – or, for that matter, on tax-rolls. They bear out the pattern seen in the United States over the same period: the accelerated income returns to human capital in certain sectors (and notably the role of finance), and the way these impact on the economies of cities.

A similar picture emerges for the Chinese cities that boasted such striking indices of inequality by the early twenty-first century. Certain deeply embedded factors remain crucial in shaping inequalities in developing economies such as China and India: in particular, unequal access to land is key in these still highly rural societies – India remains majority rural, while China's urban population share passed 50 per cent only in 2012. Rural inequality historically has been worse in China than levels of urban inequality, while consumption inequalities between urban and rural dwellers continue to grow (UN-Habitat 2008: 60, 77–8). However, a different set of factors is driving emergent inequalities as these nations' urban economies expand. Growth in manufacturing, technology and services has resulted in larger wage differentials for skilled and unskilled workers. The increasing returns to skill that Glaeser and his colleagues noted for US cities after 1980 have been paralleled in China and India since the 1990s, with higher-skilled urban workers taking the greater share of income growth in those countries, alongside accumulating wealth at the top for those groups who derive their income from capital rather than from labour (UN-Habitat 2008: 60, 66, 78; see also Liu et al. 2010; Zhang et al. 2005). It should be noted that China has been more effective than India at decreasing overall levels of poverty in the context of rapid economic growth and increasing inequality – and urban residents in particular have had access to publicly subsidized housing, health care and education (although public provision is now being eroded) – but it nevertheless maintains the highest consumption inequalities in the Asian region (Meng et al. 2005; UN-Habitat 2008: 78). The picture looks bleaker, too, when the situation of the substantial migrant population in Chinese cities is taken into account (Park and Wang 2010; see also Solinger 2006). Beijing's equality profile looks less 'Scandinavian' when its floating population is figured in, with one estimate that by 2000 the city's Gini co-efficient rose to .33 when migrant as well as registered households were included (Dai

2005; UN-Habitat 2008: 78). Moreover, consumption inequalities may be deeper even than income disparities for this group, given unregistered migrants' lack of access to public housing and social security. Such exclusion is further reinforced by the fact that children of migrant households do not enjoy equal access to the urban public school or university systems, re-embedding disadvantage for the next generation in light of the increasing importance of education and skill in Chinese income inequalities.

The intersection of these non-market factors – public provision of education, housing and social services – with market outcomes is important for how inequality is managed, mitigated or compounded. A gathering political orthodoxy across governments of notionally different stripes and in quite different socio-economic contexts has, since the 1980s, underwritten the widening of income inequality in a number of national settings, based on both hotted-up growth at the top of the income scale and the cutting of public transfers and services for those lower down. A deliberate move away from a politics of redistribution (dismissed as seeking to engineer 'equalities of outcome' by the Blairite centre in Britain, for instance), and more aggressive policies of tax cuts for the rich (as pursued most vigorously under the second Bush presidency in the United States), reinforced the inflation of incomes in certain lead sectors of the economy, as well as fuelling the growth of property-based wealth in over-heated urban real estate markets. It follows that cities will tend to concentrate the effects of such top-heavy income inequality. As cities compete to attract and retain high-skilled employees in the finance, IT and other advanced service sectors (bankers, in particular, have become bullet-proof as objects of boosterish desire), they are competing to concentrate those populations whose incomes are driving increasing urban inequality from the top of the income scale. Once it was the concentration of poverty that made cities more unequal, and the growth of the middle classes that tended to reduce inequality. Now, as urban poverty persists as a problem, and urban middle classes are subject to stubborn wage stagnation and increasing economy insecurity, the top end of earners are making cities more unequal through exaggerated *inequalities* of outcome.

These trends are not confined to the wealthier liberal and social democracies. Welfare retrenchment has been a keynote of government reforms in former Communist states following the break-up of the Soviet Union, as well as under the novel hybrid of capitalism and state centralism that the Chinese polity has become since the 1980s. Other emerging market economies are witnessing economic growth and increasing urbanization – processes that in themselves will tend to produce inequality – in contexts where the public provision that might offset their negative effects is already sparse, and has in many cases been depredated by earlier rounds of structural adjustment required under the terms of international loans and investment.

In numerous expanding cities, old patterns of inequality endure – as access to land and property, gender inequity, ethnic and racial discrimination, and various forms of legal exclusion continue to divide urban populations – while newer patterns emerge from the forms of economic and political restructuring that have run alongside recent urbanization: deepening wage/skill disparities in both services and manufacturing, increasing income returns to capital, liberalization of accumulation at the top, and welfare retrenchment and state abandonment. Urban inequality is a common story, but it is produced and reproduced through a range of different means. It is also spatialized in a variety of forms – and this, too, is linked to the ways in which inequality is racialized, shaped by legal rights of citizenship or physical patterns of cultural exclusion, entrenched in inner or outer cities, or more radically displaced beyond the urban periphery.

Segregation and desegregation

The most obvious spatial correlate of economic inequality in the city is urban segregation. The ghetto or native quarter, the township or migrant colony, the *favela* or slum, the inner city or *banlieu*, represent emblematic urban spaces of differentiation, division and disparity. Many of these spaces of segregation intercut economic and legal inequalities with racial and ethnic difference. But these stark morphologies can belie the often more complex ways in which cities organize social and economic divisions in space. In a classic essay in the field, Douglas Massey and Nancy Denton (1988) unpack the notion of 'segregation' along five different dimensions. *Evenness*, firstly, refers to the distribution of minority residents across an urban area; a relatively more even spread denoting lower levels of group segregation. *Exposure*, secondly, reflects the extent to which these residential distributions bring members of different groups into proximity with each other – with integration or isolation indices measuring the degree to which different groups live alongside others, or in neighbourhoods dominated by members of their own (racial, ethnic, cultural or socio-economic) group. These two dimensions of segregation – in terms of spatial distribution, and proximity or exposure to others – are the standard measures for the study of segregation, but Massey and Denton add three further factors which have to do with the spatial morphologies of urban segregation. *Concentration* refers to the spatial density of minority settlements in particular urban areas. *Centralization* indexes the tendency of minorities to live closer to the centre of the city as compared to other groups – or alternatively, further away: racial and ethnic minorities in many US cities may be more centralized than majority groups, while the reverse is true of disadvantaged and minority groups in certain South American or European cities. Finally, *clustering* indicates the extent to which minority neighbourhoods border each other, rather than being spread across the wider city. Massey and Denton note that these various dimensions of segregation frequently overlap, but are conceptually and spatially distinct. The value of such an approach is not simply in providing a more nuanced spatial frame for thinking about the patterning of urban segregation, but in opening out the different ways these patterns of segregation are experienced in both social and spatial terms.

Conventionally, residential segregation is measured using the *dissimilarity index*, which corresponds to Massey and Denton's notion of 'evenness': this calculates the distribution of minority residents across an urban area relative to that of another (usually the majority) group. Expressed as a figure between 0 and 100, where 0 indicates perfect integration and 100 complete segregation, it denotes the percentage of this group that would need to relocate in order to achieve an equivalent spread across the city relative to the other group. A zero value for black–white dissimilarity, for instance, would indicate that the black and white populations of a city were distributed in exactly the same proportions across different neighbourhoods, and no-one would have to move in order to even out the spread. American cities offer critical contexts for thinking about forms of segregation, given their histories of producing these forms both through definite patterns of racial and ethnic exclusion, and through more 'voluntary' effects of group clustering: urban segregation in the United States today reflects a cross-cutting of these patterns of ghettoization and ethnic enclaving over time. Moreover, it involves current trends of both desegregation (especially of primary cities and suburbs) and *resegregation* through exurban development. The 2010 US Census showed racial segregation declining for the nation's 100 largest metropolitan areas, with levels of black segregation relative to whites (measured by the dissimilarity index) falling across nearly all urban areas with populations over 500,000, and Hispanic segregation decreasing between 2000

and 2010 in two-thirds of these large metros (Frey 2011b). Levels
of segregation remain high, however: more than one-third of the 100
largest metros had 'high' (over 60) black–white dissimilarity measures in 2010; with the Milwaukee metro evincing the highest degree
of black residential segregation (81.5) followed by the greater New
York, Chicago, Detroit, Cleveland, Buffalo and St Louis metros, all
with 'extreme' indices over 70, and a metropolitan average of 55.
Hispanic Americans now represent the largest minority group in US
cities overall, and levels of Hispanic–white segregation are generally
lower, peaking at around 62 in both Los Angeles and New York, and
averaging at 44 across all metros. Asian Americans remain the least
segregated urban minority in respect of whites, with an average dissimilarity value of 40 (Frey 2011b; Frey et al. 2011).

The picture that emerges from the 2010 Census is an urban
America where the primary cities – the biggest centres within a wider
metropolitan area – are disproportionately black and Hispanic; the
suburbs reflect a more even share of the nation's ethnic breakdown;
and the low-density urban periphery is disproportionately white.
White Americans are significantly under-represented in primary
cities – non-Hispanic whites account for just under 66 per cent of the
population as a whole, but only 41 per cent of the population in these
urban centres. Black and Hispanic Americans are over-represented in
cities, with respectively 12 and 16 per cent shares of the national population, but 22 and 26 per cent population shares in major cities – by
2010, 58 of the 100 largest US cities were 'majority minority' (Frey
2011a: 5). However, the 2010 Census also revealed an increasingly
balanced suburban America: more than half the urban populations of
all major racial and ethnic groups (including those who self-identify
as mixed race) live in the suburbs – Hispanic Americans living in metropolitan areas were majority suburban by 2000, as were black urban
Americans by 2010. Nevertheless, it would be an error to assume this
suburbanization of difference equates to spatial 'mix' or diversity at
more local scales. At neighbourhood level, many US suburbs remain
highly segregated along racial and ethnic lines. At the larger scale,
though, suburban America does not display the skewed profiles that
characterize the racial and ethnic geographies of the central cities:
with around 35 per cent minority residents overall, the suburbs of
large US cities now mirror the minority share of the US population
as a whole (Frey 2011a: 7; see also Hall and Lee 2010). Meanwhile,
suburbanites remain a 'supermajority' among non-Hispanic whites
in US cities (around four out of every five white metropolitans live in
the suburbs), with especially high concentrations in the 'peripheral,

low-density portion of large metro areas' – or 'exurbs' (Frey 2011a: 11–12). While these peri-urban developments account for only a tiny share of the total urban population (with just 2.5 million residents, or 1 per cent of metropolitan America), they are growing much faster than the population as a whole, and that growth is largely driven by white Americans. In contrast, non-white minorities and Hispanics accounted for nearly all growth in primary cities during the same period. As William H. Frey notes (2011a: 12), the white population grew nationally by just 8 per cent in the decade up to 2010, but by 73 per cent in these low-density suburban counties. This now rather far-flung version of white flight appears increasingly anti-urban – both as a spatial strategy and insofar as it anticipates, as Henri Lefebvre (2003 [1970]: 96) put it, 'the disappearance of differences'.

Taken as a single measure, the dissimilarity index can tell us one big thing about a city, but offers only an initial level of insight into how ethnic, racial or economic difference is spatialized in that context. New York's high dissimilarity index for black Americans relative to whites suggests that the city's black residents are heavily concentrated in certain (largely non-white) areas, but doesn't tell us where these are, or who else is living there. A further dimension of segregation, which has more to do with the nature of residential *mix*, is captured by the 'exposure index'. This measures the average neighbourhood composition for members of particular groups. In 2000, for instance, the average black resident of New York City lived in a neighbourhood that was around 61 per cent black, 23 per cent Hispanic and just 9 per cent white. A white New Yorker, in contrast, was most likely to live in a neighbourhood where 67 per cent of other residents were also white, 14 per cent Hispanic, and fewer than 6 per cent black. Hispanics tended to be more 'exposed' to a mix of other New Yorkers, with the average resident living in a neighbourhood that was half Hispanic, but also included over 20 per cent blacks, just under 20 per cent whites and around 8 per cent Asian Americans (Frey and Myers 2002: 18). Segregation is generally thought of as something that 'happens' to non-white minorities, but in this diverse city it is the white minority that appears *most* segregated, as measured by exposure to others in a typical neighbourhood setting.

The exposure index is often taken to be a more sociological measure of interaction, as compared to the geographical spread of differences across a city. However, it is not clear that we can simply assume 'a direct equation of spatial and social patterning', whereby '[s]egregated groups are unassimilated [while] spatially dispersed groups, that have the same distribution as the majority population, are assimilated' (Peach 1996: 380). By the same logic of reading social facts off from spatial arrangements, one could reason that in New York – a city with no single racial or ethnic majority – whites are the most poorly integrated and most 'enclaved' ethnic group, least likely to live in neighbourhoods with a mix of other residents. This might well be so – one of the salutary effects of urban diversity is that it becomes difficult, and often arbitrary, to determine what 'normal', 'typical' or 'mainstream' looks like.

As with inequality itself, segregation is a long-standing – and very widespread – urban phenomenon; and like inequality, it is not simply or necessarily a bad thing. As Ceri Peach (1996: 379) contends: 'Segregation, is in fact, one of the key methods of accommodating difference' in the city. What is noticeable in the US figures is that those cities with high levels of segregation – especially black–white segregation – are also highly diverse. Lefebvre asserts in the opening epigraph to this chapter that segregation 'complicates and destroys diversity', but this is true only up to (or perhaps beyond) a certain point. Diversity is complicated in itself, and it is not inevitably 'destroyed' by segregation. The socio-spatial clustering of groups in cities is a regular fact, and may be a substantive benefit, of urban life. The key issue here is the degree to which segregation is coercive, constrained or compulsory, as opposed to more or less 'freely' chosen. Alongside Massey and Denton's socio-spatial dimensions of segregation, we might add the distinction between voluntary and involuntary modes of segregation, as exemplified by the differentiation of the ethnic enclave from that of the ghetto (see Smets and Salman 2008; Varady 2005). This is where Lefebvre's point is sharp: differences that are expressed, produced and lived spatially are not simply reducible to segregation as a spatial life sentence.

The American cities with the most extreme levels of black–white segregation are cities in the northeast and midwest that were the major destinations of urban migration for blacks from the southern states during the twentieth century. Successive waves of this Great Migration saw black Americans settling in industrializing cities, and notably in those – Chicago, Cleveland, Detroit, New York – that evince such high levels of residential segregation to this day. The housing markets these black migrants moved into were skewed by discrimination, redlining, overt and covert racism, and reinforced over time by income inequalities, 'informal' racism, urban and industrial decline. These histories are embedded as long-standing patterns of neighbourhood segregation; in more recent decades the relative lack of new housing development inside these primary cities and the tailing-off of black population growth have made for little black population churn into new neighbourhoods or few new arrivals moving into different parts of the city. Black suburbanization, the gentrification of certain black and low-income neighbourhoods in some of these cities and new minority populations moving in all contribute to declining trends in segregation. But the US cities with the lowest levels of black–white segregation are smaller and newer cities in the Mountain States with growing black populations – including Las Vegas – while southern cities are seeing declining rates of black–white segregation together with a reversal of older migration trends, as significant numbers of (notably middle-class) black Americans move 'back' to the South (Frey 2011b: 14–15, 10).

These entrenched spatial histories of segregation contrast with patterns of group clustering that may emerge out of labour and housing market constraints, but also involve issues of cultural preference, economic opportunity and social solidarity. Ethnic neighbourhoods are shaped not simply by patterns of exclusion, but around social, economic and cultural networks that provide spatial resources for both livelihoods and lifestyles. First-mover migrant populations, religious and cultural associations, political networks and civic institutions, welfare and support services, small businesses, shops and restaurants all represent socio-spatial anchors around which ethnic enclaves are formed not simply as points of arrival but as embedded places in the city. A standard distinction between 'voluntary' and 'involuntary' forms of segregation does not entirely capture the degrees of choice and constraint involved in any pattern of urban settlement – and which may be experienced very differently *within* households as well as across neighbourhoods – but it does point to the various benefits of degrees of segregation for minority groups. Information networks and job openings; social solidarity and mutual aid; opportunities for enterprise as well as for consumption; cultural and religious association and expression; political mobilization and community organization – ethnic enclaves are pre-eminent urban cases of the spatial expression of social capital.

In these ways, forms of segregation can be productive as well as protective, offering opportunities for employment and enterprise that may work to mitigate wider urban inequalities rather than simply reflecting them. Segregation, however, is both reflective of urban inequality and also reproductive of it when it serves spatially to reinforce inequalities in access to employment, financial, social and public services, transport and urban amenities. While there may be powerful arguments for the social benefits of group clustering – as much as there are critiques on the other side of 'ghetto cultures' – the major disadvantages of segregation tend to be material ones. Racial segregation is a critical factor in poor labour market outcomes for many urban black Americans (Stoll and Covington 2012), with the spatial mismatch between areas of employment growth and areas of black residential concentration compounded by ongoing effects of 'job sprawl'. The suburbanization of employment in this way runs counter to the disproportionate 'centralization' of black urban minorities highlighted by Massey and Denton in the 1980s and persisting into the next century. Meanwhile, patterns of spatial 'concentration' that squeeze minority or migrant populations into tight spaces in the city, or the 'clustering' of minority neighbourhoods in particular urban areas, may underpin the effects of environmental racism which relegate disadvantaged and minority groups to the most polluted, contaminated, fragile or unliveable parts of the city.

The analysis of urban segregation tends to focus on lines of ethnic and racial difference, but patterns of segregation in the city are not organized solely in terms of racialized divisions. While race and class often intersect in the structuring of urban space, the spatialization of economic inequality clearly is not limited to differentiation along lines of race. Economic or class divisions striate cities in both crude and complex ways. Moreover, economic segregation is not simply and always an urban problem – Peach's dictum, that segregation is 'one of the key methods of accommodating difference' in the city, is as true for class and economic differences as it is for racial or ethnic difference. Urban land and housing markets intersect with employment markets and transport infrastructure, amongst other factors, to produce higher- and lower-rent areas, with local services and retail catering to these segmented populations. Economic segregation in this way makes it possible for cities to support populations that are highly differentiated in class terms – including the income extremes that routinely structure cities as sites of higher inequality. Indeed these forms of spatial and market segmentation, Glaeser and his colleagues (2008: 9) suggest – not altogether implausibly, if somewhat ironically – means that living in a city such as New York 'may be much more expensive for a relatively rich person than it is for a relatively poor person'.

Notwithstanding the distressed rich struggling with exorbitant rents, over-priced restaurants and extortionate valet parking, the notion of 'choice' tends to be less powerful – or at least more one-sided – in accounting for economic segregation than it is for racial or ethnic divides. Paul Cheshire (2007: ix) expresses the economic logic very clearly: the various positive and negative 'characteristics of neighbourhoods are effectively capitalized in house prices and rents' such that it simply 'costs more to live in nicer neighbourhoods'. It follows that '[t]he poor do not choose to live in areas with higher crime rates and worse pollution: they cannot afford not to. That is, the incomes of people determine the character of the neighbourhood they can afford to live in. The problem is poverty, not where poor people live.' It is difficult to argue with the central point – on which orthodox economists and Marxists ones are likely to be in full accord. However, poverty is a relative concept, as is urban deprivation. The condition of the urban poor is not a universal fact, and degrees of difference between rich and poor are subject to a range of extremes in different cities. Moreover, the spatial environments of urban poverty, while they do not determine the economic conditions of their inhabitants, can do much to entrench, deepen and reproduce them. Housing markets are a primary, but they are not the only, factor at work in shaping economic inequalities in cities; and the solution to 'higher crime rates and worse pollution' is not simply the individual strategy of getting richer and moving somewhere *nicer*. The incomes of people determine the character of the neighbourhood they live in to a significant degree, but this character is influenced in important ways by public and collective provision and intervention. It may be that poorer neighbourhoods tend to have higher rates of crime and victimization, for instance, but there is no good reason – outside a total market model – why they should have worse policing services. Similarly, house prices and rents will reflect levels of pollution in the local environment, but environmental regulations and protections do not (or should not) simply reflect ability to pay.

    Economic enclaves clearly provide certain benefits to the affluent – including a sense of security, identification and spatial distinction – but can also be seen to provide resources of solidarity and opportunity for the residents of lower-income neighbourhoods. Economic segregation accommodates difference in allowing people on low incomes to live in the cities in which they grew up, where they work or simply where they want to be. It offers certain 'welfare benefits' in the form of relatively more affordable housing, collective and consumer services, opportunities for employment and enterprise in lower-value markets, and can generate spatial solidarities around neighbourhood and economic identities, whether this is understood in terms of 'turf', 'territory' or 'community'. Segregration can also be seen to make divided cities more 'liveable' in a psychological sense, with certain analysts suggesting that economic inequality is experienced more negatively when the better-off live in closer proximity – and on fuller display – to those who are doing it harder (Luttmer 2005). Such a model of class consolidation, however, needs to be set alongside the way that poorer neighbourhoods offer cheaper points of entry for urban incomers, creating neighbourhood instability and higher rates of population churn. While poorer areas may in this way play a key functional role in the wider ecology of the city, they themselves are often subject to the corrosive effects of population instability and weaker patterns of long-term residential and commercial investment.

Massey and Denton's dimensions of segregation are as relevant to the distribution of higher- and lower-income groups across the city as they are to groups marked by racial or ethnic difference. In a city such as London, for instance, histories of public housing have made for a certain degree of both *evenness* and *exposure* in the spatial organization of different income groups. The most affluent areas contain a share of social rented housing, although this stock has been eroded by the gradual privatization of public housing since the 1980s. Poorer neighbourhoods have tended to be more consolidated in income or class terms – a condition that in its turn has been eroded over the same time period by widening effects of gentrification. It is important to note that spatial 'exposure' does not equate in any simple way to social encounter; in an urban landscape such as this, rich and poor may live in relatively close proximity while preserving sharp degrees of social distance. Such an effect is even more pronounced in cities with embedded histories of segregation. In her analysis of Muizenberg, a desegregating area in Cape Town, Charlotte Lemanski (2006a) explores the ways in which policies and processes of residential desegregation may work to 'mask' enduring patterns of social segregation. While neighbourhood change in the post-apartheid era has produced a racial and class mix in the area, she suggests there is more limited sharing of local facilities, desegregation of civic institutions or social interaction across lines of class and race.

Other dimensions of segregation are also relevant to thinking about economic divisions in the city. Degrees of *concentration* vary across different urban contexts. Poorer populations in many cities tend to live at higher densities, and at super-densities in urban slum conditions. The rich, however – as much as they may be associated with deconcentrated living, especially on urban peripheries – are not necessarily averse to living at relatively high density, as suggested by the density peaks of Manhattan's Upper East Side or the central areas of west London (Burdett et al. 2005). Similarly the *centralization* of

lower-income groups in inner cities, which had been a long-standing
trend in older European and North American conurbations as well as
in the central slum areas of cities such as São Paulo or Delhi, has been
diluted in many urban contexts by the hollowing-out of inner cities
in 'advanced' urban economies as a result of capital and employment
flight from the 1970s, followed by the in-migration of gentrifying
households from the 1980s; and by more aggressive programmes of
slum clearance in the centres of developing cities. In other contexts,
the spatial experience of the urban poor is one of decentralization – as
evident in the post-apartheid geography of a city such as Cape Town,
with its affluent, white central suburbs and poor, black periphery
(Lemanski 2006a; Turok 2001), or in the peripheral slums of many
cities created by rural–urban migrations and land invasions. Finally,
lower-income groups are subject to various patterns of *clustering*
across urban environments: from the cheek-by-jowl character of some
US cities that set working- and upper-middle class neighbourhoods
alongside each other (the border at 96th Street between Harlem and
the Upper East Side long marked a stark racial and income divide,
now gradually weakening through white in-migration and gentrification to the north of the border), to the clustering of poverty 'clumps'
across extended areas in Britain's former industrial cities and in inner
East London (including a 'single uninterrupted stretch of adjacent
poverty areas' in Liverpool with a population of more than a quarter
of a million people – see Glennerster at al. 1999).

At the other end of the income scale, the concentration of affluence
and forms of elite enclaving produces distinctive patterns of economic segregation around concentrated spaces of wealth. Economic
segregation conventionally has been associated with the ghettoization
or marginalization of the poor, but the distended relations of income
inequality that many cities now support is spatially reflected in the
advancing segregation of the rich. Where high-income neighbourhoods become increasingly homogeneous in terms of both rental
values and urban amenities; where they are physically secured by
gates or manually secured by private guards; where elite enclaves are
inaccessible not only to lower-income residents but also to lower-
income consumers or even pedestrians: under such conditions, the
spatial arrangement of exclusion reflects but also intensifies social and
civic segregation. Writing of the spatial and economic trends shaping
US cities by the end of the twentieth century, Douglas Massey and
Mary Fischer (2003:2) suggest that 'the simultaneous occurrence
of rising socioeconomic inequality and growing class segregation
portends a society that is divided not only geographically, but also

socially and politically as well.' They describe this as a 'pulling apart' of rich and poor in these cities, where economic segregation is both the spatial expression of, and the spatial stimulus for, dissociation and dis-identification across physical and socio-economic distance.

There are, as we have seen, important arguments for degrees of economic segregation, where this ensures access to cheaper housing, opportunities for small-scale and independent enterprise, forms of collective provision, and defensive or protective identities around class and locality. It would be difficult to claim in any sustained way that these pluses outweigh the minuses of poorer housing and environmental conditions, residential instability and population churn, concentrated unemployment and spatial discrimination, poor transport access and urban service provision; but they do suggest that the 'do without' parts of the city do not simply constitute an urban *problem* (Mumford 1938: 249). The increasing segregation of the rich, however, may represent a different kind of socio-spatial problem. Segregation works spatially to compound the material effects of relative deprivation when it entrenches inequities in access to jobs, transport and other urban services, and environmental and cultural amenities. In a social and political sense, moreover, segregation may be seen to promote urban relations of mistrust, hostility and fear; to fragment the social base for and political legitimacy of collective provision; and to reinforce social exclusion or economic marginalization by spatial distance (see Atkinson 2006: 830). The separation of the over-advantaged parts of the city from the 'do without' areas simply tends to make 'privilege invisible to the privileged' (Young 1999: 242). This is not to suggest that the purpose of desegregation is to raise the social consciousness of the well-off, but it is to point to the way that spatial separation can normalize political disengagement, civil disregard and social abandonment. The consolidation of elite *sinks* in the city is a key spatial element of what Ash Amin (2012) has described as a 'cauterized society' in which the socio-economic lives of the over-privileged are increasingly insulated from those of the ordinary as well as the precarious.

In the context of deepening inequalities in the United States in the 1990s, the political thinker Iris Marion Young (1999: 237) wrote of 'an ideal of desegregation' that she called 'living together-in-difference'. This is an ideal which 'assumes that people dwell together in a common polity but are locally differentiated into group affinities. [It] both affirms such group affinity and calls for equality of life chances across space.' As anodyne as a formulation such as 'together-in-difference' might sound, the negative strength of Young's position is that it is an argument for degrees of desegregation rather than a positive claim for integration; her interest is in the formation of urban policy that recognizes realities of spatial and social differentiation, and so 'focuses more on the movement of resources than people' (Young 1999: 248). In this spatial logic, 'moving resources to people is at least as important as moving people to resources' (Young 1999: 237). Such an account, to be sure, may be a simple argument for spatial redistribution, but one that unsettles certain assumptions regarding impacted spaces of urban deprivation, or the spatial immobility of under-privileged social groups; assumptions that are especially tenacious in an American context where spatial separations have endured in spite of legal desegregations, and where social and spatial mobility are so closely associated. Housing markets sort urban populations along class lines, and within the constraints of these markets urban populations may 'sort' themselves along cultural or ethnic lines. These forms of separation harden into lines of inequality when they correspond – as they too often do – to inequities in urban services and provision; when low-income and minority neighbourhoods get worse schools, poorer open spaces, inferior transport, sparser or more punitive policing, or patchier health services. Desegregating hard-to-reach resources, in this context, may be a more important consideration for urban politics than desegregating 'hard-to-reach' – or hard-to-budge – social groups.

Elite sinks: gentrification, gating, enclaves

I have suggested that contemporary patterns of urban inequality are to be explained not only in terms of large low-income populations in cities, but also in terms of increasing concentrations of (increasingly extreme) wealth. The spatial geography of urban affluence, likewise, is characterized not simply by the segregation of the poor, but also by the sequestration of the rich. This 'bifurcated' model of urban polarization produces ghetto effects at both ends of the income spectrum (Atkinson and Blandy 2005: 180; see also Marcuse 1997). While there may be debate over the extent to which the segregation of poor or minority populations can be understood as 'voluntary', there is no such question over the spatial choices of the rich. Ideals of the city as a forcing ground for socio-economic diversity are troubled by growing trends towards separatism and secession on the part of higher-income groups. Rowland Atkinson (2006) describes these forms of elite withdrawal in terms of class strategies of *insulation*, *incubation* and *incarceration*. There are different degrees of separation at work here. At its most stark, the better-off occupy highly distinct and heavily secured territories of the city, but growing income inequality is not only played out in terms of heavily marked patterns of socio-spatial polarization. In many urban contexts, such a 'pulling apart' occurs at a finer scale through the maintenance of social distance within proximate spaces.

Atkinson's first two categories – insulation and incubation – in this sense can be seen as strategies to establish and preserve socio-spatial distinction under conditions of relative mix. In gentrifying areas, for instance, different income groups may live in close physical proximity but maintain clear degrees of social distance and occupy quite different social and economic worlds. Tim Butler's work on gentrifying areas of London speaks to these localized patterns of 'pulling apart' which can be seen to *insulate* more affluent residents against the less desirable aspects of their neighbourhoods, or to *incubate* certain locales as safe havens for middle-class investment and attachment. Both tactics work through forms of 'class clustering' based on shared consumption, housing and neighbourhood preferences (see Butler 2007). Butler highlights, for example, the educational strategies of middle-class parents who choose to send their children to 'better' schools (including private schools) outside their local areas, or alternatively choose residential locations at a cost premium in the catchment areas of the most popular local schools (Butler 2003; Hamnett and Butler 2011; see also Bridge 2006). These spatial strategies around residential and educational choice suggest 'an increasingly polarized social structure in which the middle classes and their children inhabit entirely separate social spaces from other, and more disadvantaged, groups' (Butler 2003: 2469), creating class 'bubbles' inside relatively mixed urban spaces. Such dual strategies – of residence and schooling – suggest that socio-spatial advantage is secured through interlinked patterns of fixity and mobility (Rérat and Lees 2011); whether whole households make strategic moves into more attractive school catchments, or children move on a daily basis to access better schools at a distance. The daily out-migration of children represents a middle-class 'disinvestment' – social capital flight, if you will – from local areas and their schools; in contrast, where middle-class households monopolize the most attractive school catchments, investments of economic and social capital are concentrated in the more desirable parts of local areas within an insulated and largely middle-class mono-culture.

Exercising power over position, especially in striated inner urban

housing markets, in this sense also requires the management of proximity. 'Urban-seeking' gentrifiers who choose attractive locational
positions in inner city neighbourhoods may prove to be 'urban-
fleeing' when it comes to educational choices for their children. This
means negotiating fixity and mobility in terms either of household
relocations to the most desirable local catchments (and the payment
of the associated real estate premiums), or of daily out-migrations
to more desirable schools at a distance. Such a pattern exemplifies
Patrick Rérat and Loretta Lees' (2011) argument that the effective deployment of 'spatial capital' involves a certain preferential
command over space: the ability to make spatial choices in terms
of both fixed locations *and* market mobilities; to both stay and go;
to organize one's spatial life more or less as one chooses. Similarly,
Jo Foord (2010: 60) writes of the spatial 'trade-offs' more affluent
residents are able to make in an inner London neighbourhood that
has been socially mixed through gentrification: '[W]hile the ability to
travel out of Clerkenwell makes it possible for most residents to live
in this dense mixed-use environment, many who are unable to travel
find themselves trapped in an area with limited resources and potentially a declining quality of life.' The capacity, both material and cultural, to adopt these kinds of spatial strategies is of course an index
of social power, and is exemplified and at the same time obscured
by an educational policy rhetoric of parental 'choice' in which some
parents are simply much more equal than others (see Butler and
Hamnett 2010). It suggests a 'pulling apart' of higher- and lower-
income groups that takes a less stark form than clear socio-economic
(and racio-economic) segregation, working instead through micro-
segregations in what otherwise appears as shared local space.

Thinking about the management of proximity in this way sheds
light on the 're-sorting' of urban neighbourhoods through local
housing and education markets. This re-sorting occurs alongside a
layering of gentrifying neighbourhoods in which higher- and lower-
income residents do not necessarily compete over the same housing
stock (in areas that retain significant levels of public housing, for
example, or significant levels of new-build or conversion stock for
middle-class investment), but in which different groups do compete
over places of consumption (local pubs, parks and shops), local
services (especially education) and the more symbolic ownership of
local space. Foord (2010: 60) notes that 'high tolerance of others
is only possible where households have significant economic and
social resources'. The urban ecology of inequality is a complex
and often small-grained one in which relations of proximity must

be managed and fine social distances maintained in contexts of unwanted or uncomfortable adjacency (see also Chaskin and Joseph 2013; Davidson 2010). It is in these ways that '*structures of privilege and spatial advantage* based on differential wealth and power' (Soja 2010: 48, italics in original) are threaded through the everyday fabric of cities, as well as being marked in property boundaries or cruder lines of segregation. Some of this will show up as socio-economic distributions across census tracts, but much of it has to do with the ordinary occupation and disposition over 'unmarked' space, in patterns of positionality and mobility that are much harder to track in quantitative ways. 'In short,' as Rowland Atkinson and John Flint (2004: 876) put it, 'segregation needs to be considered both in its daily dynamism as well as its static residential manifestations.'

The social, economic and spatial capacities displayed by more privileged groups in insulating themselves from the 'do without' parts of their own neighbourhoods, or in incubating safe havens for middle-class consumption, can of course be traded for blunter instruments of spatial separation. Atkinson's third category of elite withdrawal – incarceration – suggests a more frontal strategy for demarcating the urban geographies of rich and poor. In the mid-1990s, Teresa Caldeira (1996: 303) wrote of the development of fortified enclaves as portending a 'new model of spatial segregation', one closely linked to the fear of violence in cities such as São Paulo or Los Angeles (see also Caldeira 2000, 2011). In the period since, walling and gating have become standard gestures of urban separation, at times still linked to perceptions of crime (or to paranoia over difference), but always marking lines of economic distinction and social distance in the form of impermeable physical borders.

The notion of the 'gated' enclave translates into a number of different built typologies and legal forms. These range from the secured-entry building (augmented to various degrees by closed-circuit surveillance, security guards, underground parking, etc.) to the walled housing development to the fully privatized and fortified neighbourhood or 'security village' (Atkinson and Blandy 2005; Grant and Mittelsteadt 2004; Landman 2004; Lemanski et al. 2008; Low 2003; Webster et al. 2002). As Caldeira's early work suggests, the fortified enclave as a new international style has migrated between low- and high-income cities, and between urban contexts of very high and relatively low degrees of inequality. If the extreme version of the gated development (São Paulo or Johannesburg, say) sought to secure its inhabitants against fears of gun crime, home invasion, carjackings or kidnappings – and the exemplary version in US cities crystallized a more abstract 'discourse of urban fear' encoding insecurities around class and racial diversity (Low 2001) – its derivative versions may have less to do with any actual or perceived risk of serious crime than with the anti-urban 'desire to avoid day-to-day incivilities and random social contact' (Atkinson and Flint 2004: 880).

The impulse to enclave, then, is not a simple index of levels of violence, crime and insecurity in different cities, but may be a more straightforward indicator of the degrees of 'mixophobia' among more affluent segments of urban populations (Bauman 2003). Low (2001: 47) points to the strong 'psychological lure of defended space'; as this is built into locked-down housing and neighbourhood typologies, the urban neighbourhood is re-imagined as one big panic room. These defensive typologies form a critical part of the 'architectural policing' (Davis 1990: 223) of social and economic divisions in contemporary cities. The spatial patterning of incarcerated affluence, insulated advantage, residual mix and 'neighborhoods of urban relegation' (Wacquant 2008) produces fragmented urban morphologies around defended lines of social difference, economic differentiation and cultural distinction.

Diversity by design: social mix and spatial form

Social separation is designed into the fabric of cities by a variety of means: the sorting of space by urban land markets, legal segregations and informal exclusions, socio-cultural enclaving and defended spaces of elite withdrawal. But is it also possible to 'design in' social and economic diversity through more coordinated engineering of the 'interrelations between urban forms and human objectives' in cities (Lynch and Rodwin 1958: 201)? A range of urban policies in different national contexts have sought to produce such diversity effects through spatial strategies aiming to protect, re-instate or introduce varieties of mix into urban neighbourhoods, notably through affordable housing and mixed-tenure initiatives (Arthurson 2002; Berube 2005; Bridge et al. 2011; Cheshire 2007; Coupland 1997; Fainstein 2005; Gilmour 2012; Holmes 2006; Popkin et al. 2004; Roberts 2007; Tunstall 2003; Uitermark 2003; Wood 2003). At a basic level, measures such as the 'HOPE VI' programme or 'Moving to Opportunity' experiments in US cities, or 'mixed communities' policies in the United Kingdom, have sought to break up concentrations of poverty around specific urban neighbourhoods or housing projects, drawing on a range of tactics, including household relocations, estate renewal and tenure diversification, new-build mixed-tenure housing, planning targets or quotas for affordable housing, as well as public subsidies for housing vouchers, 'intermediate' tenures, shared ownership schemes and other quasi-market tenure forms.

The political rationale for such interventions turns around the perceived social and economic effects of mono-tenure (i.e. social housing) estates – variously linked to problems of joblessness and skills deficiencies, lack of economic opportunity, worse health outcomes, higher levels of crime and victimization, educational failure, family breakdown, poor environmental quality and sub-standard housing conditions. The other side of such critiques is a more boosterish argument for the advantages of urban mix – including economic vitality and opportunity, broader social inclusion, improved housing and urban environments, and a kind of social upgrading through aspirational uplift. Urban 'mix' is generally defined in functional as well as social terms, emphasizing the value of mixes of different uses as well as of different kinds of people in estates, streets and neighbourhoods. Policy discourses and programmes in this context raise a series of questions regarding the production of urban 'mix'. At what scale should social or functional mix obtain? The building? The block? The street? The neighbourhood? Which population should be mixed? Residential? Commercial? Working? All of them? What relation, if any, exists between degrees of spatial mix and forms of social interaction? And whose interests are served by the construction of social mix?

It is not clear, after decades of research, argument and policy, that any of these questions have been resolved in any definitive way. Debates over diversity highlight the extent to which the design of cities is always a political as well as a physical act. Emily Talen (2006) is clear about these normative underpinnings in outlining the case for urban diversity to be made on the grounds of place vitality, economic health, social equity and urban sustainability. A diversity of functions and uses produces more active and heavily used spaces offering wider choice for various users; supports a range of economic enterprises at different scales; fosters economic innovation and creative spill-overs; provides more equal access to urban opportunities and amenities for different groups, as well as enhancing possibilities for social encounter and interaction; and makes for more efficient land use by mixing functions and reducing transport distances. While such outcomes may be impossible to engineer, design and planning might help enable the conditions for them through the use of different housing

typologies and sizes, the design of urban amenities for diverse populations, the integration of commercial, residential, civic and cultural
functions at accessible urban scales and grains, and the creation of
non-exclusionary public spaces that accommodate differences in
shared space. In truth, the elements of designing for diversity are
fairly well known – the larger problem is how to support or maintain
a diversity of users in such spaces, given that a 'diversity premium' on
varied and vital parts of the city so often leads to processes of incubation and colonization by more privileged socio-economic groups.
If approaches to urban diversity are driven by critiques of impacted
deprivation or ghettoization on one side, they are threatened by risks
of gentrification on the other.

Indeed, it can be argued that market-led processes have been more
effective in diversifying urban areas over recent decades than any
number of well-intentioned government programmes. The restructuring of low-rent areas through colonization by higher-income
residents has had far more significant impacts on geographies of
socio-economic diversity than public programmes to diversify and
re-distribute tenures and incomes through housing interventions.
Steve Belmont (2002: 339) makes the case for gentrification with
rare clarity: 'Until cities no longer house inordinate numbers of
low-income households,' he writes, 'the pursuit of income diversity
should focus on the gentrification of distressed neighborhoods rather
than the introduction of poverty to middle-class neighborhoods.' He
goes on to argue that urban policy-makers should be more concerned
with attracting middle-class incomers to low-income areas than with
redistributing poorer households. Such a position underlines the fact
that gentrification is not simply a 'market' effect, given the extent to
which it is facilitated by relaxations in zoning and planning regulations or abolition of rent controls, or fostered by public interventions
in transport provision, urban amenities or environmental services.
The distinction between market-led and state-driven diversification
is difficult to sustain in practice: a key measure to 'diversify' tenure in
British cities, for example, was the Thatcher government's institution
in 1980 of the right for public housing tenants to buy their properties,
a policy that has seen the transfer of up to three million homes from
public to private ownership in the three decades since. Similarly,
Gary Bridge, Tim Butler and Loretta Lees (2011) argue that more
recent UK policies aiming to introduce social and tenure mix
through estate renewal and affordable housing targets for new development can be seen as a form of 'gentrification by stealth', producing
housing environments that are oriented to the needs and preferences

of higher-income owner-occupiers, and reinforcing the displacement of lower-income residents and users from spaces of urban regeneration (see also Davidson 2008; Lees 2008). Any volume of housing produced at affordable rents in mixed-tenure developments may be outweighed by the market effects such renewal efforts have on the larger stock of lower-rent housing in the local area, particularly in the private rental and ownership sectors, which falls outside the purview of policy controls and affordability targets and becomes vulnerable to rent-gap pressures. Alongside these pressures for indirect displacement, and even where groups do not compete for housing, more everyday displacements occur in public and consumption spaces, in the provision of social services and in the symbolic ownership of local territories. Through forms of economic and environmental upgrading, interventions aiming to promote social mix in these ways are often implicated in the 'unmixing' of the city.

The interaction of real estate effects and public policies in this field – in relation to both gentrification and policy-led renewal – makes it difficult and often erroneous to separate out the sortings of the market from the spatial programmes of the state. In like manner, it can be hard to differentiate in very clear ways between 'designed' and 'unplanned' mixed income areas (Kleit 2005), given the unplanned consequences of policy design, on one side, and the purposeful strategies of developers, realtors and gentrifiers, on the other. These interrelations between public and private designs and objectives are basic to the making of cities and the organization of socio-economic differences across space. The enabling role of city governments and planning authorities is especially pronounced in the 'sharp-edged forms and processes of socio-spatial upgrading' characteristic of gentrification processes in developing and transitional cities (Harris 2008: 2423 – Harris is referring to the case of Mumbai in particular; see also Badyina and Golubchikov 2005, on Moscow; He 2007, 2010, on Shanghai; Lopez-Morales 2011, on Santiago de Chile; Visser and Kotze 2008, on Cape Town). The modes of 'mega-gentrification' and 'mega-displacement' that are at work in slum clearances and household relocations in cities such as Mumbai or Shanghai operate at a vastly different scale from even the most revanchist programmes of class reclamation in the cities of the global north (Lees 2012: 164). This 'new urban colonialism' (Atkinson and Bridge 2005) works through a combination of permissive and aggressive state strategies for the re-making of space around increasingly elite private interests.

Below the scale of visibility of large state-led clearances, or the colonizations of big capital in major urban redevelopments, more local and uneven patterns of mixing and unmixing take place. Charlotte Lemanski (forthcoming) describes the mutated or 'hybrid' form of gentrification configured by the movement of certain middle-income households into 'slum' areas in South African cities as they are priced out of more formal property markets (see also Fawaz 2009, for the case of Beirut). She argues that these kinds of 'downward raiding' in Southern cities are rarely analysed in terms of gentrification, but the socio-spatial effects of such incursions are comparable. How far the concept of gentrification can or should stretch to take in the various scales and strategies of neighbourhood restructuring, housing renewal, tenure mixing, state-led slum clearance, real estate development, social upgrading and downward raiding in different urban contexts is open to debate (see Butler 2007; Lees 2012), but these processes and settings point to the many ways in which socio-economic 'diversity' is *designed in* to cities through varying 'inter-relations between urban forms and human objectives', to use Kevin Lynch and Lloyd Rodwin's terms.

Gating is often seen as the antithesis of principles of urban diversity, yet there is a case to be made for enclave urbanism as a basis for securing socio-economic mix at both neighbourhood and city scales. When set against trends for elite withdrawal and middle-class suburbanization, it is arguable that gated developments within the city can mitigate spatial segregation *through* the device of the wall. In the context of Santiago de Chile, for example, Rodrigo Salcedo and Alvaro Torres (2004: 28) contend that 'gated communities reduce the scale of segregation in the city, acting as a semi-open border between different social groups.' While it may be difficult to argue for this sort of 'good gating' on the grounds of social cohesion or inter-action (see Lemanski 2006b), there is a more basic case to be made that such housing geographies retain middle-class investments within the city, creating jobs and economic demand for services. While most urbanists might want to see such diversity effects produced in a context of permeable neighbourhoods and open borders, in cities of extremes it may be that defended territories such as these are a pragmatic means of preserving some degree of economic and social mix in contexts where the alternative is spatial and economic segregation at greater scales and across larger distances. In such settings, of course, 'it is uncertain what contiguities in place actually mean. . . . What does it mean for particular kinds of built and social environments to be "next to each other", enjoined in a common designation of being part of the same city or urban region?' (Simone 2011: 358). The meanings of contiguity will depend on its socio-spatial contexts, but these different forms of contiguity, co-location and colonization suggest that there is more than one way to diversify a city.

Conclusion

Henri Lefebvre saw segregation as the spatial 'caricature' of difference. It interposes separation where the category of difference supposes a relationship. 'When we speak of difference,' he wrote, 'we speak of relationships, and therefore proximity relations that are conceived and perceived' (Lefebvre 2003 [1970]: 13). In referring to these proximity relations as both 'conceived and perceived', Lefebvre is pointing to the way that they are both *designed* in cities – by planners, architects, policy-makers – and *lived* in cities as experiential realities. The ways in which relationships of difference are designed and lived are put under serious pressure given the 'scale and intensity of disconnection' in contemporary cities characterized by 'super-diversity' and 'mega-gentrification' (Amin 2006: 1015; Lees 2012; Vertovec 2007). Many cities today exist in a fraught space between the ordinary diversity of 'mongrel cities' (Sandercock 2013) and the divisions and disorder of the 'feral city' of paranoid urbanism (Graham 2007: 122). Inequality and diversity produce edge conditions in the city, at times as lines of segregation, or through the brute fact of defensive walls. But the stark conception and violent perception of these edge conditions can belie the many ordinary border crossings that take place in everyday urban life; the various kinds of 'trespassing' that the interplay of spatial contiguity and social difference entails (Simone 2011: 358; see also Sennett 2011).

Economic inequality and social distinction have material consequences, carving out the city as a geography of division and difference. But these urban spaces in turn are consequential for the reproduction of inequity, the reinforcing of social distance, the stunting of life chances. The accident of geography *can* come to be a kind of social fate, as poverty, crime or environmental blight stick doggedly over time to poor, unsafe or degraded spaces. This sticky geography of economic and social injustice consigns certain bodies to certain places, and then makes it hard for them to get out. In such a context, desegregation might well be necessary for attempts to redress urban inequality, but it is not in itself a sufficient condition for the mediation of race and class inequalities through social interaction or spatial commonality. Economic inequality and social power are reproduced not only through formal property divisions and entitlements, but also through more ordinary and minor practices of occupying space, and the management of social proximity and distance. Sharp economic divisions and deep social distance can occur in contexts of close spatial proximity, and partly are reinforced through the ways quite local spaces are taken, marked and defended. The small scale of spatial inequities runs below the larger 'ecology of inequality' that has emerged since the latter decades of the twentieth century (see Fischer and Massey 2000; Massey 1996; Massey et al. 2009; cf. Gans 2010). The 'pulling apart spatially' of rich and poor can be taken to refer not only to cruder patterns of socio-spatial polarization but also to the maintenance of extreme social distance within proximate spaces.

Andriyivskyy Descent, Kiev, 2011.

4

The Contradictions of Informality

Informal urbanism is perhaps the clearest example of city-making as an ordinary practice. The ways in which people make and re-make their cities through informal processes and in unauthorized spaces exemplify the practice of city design, understood in terms of the many 'interrelations between urban forms and human objectives' (Lynch and Rodwin 1958: 201). Accelerated processes of urbanization in the twenty-first century, as we have seen, are largely concentrated in cities in developing countries, and the bulk of these new urban denizens are living in informal or illegal developments. The argument in this chapter, however, is that informality should not only be equated with practices of 'urbanization from below'. Rather, processes and practices of informality are a systemic feature of rich and poor world cities, and numerous spatial claims and formal outcomes are the effects of powerful modes of informality 'from above'. The discussion that follows explores these interactions between legitimized and de-legitimized forms of urban informality. It explores some of the contradictions of informality in respect of the productive and corrosive dimensions of informal urbanism; the capacities of unofficial and extra-legal practices to meet urban needs, organize urban systems and shape the city in inventive ways, as well as to exploit urban inequalities and entrench urban power.

The urban world as jerry-built

My friend in Egypt says to me: 'People come to Cairo thinking they're going to see the past, and they find the future.' Here, the future of the city has already taken shape. In Cairo, millions of people live with only the most elemental condition of settlement: bare shelter. No power, no streets or sewerage, no water. In the centre of the city is the carcass of the Paris of the east. Boulevards, apartment buildings, squares and circuses. Predicting the urban future is a fool's game; planning for it has come to be seen as an hubristic error. Yet in old cities such as this, the future of the city has already arrived.

The future of Istanbul was America. Glassy high-rises have gone up, apparently randomly, always speculatively and often illegally. These high-end squatters have made a ramshackle big end of town, including the tallest residential tower in Europe, inaugurated in 2011 after various delays – whether by the credit crisis or some more local difficulty is unclear.

On the West Bank and in East Jerusalem, over half a million Israeli settlers live in houses built on territory illegally occupied under the terms of the Fourth Geneva Convention. In adjacent urban territories, many more Palestinians live in decades-old refugee settlements that have become embedded elements of urban morphology. In 2012, HSBC bank was sued in US courts for 'illegally transferring monies' for the purchase of holiday homes in Northern Cyprus, in the knowledge that the underlying land titles were untenable because the occupying Turkish Republic of North Cyprus does not have sovereign power to issue them.

In West London, a former military barracks is redeveloped as the city's most expensive residential site. Acquired by the property investment arm of Qatar's sovereign wealth fund at the 2007 peak of the real estate market for a sum just short of £1 billion, the developers planned a scheme for 552 'modernist' flats. In 2009, the Prince of Wales wrote to the Qatari prime minister (the emir's cousin) regretting the design, followed by tea with the emir himself, and meetings with the city's deputy mayor and a local planning official. The scheme was withdrawn, relevant emails were deleted, a court case for breach of contract ensued, and a new set of designers eventually was engaged.

Whether in terms of subsistence urbanism in the poorest urban neighbourhoods, the knock-ups of opportunistic developers, the colonization and commoditization of occupied lands, the impacted spaces of refugee settlement, the grey economy of major banks or the off-the-record interventions of elites, cities get made through different degrees and kinds of informality. Informality is a category that reverses the usual colonialism of the urban imagination. It has travelled across the old geographies of urban power – from global south to global north, from margin to centre, from periphery to core. At the broad scale, this is due to the fact that the major plot-line in the big story of contemporary urbanization is one of informality. In terms of both the material making of cities and the social organization of urban economies, most of the rapid urban growth of the early twenty-first century is happening informally, partly or wholly beyond the reach of governments and more or less outside the shadow of the law. Even the state-driven city-building of the Chinese boom relies on the economy's extended informal sector, especially in unregistered and unprotected migrant labour. At more local scales, the persistence and prevalence of urban informality has forced a recognition of how many aspects of urban life are done off-the-books, without planning permission, in defiance or ignorance of regulations. From a sociological standpoint, informality is something of a non-concept. A lack of legal 'formality' does not mean either an absence of form or a lack of organization. Whether or not they are regulated by explicit or legal rules, socio-spatial practices and forms of human settlement are always modes of social order. Indeed tacit rules, cultural norms, social convention and routine practices can be far more effective in organizing behaviour and ordering social spaces than can legal codes. The formal and the informal may or may not be categorical distinctions in law, but they are rarely clear distinctions in social life. Moreover, these categories intersect in material ways in the ongoing re-design of urban space through improvised inhabitations, pirate augmentations, informal infills, crafty *détournements* and extra-legal usurpations.

The analysis of urban informality has usually been associated with cities in the developing world, but questions of informality are issues not only for the urban poor. The latest round in the ongoing retreat of the state has animated political debate and steered urban processes around informality (or less formality, or *anti*-formality) in many high-income economies. While the language of informality is one that now translates widely from poor- to rich-world cities, it is accented rather differently in these contexts. What once was seen as a matter of subsistence or survivalist urbanism is now more often seen as a key driver of urban growth in the developing world; whether growth is defined in economic terms, in respect of population increase or by the expansion of the city's physical footprint. Much emerging economic trade is 'unconventional', many incoming urban residents are undocumented, most new building is illegal. Informality has a rather different relationship to urban growth in many advanced capitalist cities. While working or living in the cracks between the formal and informal

Kurskaya Station, Moscow, 2011.

has long been understood as what some migrants, many chancers or a few anarchists do, informality has taken on a critical new meaning given the global downturn in growth, as governments retrench, jobs dry up and development sites lay empty. As Saskia Sassen (2005a: 85) notes, 'after a century of efforts by the regulatory state, we see an expanding informality in the global North' that should be understood as a 'systemic feature of advanced capitalism, rather than an importation of the Third World'. In parallel, 'in the major cities of the global

South, this new informality has also appeared, though it exists along-side older forms and is often obscured by them.'

Such older forms of informality are typified in the urban landscape by slum housing settlements. If this remains the dominant grammar of contemporary urbanization, however, a significant portion of new residential territories – in low- and middle-income as well as high-income cities – is the private or enclave development, secured within the existing boundaries of the city or expanding outward on the urban periphery. There are critical parallels to be drawn between the low and the high road to urban extra-legality. The informal settlement and the secessionary spaces of private development both have exceptional legal status in relation to the public city. Each entails forms of segmentation from municipal services and provision, being excluded or electively seceded from public infrastructure, including roads, services and utilities. While city governments variously respond to the low-income slum through gestures of abandonment or strategies of clearance, there are perverse incentives for allowing or even facilitating private developments, especially on urban peripher-ies, for municipalities unable to provide adequate urban services or extended urban infrastructures. The legal exceptionality of the seces-sionary enclave is legitimized, and even encouraged, while that of the slum is illegitimate, ignored or excised.

In the official parlance, 'slum areas' in cities are those where half or more of all households experience at least one of the standard dimen-sions of shelter deprivation: lack of access to improved water; lack of access to sanitation; non-durable housing; insufficient living area; or insecurity of tenure. UN-Habitat (2008) distinguishes between various degrees and patterns of slum prevalence in different cities. 'Slum cities', firstly, are urban contexts with high slum prevalence, where slum areas account for a substantial part of the urban fabric and living in slum conditions is the majority experience of urban households (as in parts of sub-Saharan Africa: see UN-Habitat 2008: 113–14). In other contexts, secondly, slum conditions are associ-ated with an 'isolated underclass' and slum areas are more clearly segregated, constituting 'highly visible and concentrated settlements in capital and large cities' (UN-Habitat 2008: 114): such a pattern is evident in a number of Central American cities, and in cities of Central and South Asia – in Pakistan, for instance, the UN agency estimates that 90 per cent of slum households live in slum areas. A slum geography of 'poverty at the margins', thirdly, is typical of coun-tries with lower overall levels of slum prevalence, where slum house-holds live in conditions of shelter deprivation in what are otherwise 'non-slum areas' (UN-Habitat cites the examples of cities in Brazil or Ghana – see 2008: 114).

A focus on slum settlement as a crucial part of the urban experience of a significant minority of city-dwellers can be an important move in decentring urban studies, rendering the concept of the modern city that has dominated the urban imagination more 'exotic' or 'strange' in itself. A number of thinkers have criticized the language of the 'slum', and have stressed the need to differentiate modes of informality in more nuanced ways (e.g., Gilbert 2007; see also Arabindoo 2011; Simon 2011). These are important arguments, but it might also be important to underline some of the commonalities in play in this context, not least to bring into the critical frame the normalized practices of 'informality from above'. Ananya Roy (2011: 225) writes that the figure of the slum has become one of the primary ways in which the Third World city has come to be 'worlded', that is to say, made recognizable within a global urban imaginary. Slum aesthetics – 'poverty pornography', as Roy puts it – have become prevalent in representations of developing world cities, but one way of responding to this critically might be to think about the work of 'worlding' in a different sense: to recognize, and to de-fetishize, the extended worlds of informality which go well beyond a discourse of 'urbanization from below' (see Jones 2011; Mbembe and Nuttall 2004; Roy and Ong 2011). This is a question, then, not only of 'worlding' the informality of the low-income and no-income city, but also of rendering the informality of the rich as part of the same urban *world*; and of asking why the informality of the rich is so often unseeable, unrecognized, legitimized.

Informality has a complicated relation to visibility. In economic settings, informality is generally imagined as invisible: under-the-counter trade, unaccounted income, clandestine workplaces. The informal sector takes a major, if largely hidden, share of urban economies, but these informal practices all take place somewhere, and they shape patterns of urban settlement and urban form in more observable ways (see Dovey and King 2011). As urban informality gets *built out*, it becomes legible in the physical order of the city, whether or not informal settlements show up on official maps. The informal city is subject to its own spatial logics. In some cases the logic is that of densification – especially the infill of tight margins or void spaces to allow settlers to live close to sites of work and livelihood. A counter-logic is that of sprawl, the spread of peripheral developments on the outskirts of the city, whether at points of arrival, along arterial road or rail networks, or in zones of exclusion at the city limits. Geographies of 'marginality' in the city can be found at the centre as much as on the edge. Matthew Gandy (2005a: 52), writing about Lagos, speaks of a kind of 'amorphous urbanism': the mutable form of a 'city that is simultaneously growing, dividing, polarizing and decaying', in which lines of formality and informality are threaded through the complex fabric of the city. In contrast to the broad classifications of slum areas by official agencies, Kim Dovey and Ross King (2011) trace some of the diverse morphologies of informal settlement: sometimes *settling* in more coherent districts, but also *inserting* laterally along waterfronts and escarpments, on easements or pavements; or *attaching* through adherences to existing structures, in backstages and enclosures – these patterns variously shaped by urban topographies, circulation routes, built forms and the interfaces between public and private infrastructures.

If, as David Harvey (2008: 37) has suggested, accelerated urbanization has re-made 'the planet as building site', it is one that is largely undocumented, casualized, cash-in-hand. The urban world is jerry-built. Informality is not only 'an idiom of urbanization' (Roy 2009: 9), but now its first language. Neither is this solely due to the growing urbanization of and by the poor. Informality, in such cities as Karachi, Istanbul or Cairo, 'has become a primary avenue for home ownership for the lower-middle and middle classes' (AlSayyad 2004: 20), as well as a significant resource for the landlord class everywhere. The jury-rigged city is necessarily an inventive one. Outsider urbanism, or urbanization from below, increasingly is celebrated for its tactical and resourceful colonization of space, its clever economies and its unruly sociability. Informal spaces become test beds for 'new ideas unfettered by law or tradition', as the environmentalist Stewart Brand has argued (2010: 40): 'Alleyways in squatter cities, for example, are a dense interplay of retail and services – one-chair barbershops and three-seat bars interspersed with the clothes racks and fruit tables.' Such make-do inventiveness might offer a model for the dead spaces of the formal city. Brand cites Jaime Lerner, former mayor of Curitiba and poster boy for urban innovation: 'Allow the informal sector to take over downtown areas after 6pm. . . . That will inject life into the city.'

Drawing the lessons of informality – 'learning from Tijiuana', as Teddy Cruz puts it (see Ouroussoff 2008) – is partly about crediting the intensity of activity and interaction that Cruz (2008) proposes as a better measure of urban density than raw count of bodies at work or sleep. Informality is productive, not only in terms of the alternative possibilities that it opens up in over-programmed and over-capitalized cities in the rich world (whether injecting life into downtowns or finding designs for living in saturated property markets and depressed labour markets), or simply because this is the way a very great number of people in this majority urban world *do* cities. 'One hesitates', Kim Dovey (2011: 351) writes, 'to call it urban planning but it is the emergent effect of millions of small-scale designs.' But one needn't be an unreconstructed Hayekian to see these countless designs on space as a mode of 'spontaneous' or improvised planning that produces the kinds of substantive goods with which formal planning systems are concerned: providing housing, workplaces and retail space, distributing resources, allocating services, supplying transport and other infrastructure (see Gordon 2012). Moreover, these practices intersect with more formal planning processes in numerous ways – as nicely suggested by Lerner's proposal that city authorities might 'allow' informality to take place at various times. 'Planning for informality' implies an approach grounded in existing urban conditions rather than ideal end-states: admitting some latitude in the regulation and licensing of business and trade that offers some protection for hawkers, street-vendors, informal market traders and hole-in-the-wall businesses; legitimizing 'irregular' (including collective) tenures so as to provide a degree of security for those living outside formal property relations, including basic protections for the shelter rights of squatters and land invaders; supporting or underwriting micro-systems of credit for those reluctant or unable to access financial institutions, or vulnerable to loan sharks and other predatory lenders; providing collective infrastructure and upgrading of existing informal supplies – of roads, sewers, drains and waste management, water and electricity – as a backbone for informal settlements; recognizing undocumented, 'invisible' and community actors as parties to participatory and deliberative processes of planning and provision (see UN-Habitat 2012b: 50–1). These strategies of planning for informality in most cases require only fairly modest government capacities, and will nearly always entail fewer economic and social costs than more frontal approaches to the informal city based on policing, evictions, demolitions and clearances.

Informality from above

Spaces of informality may be linked with practices of insurgency, of resistance, or with the 'quiet encroachment' of the poor and unre-

garded into the city (Bayat 2000; see also Roy 2009; Sanyal 2011).
But the recourse to informality is also a routine tactic of the powerful.
The rich, we know, are not given to paying tax; and the off-balance-
sheet activities of the 'advanced' financial sector have in recent years
proved a match for the murkiest underground economy. Arguments
for advocacy or equity planning are based on the idea that adjustments must be made in 'normal' planning practice to recognize the
particular needs and claims of minority or marginalized groups. The
other side of this demand is a routine kind of 'inequity planning' in
which a skewed form of planning for elites passes as formal neutrality
in the governance of space. Urban-planning-as-usual is frequently a
version of advocacy planning for the largest speculators and developers, nodded through by captive officials and occasionally eased on
its way by sympathetic politicians and princes. The routine ways in
which social power is translated into spatial outcomes through elite
strategies ranging from extra-legal settlement, appropriation and
enclosure to the gaming of planning systems are helpful in unpacking
any simple distinction between formal and informal urban processes.
Are corruption, cronyism and backhanders so 'informal' if they are a
normal and even necessary part of urban development and planning
in London or Chicago as much as in Moscow or Almaty? Manuel
Castells (1998: 2) suggests that under any sane definition of urbanism, 'the informal economy would be treated as the real economy',
given the share it takes of overall economic activity, but this argument has to cut both ways – referring not only to unconventional
trade and unregistered labour on the part of the urban poor, but
also to the embedded, indeed systematic, informality of the urban
rich.

Law is not necessarily a straightforward arbiter of which urban
claims are to be permitted or proscribed. Different urban legalities
are produced through systems of law pertaining to property and
planning, constitutional, civil or human rights, and these come into
conflict in disputes over tenure and territory. Charlotte Lemanski
and Sophie Oldfield (2009: 635) contrast the very different responses
of the South African state to land invasions and the gating of security
estates as different ways of claiming and making residential territories in the city: '[W]hile residents of both gated communities and
land invasions are driven by similar desires for a secure home and
autonomy, the state legitimates gating while prohibiting invading.'
They argue that the legal status of these spatial acts, however, is
more complex than the uneven relations of legitimacy would suggest.
The South African constitution enshrines a principle of freedom of

movement, which the authors argue is frequently negated by the enclosures of public land (including public roads) that gated estates entail. Conversely, the post-apartheid nation has been founded on a commitment to housing as a universal right – a principle that can be seen to underpin the spatial claims of the land invaders. It follows that, while the political 'vision of a unified city is thwarted by "legitimate" gated communities, the latter goal of universal housing is in fact facilitated by "illegitimate" land invasions' (Lemanski and Oldfield 2009: 635). There is therefore a deep contradiction in state responses to these territorial claims, and in the policing of 'legitimate' and 'illegitimate' land uses.

In another context of stark spatial injustice, writing on Israel/ Palestine, Oren Yiftachel (2009) speaks of the 'stratification' of informalities; the determination of which illegalities can be condoned and which cannot. This is again to draw a distinction between the 'informality of the powerful' – the extra-legality that allows for the arbitrary exercise of spatial control – and the illegality of the powerless. Your claims to space are unrecognized, undocumented and illegitimate; my occupation of space is a reality on the ground. Similarly, Ananya Roy (2004a), writing in the context of Kolkata, refers to the power to make and re-make space as lying not only in formal zoning processes but also in the summary 'unmapping' of existing land uses, property and development rights. I have suggested that informal economies are often imagined in terms of activities that happen out of sight, but it is harder to account for the ways in which entrenched spatial settlements and built forms are made invisible. Official mappings frequently excise geographies of informality: the 'spectral housing' (Appadurai 2000), 'invisible land' (Gandy 2008: 124) or 'blind' topography of the informal city (Gandy 2006b: 389; see also Dovey and King 2011). How it is that material forms, inhabited spaces and even human bodies can be rendered *unseeable* as features of the ordinary city, even while informal settlements are made visible in sensational, spectacular or violent ways – whether through the 'poverty pornography' of popular culture, or the sanitizing lens of clean-up and clear-out political programmes (Roy 2011; see also Ghertner 2010; Jones 2011)? 'Seeing like a state', in these contexts, variously can involve *not seeing* material spaces of settlement and livelihood as legitimate urban forms and morphologies, or alternatively seeing such territories solely as spaces of pathology, criminality or blight (Scott 1998). Logics of invisibility are relevant, what is more, not only for the illegal or extra-legal settlements of the urban poor; the informality of the rich frequently passes below the threshold of the visible,

North Kolkata, 2010.

whether in respect of permissive planning regimes, behind-the-scenes deal-making or blind-eye policing and financial regulation. Recourse to the rule of law in cities is or should be not only about giving the ordinary, the vulnerable and the marginal a basis for making claims upon formal institutions, both public and private, but also about protecting them against the casual prerogatives of informality from above (see Frug 2007).

As an idiom of urbanization, then, the language of informality translates only crudely from Cairo's City of the Dead or Kibera in Nairobi to Christiania in Copenhagen; between the 'informality' of Israeli settlement-building in the Occupied Territories and that of squatters in Palestinian refugee camps in Jordan or Lebanon (see Sanyal 2011); from the 'quiet encroachment of the ordinary' (Bayat 1997, 2000) to more invasive assertions in space. Herein lie some of the contradictions of informality: the dual edge of a set of economic and spatial processes that might help us both to trace the shape of 'the city yet to come' (Simone 2004a; see also Neuwirth 2007) in the contours of contemporary urbanism, and to examine the conditions that entrap too many urbanites in spaces of exception and exclusion. Ananya Roy (2009: 8) argues that 'in the ever-shifting relationship between what is legal and illegal, legitimate and illegitimate, authorized and unauthorized, informality is a state of exception and ambiguity.' In what follows I identify some aspects of this ambiguity; the series of double-plays that runs through informality and its discontents.

The contradictions of informality

Organic settlement/slum

A conventional opposition in the study of urban morphology distinguishes 'organic' patterns of settlement from planned settlements. The former are understood as flexible, responding to environmental conditions and limits, organized around habitual patterns of movement, and expressive of social solidarities, usually around family or kinship networks. One of the key defences for informal modes of settlement is their adaptive qualities, their capacity (usually born of necessity) to support different uses, as well as the physical flexibility that allows for extension and conversion. It is a line that runs from John Turner's (1976) advocacy of the 'supportive shack' over the 'oppressive house' in meeting the needs of the urban poor in Mexico City, to more recent arguments concerning the redevelopment and resettlement of Dharavi and other settlements in Mumbai, where intricate living, working and trading environments are being replaced by maladapted mass housing blocks (see Anand and Rademacher 2011; Arputhan and Patel 2007, 2008, 2010; Nijman 2008).

These are compelling arguments, and they turn on the 'ambiguity' of *porous* housing environments that in one sense support diverse uses and allow for adaptation but at the same time are physically permeable and legally vulnerable. The UN definition of the slum, we have seen, is based on five simple conditions of 'shelter deprivation': lack of access to improved water; lack of access to sanitation; non-durable housing; insufficient living area; and insecurity of tenure. There are certain things to notice here. The first is the way these measures combine environmental, physical and legal forms of insecurity – slum housing refers to both legal and material conditions. The second point to note is that these measures are hardly confined to informal housing in the poorest urban environments. Overcrowding (more than three people to a room), insecure tenure and poor housing quality are common conditions in even the wealthiest cities – a modern narrative of progress in terms of the improvement of urban housing conditions has stalled in cities such as London, Paris or New York as public housing has been privatized or degraded, and private property markets have spiralled out of the reach of those on low incomes. The UN's fifth criterion of shelter deprivation – insecurity of tenure – is hardest to define, especially where legal systems (private property, communal or traditional rights) overlap, where property and possession stake out different claims to space, where the right to housing is understood outside the letter of legal title.

Self-help/abandonment

It has become conventional to argue that the informal economy should be seen not as a residual or marginal sector, but rather as the most dynamic part of rapidly growing economies. Moreover, informal economies take the vast share of economic activity in most developing economies, and a significant – if unaccounted – share of 'organized' capitalist economies. If the concept of informality in the realm of housing is contentious, the distinction between the formal and informal economies is even harder to sustain. 'If people mattered,' Manuel Castells (1998: 2) has written, 'the informal economy would be treated as the real economy,' given the numbers it supports, the range of goods and services it provides, and its functional relationship to the 'formal' sector. Neither is formality and informality a meaningful way of differentiating 'developed' from 'developing' economies: a great part of many people's material needs in advanced economies are met through informal and largely undocumented activities in caring and domestic labour, in self-provisioning and mutual aid, doing favours and lending money, cadging, hustling, and so on. The economics of self-help has a long history among poor urban populations, and in particular those groups who experience systematic forms of economic exclusion, notably women and minorities (see Arunachalam and Landwehr 2003; Butler 2005; Portes et al. 1989; WWF 2000). But in this sense the recourse to self-help can be seen as a survivalist response to economic abandonment by groups barred from mainstream labour or credit markets through discrimination or disregard. It is the enterprise of exclusion.

The economics of self-help can serve to reinforce these kinds of exclusion, to embed social abandonment, as the self-employed and self-sufficient continue to lack access to welfare rights, reliable credit, labour protections or licences to trade, while continuing to supply goods and services – as street-vendors, petty producers, sweated labour, service providers or domestic workers – to the formal economy. Self-help forms of micro-credit offer a key instance of how livelihood strategies from developing economic contexts have travelled to become an international model for small-scale economic development. Systems of mutual and rotating credit are an important resource for those who lack access to formal institutions of finance, but then so is the loan shark – a largely 'informal' mode of financing that operates according to codes, sanctions and coercions that are often at least as effective as legally regulated credit. Hernando de Soto (2001) has convinced as many as he has antagonized with his analysis of the 'dead capital' sunk into the informal city – the latent value of housing and other physical assets in informal settlements that cannot be realized because they are not based on formal property rights, and therefore cannot be used as a basis for investment or improvement by providing collateral for a loan. A key anti-poverty strategy is thus to be found in the formalization of latent capital assets, the conversion of extra-legal housing into legal property titles (see also Mukhija 2003). Ananya Roy (2011: 229) refers to these strategies in terms of the exploitation of a kind of 'poverty capital': an alchemical conversion between poverty and capital where 'the slum, in its territorial density, represents a crucial space for bottom-billion capitalism, one where poor populations can be easily rendered visible for global capital.' And Charlotte Lemanski (2009) writes of the 'augmented informality' by which rents can be derived from the

uncertain space between property and informality, in this case referring to the backyard rentier capitalism of South African householders
who have gained housing rights through public programmes; a real
estate strategy, it might be said, exploited in South African cities
some time after London property-owners had cottoned on to the
rents to be made from their backyard sheds and lean-tos.

'Third World urban life', Asef Bayat (1997: 61) writes, 'is
characterized by a combined and continuous processes [*sic*] of informalization, integration and re-informalization.' His account inverts
the discourse of informality as one of abandonment and disempowerment: 'Popular control over contracts, regulation of time, space,
cultural activities, working life – in short, self-regulation – reclaims
significant political space from the state' (Bayat 1997: 63). In turn,
governments may have an interest in capitalizing on these extended
networks of social and welfare provision, vacating the space in which
'informal' organizations offer services and provide forms of regulation beyond the capacities of under-resourced or retreating states.
Such a politics of abandonment is a feature not only of poor or inef-
fective states, but also of the roll-back retrenchments of advanced
welfare states that cede social and public services to voluntary effort
in cities at the 'bleeding edge' of austerity policies (see Peck 2012).
Informal solutions and channels can enhance access to economic
resources, social protections and spatial securities in the face of state
abandonment and dereliction. The 'ephemeral social formations' of
the informal sector may in this context prove more durable and more
responsive than the formal agencies of the state (Simone 2001: 104).
Moreover, state formations in many urban settings do not constitute
coherent 'organized' sectors, but rather are imbricated with the fabric
of the informal in various relations of corruption, co-optation, cooperation and compensation.

Social capital/racketeering

Economic strategies of self-help frequently rely on social networks to
access resources – credit, information, land, physical capital, protection, labour, work opportunities – that cannot be accessed through
formal means. The mobilization of social capital in this way allows
things to happen – people get work, build shelter, borrow money,
stay safe, acquire goods – that would not be possible if individuals
had to rely on formal credit, consumer or labour markets, formal
private or public housing provision, police and welfare systems. The
use of social ties for economic purposes, like so much else in the

field of informality, is hardly confined to a tactics of the poor. Urban elites are probably most adept at capitalizing on their social networks outside formal systems of employment and preferment, contract and finance. Reliance on informal networks becomes more important for greater numbers of people, moreover, as increasing privatization in both low- and high-income economies sees the public services which provide some measure of social security and 'public goods which provide formal security disappear, and for the great majority informal provision of formerly public goods becomes a condition of survival' (Altvater 2005: 53). In these contexts, informal and 'passive networks' represent latent resources of solidarity, collective action and security (see Bayat 1997: 66).

That social capital has a 'dark side' is now a commonplace. Forms of closure, exclusion and coercion – the often rigid hierarchies that structure 'informal' networks – tend to bear most heavily on the poorest, for whom informal strategies are not an alternative to formal markets, contracts and institutions, but the only economic option (to spin Castells' phrase in a different way, this is the 'real economy' in money, work and land). Social networks that are not regulated by law – even more so than those that are – are subject to capture, compulsion, intimidation and stand-over tactics. As Matthew Gandy (2005a: 46–7) argues, any serious account of the informal economy cannot 'ignore its highly hierarchical, often coercive structures' or fail to 'differentiate between the mini (or even major) entrepreneurs and traders on its summits and the mass of those barely surviving at its base'. The line between an informal network and a property or protection racket can be a fine one, as property mafias (Unruh 2007) and various informal 'entrepreneurs and parasites' (Simone 2004a) fill the spaces of social and economic life evacuated, or never colonized, by the formal market or the state, and in which people may have little or no recourse to protection under the law or from (and often against) the police.

The mobilization of social ties in pursuit of economic resources draws in various kinds of 'slum entrepreneurialism' (McFarlane 2012) and everyday forms of 'deal-making' that must somehow hold good outside the underwritings of the law. Edgar Pieterse (2011: 19) describes such deal-making as a sort of low-level 'futures trading': 'the elaborate and intricate processes whereby agreements are forged to cooperate in order to achieve some modest access to cash, information, favours, goods, the possibility of a reciprocal turn in the future'. Such efforts may be fragile, relying on many links in a chain that are only shakily enforceable, if at all, and so many contingencies in respect of flows of money, information and confidence. This alternative sphere of futures trading involves limited returns for many, even as it secures lucrative returns to some, but it mobilizes resources and distributes risks outside formal channels of credit, exchange and investment which are often dammed up against the ordinary as well as the illicit actor. Pieterse notes that not only is this kind of deal-making 'endemic' in the African cities with which he is concerned; there is also 'a mimetic quality to it, because the generalized perception in the broader public sphere is that the state, and especially state intervention, is quintessentially about the art and violence of deal-making'. Informality from below, in this practical understanding, mirrors the prerogatives of informality from above, which – while it might be better dressed and better hidden – is no less vicious or corrupt.

Temporary use/insecurity

Informality is frequently associated with impermanence. Yet, while informal settlements represent what Jon Unruh (2007: 116) has called 'acutely insecure real estate', many slums, *favelas*, *chabolas* and *gecekondular* are long-standing parts of their urban environments, pre-dating and often outlasting legal housing developments. Basic legal insecurity can coexist with relative permanence. Squatters' rights – where these can be claimed – require the test, and the testimony, of time. Even the most bureaucratic planning system might allow you to leave a structure in place if you're not quite caught building it. One part of the idiom of informality that has translated more widely into current approaches to urbanism is the emphasis on temporary uses of space, urban improvisations that occupy and activate spaces of disuse or desertion. These tactics draw on the gestures of the informal and the provisional, finding spatial opportunities (for commerce, for art, for dwelling) in unlikely and unofficial sites (see Colomb 2012; Mayer 2013; Oswalt et al. 2009; Owens 2008; Tonkiss 2013). It is a mode of urbanism that recalls the spatial politics of squatting in contexts – London, Amsterdam, Copenhagen, Berlin – where long-established squats have been evicted and the practice itself is increasingly proscribed. In post-crisis and pre-Olympic London, 'meanwhile uses' were promoted by the city's mayor to animate stalled development sites and enliven leftover spaces at the same time as the national government passed legislation to make residential squatting a criminal offence. As temporary uses of disused or undeveloped sites moved from the realm of improvisation to that of policy – with design competitions to decide who gets the commission for the guerrilla garden – the actually informal becomes illegal. All cities produce spaces of disuse and dereliction, as well as opportunities for appropriation. The growing recognition of the informal, the temporary, the improvised, as a ground for urban innovation has provided a platform for amateur or un-commissioned designers to make space on the hop or on the sly or on the cheap: a kind of 'architecture without architects, *with* architects', if you will. But there is a great distance between the DIY urbanism of a resting creative class in the cities of the rich world and the subsistence strategies of get-by urbanism in the cities of the poor. New myths of marginality are generated around the aestheticization of the informal, the romance of the slum and the fascination of the urban edge (see Jones 2011; Roy 2004b, 2011; cf. Perlman 1976). There is a vast difference between pop-ups in the recessionary spaces of rich-world cities, and tear-downs in the informal settlements of the poor, but they have something in common outside the idiom of informality. Both disappear in the face of more valuable uses.

'Looseness'/disorder

If tactics of informality in the cities of the poor are often a response to the abandonment or absence of the state, in rich-world cities the idiom of informality is more often one that challenges the excessive regulation of space. In over-planned and over-programmed cities where zones of public and private use are clearly demarcated, lines of ownership and access highly secured, and different functions and conforming behaviours tightly prescribed, the room for spatial manoeuvre can be limited. Contemporary approaches to urbanism look to the potential of 'loose space' (see Franck and Stevens 2006) – those parts of the city that are not wholly legible; contingent spaces which have the capacity to support the unexpected, the provisional and the unplanned. This draws on a strain of urban thinking and urban practice that is open to the 'uses of disorder' in the city (Sennett 1970): the social value and urban freedoms afforded by unlikely encounters and unruly spaces. Kevin Lynch (1995b [1968]: 779) loved these spaces, too: 'the uncommitted complement to the system of committed uses which make up an urban region – the ambiguous places of ill-defined ownership and function'.

The legibility of space may have been over-emphasized in conventional approaches to urban design – in part owing to Lynch's own influence – but the double edge of disorder sharpens as spaces become unreadable. It is an urban skill to read situations that are uncertain or volatile, but the glamour of the margins – as this appears in urban theory – can be experienced simply as danger by those who fall on the wrong side of whichever codes (of gender, age, race, culture) are working to structure apparently 'loose' space. Social space, it is worth repeating, is always subject to some version of order, however provisional, precarious or informal. In the absence of explicit and enforceable rules, tacit rules can support different uses and bear different bodies in space, or can reinforce lines of exclusion that are no less punitive for being 'informal'.

Commonalty/invasive publicness

Spaces of informality put into question conventional distinctions between public and private in the ordering of social environments. As an ideal and in practice, the politics of informality subverts both the appropriations of private property and the spatial prerogatives of the state. It expands the range of land, things and resources that may be made *commonable* – whether through collective occupations of space, shared access to goods or illicit 'de-privatizations' of water, electricity and oil by tapping into formal networks. This is perhaps the most critical register in the idiom of informality: the reminder that there are alternative and more basic ways of organizing space and distributing urban resources than through the division between public and private. The contradictions of informality are also particularly acute here, as spaces that are shared but not owned are vulnerable to various tragedies of the commons – theft, blight, conflict, over-consumption, neglect.

The other side of commonalty is an invasive publicness that allows no space for even minimal privacies. Some fifty years ago, Charles Abrams (1964: 5) despaired that 'in the age of the atom, the disposal of human feces remains one of the stubbornly persistent problems of urban man.' It's even worse for urban woman. The enduring 'politics of shit', as Arjun Appadurai (2002: 37) has put it, is the most basic version of the challenge of living outside the legal and physical infrastructure of public and private. This is true not only in urban contexts where a significant proportion of the population lives in slum settlements with limited access to basic services, but is also evident in conflicts in rich-world cities over the provision of places for public urination and defecation for rough sleepers (Blomley 2009). How is it possible for individuals and households, especially women and their dependants (see Bapat and Agarwal 2003), to protect their privacy and their property in conditions of radical commonalty?

In such situations, 'the poor have a lower capacity to conceal their failures' – as well as their basic functions – 'making their "dignified life" more vulnerable' (Bayat 1997: 62). It must be possible, *contra* de Soto, to take both rights of privacy and rights of property seriously without invoking commoditized private property as the solution. For households living in conditions of acute overcrowding, with minimal or no sanitation, or in states of extreme shelter deprivation such as pavement-dwelling or rough sleeping, the distinction between public and private is collapsed.

Simply rendering these spaces of inhabitation 'public' is not necessarily a solution in this context. Actual sites of settlement, the political claims and material appropriations that they entail, call upon a means of thinking about spaces of occupation 'somewhere between individual private property on the one hand and the tragic commons on the other' (Rose 1994: 292; 1998). As Nicholas Blomley (2008: 316) notes, one of the effects of 'urban conflicts and struggles is that they force us to go beyond an exclusive focus on the workings of private property and to acknowledge the existence of counterposed property claims that are collective in scope'. Under such a conception of extant property rights, for example, a 'developer's right to exclude is countered by the claim that the poor have a right to not be excluded.' The embedded claims of 'property' that is occupied and appropriated, however, are difficult to articulate in face of the 'dominance of certain notions of property in which the commons, a space of not-property, is imagined as inherently disordered and dangerous' (Blomley 2004: 636).

In these dominant understandings, property 'comprises two categories . . . : private or state property. If commons appear at all, they are deemed anomalous and dysfunctional' (Blomley 2008: 317). And yet, it is possible to evidence the persistence of social actors in different contexts in developing and maintaining 'institutions resembling neither the state nor the market to govern some resource systems with reasonable degrees of success over long periods of time', including collective property regimes, productive commons, collective water and irrigation systems, and common forms of security (Ostrom 1990: 1). Commonalty, publicness and privacy exist in this field as 'zones of indistinction' (Agamben 1998: 9); spaces where any distinction between interior and exterior, inclusion and exclusion, inside and outside – certainly public and private – is hard to sustain. Such zones of indistinction may represent sites of abandonment, invisibility or social dumping; but may also be inhabited as spaces of resource, invention and refuge.

Informality and its discontents

As an idiom of urbanization, informality translates more or less well into different contexts. Against the distant background of subsistence strategies in cities marked by stark inequalities, deep exclusions and radical abandonment, using the language of the informal to think about 'creative' incursions in spaces of urban privilege can be a kind of absurdity, if not obscenity. And yet the withdrawal of the state and the selective advance of privatization produce in both developed and developing cities spaces of desertion as well as potential. The question goes beyond one of how to find spaces for informality in the tightly regulated cities of the rich world, and how to secure the urbanism of informality in the cities of the poor, to one of how different spaces of commonalty might work, in different sites, 'creatively, logistically, politically', to recall Rem Koolhaas' (1995: 961) construction. The uneven spatialities of informality and its discontents mean that those who seek to act on the city, or try to influence it, must deal with the shifting tensions between improvisation and insecurity, creativity and contingency, the provisional and the precarious.

The social and spatial forms of cities of slums, struggles to access services and infrastructure, to claim rights to city spaces and to habitation, and to formalize property rights against programmes of slum clearance and dispersal, all represent critical arenas of contemporary city-making. Informal urbanization raises issues of spatial rights, unsafe or inadequate habitation, social and economic marginalization, but is also an important site for urban mobilizations, the politics and practice of self-help, and alternative urban designs. It is, furthermore, a critical realm for the reproduction of power and privilege. The argument in this chapter has been that informality should be seen not simply as a marginal or subsistence mode of urbanism, but also as a core means of ordering urban processes at quite different scales of income and urban power 'all cities embody a mix of informality/ formality and urbanity requires informality' (Dovey 2011: 351). Between the secessions at the top and the informalities at the bottom, urban lives and urban forms are improvised and enacted in more or less durable, and more or less legal, ways. The codifications of law and the prescriptions of planning are only the most explicit, and not always the most effective, designs for organizing social life, governing physical forms and regulating spatial processes in the city.

How far this can be seen as a mode of planning or design may be open to contention, but as a powerful and prevalent form of city-making it cannot be gainsaid. Insofar as urban politics and planning fail to recognize the formative powers of informality, they become exercises at various degrees of control, proscription, exclusion and expulsion; or alternatively of complicity or abandonment. Planning and design for informality is one of the critical challenges for contemporary urbanism – and certainly for majority world urbanism. And effective strategies for responding to informality will tend towards formalization, whether these strategies are carried out by state or non-governmental actors. Legitimizing illegal tenures and licensing unconventional trade, permitting temporary structures, underwriting informal credit, extending services to the un-entitled, providing bulk infrastructure to support unofficial settlements, institutions and businesses, or including unauthorized voices in processes of representation and deliberation: all such measures respond to informality through gestures of legitimation, incorporation, entitlement and authorization. Different state and non-state actors will have varying capacities to undertake any of these measures, but the minimal social and economic costs of licensing trade, living with the jerry-built or listening to squatters – as well as the heavier political and economic costs of allowing illegal land uses or providing infrastructure – are still likely to exact fewer costs than heavy-handed efforts to clear, police or enclose spaces of informality. The relationship of formality to informality in cities is not an either/or, but a question of how to handle the mix.

5

Urban Environments: Ecology, Inequity, Mobility

What kind of environmental problem is the modern city? In current environmental debates, cities appear as both problems and solutions. Rapid and often unplanned urbanization is seen to constitute a growing environmental threat, but urban forms also offer environmental efficiencies that other patterns of human settlement do not. Urban development is resource-intensive, consumes land, produces heat and emissions effect, and places strain on both ecosystems and physical infrastructures. At the same time, economies of scale in cities create resource and energy efficiencies by concentrating larger populations of users (of transport and infrastructure, energy and other resources, buildings and unbuilt spaces) over a denser territory. Such environmental efficiencies can also promote environmental equity: the economies of scale that make collective forms of provision, consumption and reprocessing viable in turn may produce *equities* of scale, extending access to environmental resources and services of higher quality and greater reliability to more people at cheaper per capita cost. The discussion that follows is concerned with this relationship between urban form and process, environmental efficiency and environmental equity. It considers how issues of urban form – settlement patterns, built environments, transport and resource infrastructures – intersect with urban practices of production, consumption, inhabitation and mobility to structure, mediate and distribute environmental risks and outcomes. Urban environments are shaped by variable interactions between design, technology and behavior, such that efforts to mitigate environmental risks and moderate environmental outcomes are as much about steering patterns of social behaviour as they are about composing physical forms.

A core focus of the discussion is the distribution of environmental risks and costs across and between cities. Like other social systems, cities 'are capable of distributing, redistributing, exporting, and concentrating risk and losses among individuals, groups, and places through a variety of mechanisms' (Dow 1992: 430). These urban mechanisms of distribution and redistribution work more or less efficiently, and more or less equitably. The urban environment can be seen as a *distribution* problem in a number of connected senses. Firstly, it concerns the distribution of *resources* – water, energy, land, materials, open and green space, produce and food. Secondly, it bears on the distribution of *risks* and *costs*: environmental hazards, environmental degradation and environmental change – including natural and climatic hazards, the risks and costs associated with pollution, despoliation and problems of scarcity and over-use, and the effects of changing climates and ecosystems. Thirdly, urban environments are shaped by the distribution of *spaces* and *things*: networks of settlement, industry and extraction; energy, resource and transport infrastructures; sites of waste, disposal and reprocessing. Fourthly, urban environments are composed around the distribution of *people* at different scales: global patterns of land use and occupation; the relationship between cities, their hinterlands and non-urban settlements; the concentrations and distributions of people within urban areas; and movement patterns from large-scale migrations to everyday mobilities. Fifthly, urban environments involve distributions of *vulnerability*: the uneven geographies in which different people in different places are able to control, withstand, respond to and recover from environmental risks and impacts. Environmental risks in this sense are mediated not only by biophysical conditions and technical responses but also by social capacities and inequalities.

As a technical problem, approaches to environmental sustainability and unsustainability centre on certain key issues: resources, carbon, emissions and biodiversity. For urbanists, the challenge is to think about how these elements are distributed, consumed, produced and managed across complex urban systems, and through the interplay of three critical factors: design, technology and behaviour. Building and systems design, transport and infrastructure technologies, are clearly crucial to the management of urban environments. A great deal of urban environmental science is focused on creating innovative technical solutions for resourcing, engineering, designing, building and mobilizing cities in more efficient and sustainable ways. Perhaps the more complex part of the problem, however, is social behaviour. Design innovation and technological change can be easier to achieve than shifts in individual and collective behaviour. Most technical solutions to urban environmental problems must engage at some level with social practices: around patterns of residence and work, mobility and consumption, re-use and waste – both in terms of how these social practices scale up to the level of urban form, and how they are played out in routines and conventions of individual behaviour. There is an argument to be made that urban residents – used to living in dynamic and changing environments, with increased access to information and social education – may be more amenable to individual and collective behaviour change than people living in less information-dense environments. However, cities also represent sedimentations of *sunk* behaviour, as entrenched social practices are embedded in buildings and neighbourhood morphologies, street layouts and transport infrastructures, spaces of production, consumption and waste. Cities in this way are an exemplary form of the 'practico-inert', an objectified outcome of social practice that in turn conditions and is resistant to human agency (Sartre 2004 [1960]). Moreover, established distributions of environmental goods and bads work to the advantage of certain social groups, and systematically disadvantage, deprive and endanger others, in ways that provide disincentives for the most environmentally privileged to change their behaviour.

The discussion that follows begins by considering the city as a form of 'socio-nature' – a complex ecology of human, built and natural forms that distributes, concentrates and transfers resources, risks, spaces, things, people and vulnerabilities. It goes on to explore how the distribution of environmental resources and risks across this socio-natural system works to reproduce structures of social and spatial inequality. The focus here is on both the causes of environmental harms – specifically the consumption practices of a global minority and the systems of production they sustain – and their effects, which tend to have quite different spatial and social contours. It raises the question of how culpable cities are in the production and distribution of environmental bads, but also their capacity to transfer these between urban populations. While cities may perform relatively well in managing and mitigating environmental risks, their internal economies of risk are often skewed around geographies of disadvantage. The final part of the discussion considers the urban environment as a problem of distribution in terms of mobilities in the city, as a critical point of intersection between elements of urban form – transport infrastructures and patterns of land use – and social behaviour. A city's 'movement system' (Lynch 1965) is composed by the distribution and interaction of hard infrastructures and mobile bodies, in ways that shape urban environments, order everyday practices and variously reinforce or redress urban inequalities. In considering these systems of distribution – of consumption and emission, goods and risks, spaces, people and things – within and between cities, the discussion explores the intersections of design, technology and behaviour in the production of urban environments.

Urban ecologies

Cities are crucial sites for the social production of nature. While the modern city has frequently been reviled for the urban 'defacement of nature' (Mumford 1938: 252), contemporary critics are more likely to understand the city as an exemplary site of 'socio-nature' – the production and reproduction (including, at times, the despoliation) of the natural through social action and interaction. Cities are synthetic constructs that can be seen to play a central part in the *de-naturing* of environments and habitats: in debates over the human causes of climate change, after all, things don't get much more 'man-made' than a city. At the same time, as a form of human settlement, cities must at some level be understood as themselves *natural* environments – it's not entirely clear, for instance, why we would think of bee-hives, ant-hills or termite-mounds as natural forms, and not these 'superorganisms' (Park 1936: 4) that integrate human actors with other organic and inorganic matter in more or less purposive, stable and functional ways. Resource ecologies – as well as resource economies – flow through cities, and urban forms in turn help to constitute, to regulate, to enhance or degrade these systems. A critical strand of environmental thought in recent years has come to understand environmental systems in terms of the complex interaction of the natural, the technical and the social; this is also a good rubric for understanding the kind of realities that cities are. Cities are complex systems that sit within and in turn shape larger and more complex environmental systems. Viewed in this light, 'urbanization is not simply a linear distancing of human life from nature, but rather a process by which new and more complex relationships of society and nature are created' (Keil 2003: 729). Rejecting simple distinctions between the natural and the artificial, the environmental and the urban, the wild and the built, an emergent body of work has come to understand the city in terms of urban ecologies, political ecologies or urban metabolisms (see, *inter alia*, Brunner 2007; Gandy 2004; Grimm et al. 2008; Haughton and McGranahan 2006;

Heynen et al. 2006; Swyngedouw 2006; Swyngedouw and Kaika 2000).

There is a long history of the use of 'bio-analogies' to describe human societies, and these neo-organicist approaches to the city take their place in this tradition. The Chicago School sociologists were to come under heavy criticism for their use of organic metaphors to characterize the human ecology of the modern city, but in recent years biological metaphors have become prevalent in the analysis of urban settlement. The concept of 'urban metabolism' takes natural systems as a model for understanding how cities do or don't work. It emphasizes the different kinds of flows that traverse and configure urban forms: resources, weather systems, materials and commodities, emissions, people and other organisms. The keynote work in this field was Abel Wolman's (1965) essay on 'the metabolism of cities', but there are other links back to Lewis Mumford's (1956) work on the 'social ecology' of cities and their relationships of interdependency with their hinterlands, as well as to Jane Jacobs' (1961) conceptualization of the city in terms of 'organized complexity'. There are also clear antecedents in the work of Chicago School sociologists, including their explicit recourse to concepts of metabolism and ecology to understand urban forms and processes (see Burgess 1925; Park 1936; Wirth 1945). In his approach to urban political ecology, Roger Keil (2003: 726) warns that it remains 'necessary to suspend all lingering notions of Chicago-style urban or human ecology', but while these earlier accounts remain unfashionable, it is not so easy to draw a categorical distinction between the Chicago sociologists' conception of ecology and that deployed in current critical accounts. The conceptualization of human ecology in the 1920s was directly informed by developments in the natural sciences, notably in plant and animal ecology (see Park 1936), and might be seen to represent an earlier moment of encounter between the biological and social sciences that is at least analogous (if not identical) to the interdisciplinary impulses of contemporary approaches. Where there are clear distinctions to be drawn is between the strongly human-centred approach of the early ecologists and the decentring of human agency in more recent theory. Louis Wirth (1945: 484) wrote that 'human ecology was less concerned with the relationship between man and his habitat than with the relationship between man and man as affected, among other factors, by his habitat,' and while social relations remain pivotal for urban political ecology, the analytical separation of the 'human' from the 'habitat' is harder to sustain. The other very salient difference between the older and the current approaches is that between the

Chicago School's commitment to the *scientific* study of human ecologies and the *critical* commitments of contemporary theory. While human ecology and urban political ecology each are concerned with the political ordering of urban systems – defined in terms of processes of distribution, regulation and negotiation – where the former takes this only as an object of analysis, the latter sees it also as a site of critical engagement and contestation (see Kaika and Swyngedouw 2010; Keil 2003: 726).

Biosocial approaches to the study of human settlements also draw important influences from work on 'human ecosystems' developed in the 1970s and after (Burch 1971; Burch et al. 1972). This framework proved innovative in its broad understanding of the 'critical resources' that circulate within urban ecosystems, which include biophysical elements such as energy, materials, nutrients and populations, but also social and cultural factors including information, institutions, beliefs and norms. Its aim in this way was to 'integrate sociocultural and biophysical systems' (Grove and Burch 1997: 263) in understanding the flows and cycles that make up human ecosystems. Moreover, the distribution and regulation of these flows are driven by both biological and social allocation mechanisms: ecological systems and cycles, but also market and non-market forms of exchange, structures of power and authority, cultural traditions, circuits of knowledge and information. Three further principles of the human ecosystems approach are particularly relevant to a critical and socio-spatial understanding of urban environments. The first is that urban ecosystems are dynamic and open: they are neither self-regulating nor self-contained. Flows of critical resources cannot easily be territorialized within the 'boundaries' of an urban system, and relations of interdependency, impact and exchange extend beyond them. Secondly, urban ecosystems are characterized by 'spatial heterogeneity', and these patterns of difference influence and are influenced by both sociocultural and biophysical processes (Grove and Burch 1997: 266). Finally, 'differential access to and control over critical resources affect the structure and function of urban ecosystems' (Grove and Burch 1997: 260). All three propositions underline the fact that the circulation and allocation of resources in urban ecosystems is not a 'natural' or endogenous effect. Such an account re-directs our attention to the externalities and disparities, uneven geographies and unequal economies that constitute the urban environment as a distribution problem.

Toxic urbanism

Cities, I have noted, occupy a complicated position in contemporary debates over the environment, playing a dual role as environmental villain and potential environmental saviour. Urbanization offers environmental opportunities as well as environmental threats. Large settlements open up environmental economies of scale (creating resource efficiencies, reducing transport distances, providing a basis for collective and synergistic systems of energy and waste), but also and more obviously represent major resource and land consumers and polluters. In a gathering planetary crisis of food and water, energy and ecosystems, cities have the potential to provide a spatial context for more rational and effective provision, access and stewardship, but more often it seems they produce extended economies of risk, waste and damage. Environmental despoliation and exhaustion is a key factor in recent processes of urban decline, but also a push factor in the processes of rural–urban and inter-urban migration that drive the contemporary urbanization of the world, in the movements of 'climate change' or 'environmental refugees'.

It is difficult to deny the correlation between levels of urbanization and levels of emissions at a global scale. With just over half of global population share, cities have been estimated to account for 75 per cent of global energy consumption and for 80 per cent of global emissions (United Nations 2007; see also Satterthwaite 2008: 540 for a roll-call of similar claims). The big figures may be striking, but must be read with a degree of caution. Greenhouse gas emissions are difficult to 'territorialize', given complex spatial relations between their sites of production, distribution, consumption and waste. Should carbon dioxide emissions from coal-based electricity, for example, be 'assigned' to the power station where it is produced or to the city where it is consumed; similarly, should factory emissions be traced to the off-shore industrial zone where they are created, or to the distant metropolitan consumers who buy the goods? And should methane emissions be allocated to the land-fill sites where they are produced, or the urban areas whose waste they contain? David Satterthwaite (2008) suggests that a consumption-based accounting of emissions is more accurate and fairer in a context where so much of the dirty work of an uneven global economy is outsourced from the cities of the rich and clean to the industrial and waste zones of the poor and polluted. Even so, he contends that the urban share of global emissions is overstated. Drawing on the 2007 assessments by the Intergovernmental Panel on Climate Change (IPCC), Satterthwaite estimates – and such reckonings are *always* ball-park estimates, despite the routine citation of the 80 per cent figure – that cities may be more likely to account for the production of around 30–40 per cent of greenhouse gas emissions, or 60–70 per cent using a measure based on consumption.

The production/consumption disparity highlights the fact that the contribution of 'cities' to climate change varies depending on the kind of city you are talking about. Post-industrial cities such as New York or London might look pretty good on the first measure, given their relative lack of heavy polluting industries, but less good when considered as global consumers. Moreover, advanced knowledge industries in cities such as these are more energy-intensive than their 'immaterial' reputation would imply, so long as they are associated with fossil-fuel electricity, resource-hungry buildings, international air travel and high-consumption lifestyles. This points to a second key issue that Satterthwaite's analysis raises. If we are going to take the *anthro* seriously in considering anthropogenic climate change, then we have to think about cities not simply as built forms but also as systems of human behaviour. Cities' emissions will vary not only according to patterns of urban form and urban industry, but also according to patterns of behaviour for different populations both across and within cities. Satterthwaite (2008: 546) draws the distinction between a typical emissions profile of an urban slum-dweller, which will vary at every level from the profile of their more affluent neighbour in respect of capital and consumer goods, household and workplace energy use, modes of transport, and practices of recycling and re-use. The urban poor negatively 'subsidize' the emissions impact of the rich, locally as well as globally, such that 'assigning greenhouse gas emissions to cities misses the very large differentials in per capita emissions between different city individuals and households' (Satterthwaite 2008: 546; see also Jorgenson et al. 2010; Lee 2006).

Urbanization in this sense may act as a cover for a different and more decisive contributing factor: the impact of relative wealth. The relationship between increasing wealth and increasing emissions is a strong one, and urban populations tend to be richer than non-urban populations. But over-consumption and hyper-pollution in cities is not a simple or universal trend, even for large cities. David Dodman (2009) examines inventories of greenhouse gas emissions for a sample of eleven cities between the mid-1990s and mid-2000s, and finds that per capita emissions for his urban sample are lower – and often significantly so – than they are at the respective national levels. In 2005, for instance, per capita greenhouse gas emissions in New York City were estimated at less than 30 per cent of national emissions per capita; São Paulo's 2003 per capita emissions were calculated at less than 20 per cent of the Brazilian average. The counter-trend was found in two Chinese cities, Beijing and Shanghai, both with per capita estimates more than double the national average by the late 1990s, in a context where urbanization was accompanied by significant wealth disparities between urban and rural populations. Even based on the small sample he considers, Dodman's analysis falsifies any simple assumption that cities are disproportionate greenhouse polluters – he proposes rather that the spatial economy of global emissions is heavily influenced by geographies of the over-consuming rich. As he notes, the one-fifth of the global population living in high-income economies accounts for almost half of global emissions, suggesting that 'it is the high consumption lifestyles of the world's wealthiest countries that result in unsustainable and harmful levels of greenhouse gas emissions' (Dodman 2009: 197). The distributions of environmental damage are heavily determined by distributions of economic wealth. Satterthwaite (2008: 547) is just as clear on this point: '[F]ocusing on the role of "cities" in greenhouse gas emissions (or carbon dioxide emissions) draws attention away from the fact that the driver of most anthropogenic carbon emissions is the consumption patterns of middle- and upper-income groups, regardless of where they live and the production systems that profit from their consumption.' And Wilfried Wang (2003: 1) is even less equivocal: 'Global climate change results from the realities of Western, post-industrial, capitalist culture. It is embedded in unsustainable lifestyles.' As Wang argues, the most environmentally damaging patterns of life have an over-sized ecological footprint, but an even more distended 'cultural footprint', as the consumption choices of a global minority are diffused through media and marketing to become more general objects of aspiration.

On these accounts, the chief factor in explaining levels of emissions is not urbanization but relative wealth – even as cities tend to produce and concentrate wealth, there is evidence to suggest that they do better in managing and mitigating the environmental effects of affluence than suburban and non-urban forms do (see also Glaeser and Kahn 2010). Re-balancing the emphasis between cities as built forms and populations as behavioural bundles is crucial to understanding how patterns of human settlement interact with and impact on their environments. And there is a case to be made that cities represent a more sustainable socio-spatial fix than some of their alternatives, with a capacity to 'de-link' affluence from over-consumption (Satterthwaite 2008: 547). This is in part due to physical factors: the resource and emissions economies to be had from collective transit provision, combined energy sources, smaller and denser housing typologies, and proximity between spaces of residence, employment and consumption. But social or behavioural factors are also key: the power of demonstration effects, interpersonal communication and social learning in dense environments makes urban-dwellers more susceptible to behavioural change (see Newman 2010), while city governments have the capacity to institute and regulate for changes (on emissions targets, on transport initiatives, on energy and recycling, on building codes) that can take much longer to grind through the cogs of national or international government. Given that cities are a large part of the environmental problem, whichever way the figures are calculated, they are an obvious place to look for solutions, and city governments operate at a scale that can make such solutions more direct and more viable (see Kousky and Schneider 2003). While a succession of global climate conferences in Kyoto (1997), Copenhagen (2009), Cancún (2010) and Doha (2012) have ended in more or less intractable log-jams, for instance, city governments working in concert have set their own emissions reduction targets, based on a reckoning that mayoral powers in the fields of planning and land use, transport, building ownership and controls, external lighting, food and agriculture, water, energy and waste give them leverage over up to 75 per cent of urban emissions sources (Arup and C40 Cities 2011; C40 Cities 2012).

If the causes of environmental risk – especially in respect of climate change – can be mapped around geographies of wealth and consumption, however, the impact of these risks has a rather different distribution. The footprinting of environmental impacts may be complicated by the fact that rich-world economies tend to out-source their emissions in the same way that they off-shore their heavy industry or their taxable wealth, but patterns of environmental damage and despoliation have a more definite geography. This unhappy, and rigged, environmental lottery works at different scales, as 'a spatialized political economy shapes the urban riskscape' in uneven and inequitable ways (Morello-Frosch 2002: 479). The urban poor are particularly vulnerable to environmental risks, at a global level and in more local urban contexts. Pressures on urban environments are arguably more intense in developing countries, given the ways that weak governance and regulatory structures, poor collective provision and lack of access to land and other resources may induce people to 'draw down' natural assets in and immediately around their cities. Low-income countries have a growing proportion of the world's population most at risk from the effects of climate change – in low-elevation coastal zones and drought areas in particular – with urban settlers taking the larger share of these populations at risk (see Douglas et al. 2008; Hardoy and Pandiella 2009; McGranahan et al. 2007; Revi 2008; UN-Habitat 2008; World Bank 2011). At regional and metropolitan scales, severe climate events do not discriminate between rich and poor, but the skewed 'geography of vulnerability' means their impacts fall most heavily on those living in the worst housing conditions, who are isolated from urban support services, or who lack access to transport or money to get out of danger zones – such that heat waves, flooding, fires and cyclones tend to hit poorer populations hardest, in high- as well as in low-income economies (Klinenberg 2002; see also Bakker 2005; Cutter and Smith 2009; ISDR 2009; Moser and Satterthwaite 2008). In urban emergencies, a Katrina effect is produced through the toxic interaction of 'the powers of nature with those of class, gender, and ethnic relations' (Swyngedouw 2006: 118; see Cutter and Finch 2008; Neumayer and Plümper 2007).

At the city scale, ordinary geographies of inequality and informality consign the urban poor to lower-level but chronic situations of environmental risk. Economic inequality and social disadvantage are lived spatially as conditions of environmental precariousness and injustice (see Bickerstaff et al. 2009; Harvey 1996; Low and Gleeson 1997; Soja 2010; Walker and Bulkeley 2006). In his analysis of Johannesburg's recurrent 'unnatural disasters' of fire and flooding, Martin J. Murray (2009) points to the spatial and existential divide between the insulated lives of the urban middle classes and the 'distressed urbanism' of the city's poor. The uneven distribution of risk across a city such as this is produced by a number of factors. Low-income populations routinely occupy the least desirable, lowest-rent and left-over tracts of urban land, often in proximity to or on the site of environmental hazards such as mines, industrial or chemical plants, energy plants and power lines, highways and railways, salvage yards, incinerators, land-fills, dumping-grounds or sewage outlets, or in flood risk zones. Mike Davis (2006: 129) notes that it is almost as if some 'infernal zoning ordinance' was at work that located slum housing next to the most dangerous and toxic urban activities – in fact, the not-so-hidden hand of urban land markets does the job just as well. Regardless of its location, housing that is inadequate in terms of both physical fabric and overcrowding renders poor settlements especially vulnerable to environmental shocks, and tends to magnify the effects of fire, flood, storms or disease. These conditions are reinforced by weak or absent planning and building regulations, especially for informal settlements, that neglect physical vulnerability and fail to ensure sufficient space between dwellings, decent sewers and drainage, or passable roads and access routes. Davis (2006: 129) again expresses this powerfully in observing how the standard 'principles of urban planning, including the preservation of open space and the separation of noxious land uses from residences, are stood on their heads in poor cities.' Informal and unreliable energy supply – pirated and patchy electricity, paraffin and gas stoves and lamps, open fires and candles – and inadequate or unsafe water supplies constitute further environmental risks for poor households and settlements. Finally, lack of access to resources, including money, information and transport, or to health and emergency services, compounds these forms of insecurity by making it harder to deal with or recover from crisis events: as Murray (2009: 165) puts it, 'the intersection of disaster-vulnerable settlement patterns with relaxed planning regulations and building standards, lack of preparation for unsuspected calamities, and inadequate crisis management creates entirely new artificial hazards' out of apparently *natural* dangers. In sum, the uneven geography of urban environmental risk is produced at the intersection of locational, physical and morphological, social and economic, legal and policy factors that makes some environmental citizens very much less equal than others.

In this sense, urban environmental goods and bads are subject not only to disparities but also to *perversities* in distribution. It is a skewed equation indeed according to which those who contribute least to environmental degradation are most vulnerable to its effects. 'For the world's poor people,' James Woodcock and his colleagues (2007: 1078) note, 'walking is the main mode of transport, but such populations often experience the most from the harms of energy-intensive transport,' whether through road traffic injuries, exposure to exhaust emissions and noise pollution, spatial severance and segmentation caused by traffic congestion and transport infrastructure, or larger climate impacts. Government and inter-governmental efforts to respond to environmental risk are heavily invested in representing the field of environment as something that is *shared* – as most famously captured in the Brundtland Report's emphasis on 'our common future' (World Commission on Environment and Development 1987). This naturalized conception of an environment held in common is crucial to political claims for collective responsibility across space and over time. The Brundtland definition of sustainable development is well known for framing this responsibility in terms of a relationship between generations – 'development that meets the needs of the present, without compromising the ability of future generations to meet their own needs' – but much of the conflict over the (un)sustainable use of resources is between starkly different 'needs' within the *same* present. 'Environmental politics', as Erik Swyngedouw (2009: 602) argues, 'is a politics legitimated by a scientific consensus which, in turn, translates into a political consensus.' Environmental ecologies – the atmosphere and climate systems, oceans, lakes and rivers, forests and wilderness areas, fish and live-stocks, natural resources – conventionally are taken to exemplify a global commons involving mutual risks and costs (Hardin 1968). However, the biophysical distribution of environmental vulnerability does not simply map onto its social distribution. In many urban contexts, the most socio-economically disadvantaged are also most subject to different 'dimensions of vulnerability', defined in terms of *exposure* to risks, *resistance* (the ability to withstand threats) and *resilience* (the ability to recover from harms) (Dow 1992: 417). Climate change may be a planetary problem, but at the hot and wet end of things not everyone has the same weather – not even in the same city.

As William R. Burch (1971: 21) pointed out in his early work on human ecosystems, an analytical focus on large-scale environmental risks in this way can obscure the fact that 'the really real environment is that which immediately surrounds the individual.' It follows that environmental problems are *lived* very differently by different populations across even quite proximate spatial scales. Urban environmental challenges can be classified according to different conditions of economic development, and these vary across the geographies of specific cities as well as across an international economy. At the most urgent level, poverty-related issues focus on access to safe water, sanitation and waste management – the so-called 'brown' environmental agenda, or Appadurai's (2002: 37) 'politics of shit'. At a different level, production-related issues concern emissions and air pollution from factories, extractive industries, construction and distribution – shaping the 'grey' environmental agenda that has been such a source of contention as developing economies increase their carbon share. Consumption-related issues, meanwhile, are those relevant to a 'green' environmental agenda focused on issues of individual and household consumption, including passenger transport, recycling and sustainable sourcing. The conventional model of modern economic development has been one of 'grow now, clean later'

(O'Connor 1996; see also Lee 2006) – on the basis that 'only when we are sufficiently rich can we afford the relative luxury of caring about the environment' (Lomborg 2001: 33) – and as exemplified by the European countries that are diligently cutting their carbon emissions and cycling to work while much of the carbon dioxide they discharged over the nineteenth and twentieth centuries remains in the atmosphere.

The argument that environmental concerns are another of the privileges of the rich is provocative, but needs to be taken seriously. Much of the global debate regarding carbon emissions, clean technologies, renewable energy and the reduction of waste is dogged by double standards that stretch across uneven histories of economic and industrial development. However, the claim that environmental politics is a rich-world game makes two assumptions. The first is that environmental issues can meaningfully be separated out from economic processes, such that it is possible to put them in order of precedence; the second is that economic growth takes obvious priority over environmental concerns – a line of reasoning that is not just relevant to a catch-up model of comparative development, but also a standard script for corporate interests and their political placemen in the world's richest economies. Moreover, it overlooks the fact that those who are growing 'sufficiently rich' are rarely those who are most vulnerable to the environmental harms of economic growth. As is the case in efforts to allocate emissions between and within cities, abstracting these debates to the level of national or even urban economies belies the way that the advantages of economic growth and the disadvantages of industrial pollution are unevenly distributed across urban populations; and this without taking into account the fact that significant returns from economic growth in low- and middle-income cities go to foreign corporations and off-shore investors who are already rather better than 'sufficiently rich', while they bear none of the immediate environmental risks. Environmental costs – in rates of mortality, disability and ill health; degraded and dangerous living and working conditions; personal and household insecurity; and poor quality of life – are among the most injurious of non-income forms of poverty. Moreover, the relationship between poverty and environmental harm is especially tenacious in urbanized contexts, where access to basic environmental goods (water, clean air, natural light) is often harder than in rural settings, housing conditions and materials are poorer or more toxic, pollution is much worse, workplaces and transport are more dangerous.

It follows, Janice Perlman (2007: 173) argues, that there 'can be no urban environmental solution without alleviating urban poverty'. For many urban populations the 'brown' environmental agenda is both urgent – representing a highly localized, immediate and sometimes life-threatening environmental problem – and inseparable from conditions of poverty. As Arjun Appadurai (2002: 37) points out, what is delicately referred to as 'human waste management' is an issue 'where every problem of the urban poor arrives at a single point of extrusion': shelter deprivation, income and resource poverty, political abandonment, environmental degradation, social indignity and physical vulnerability – including both health risks and, especially for women, personal insecurity. It can be far easier, indeed, to see the environmental subject of the open sewer or the communal latrine as an individual whose actions are linked into a larger urban environment and political economy, than it is to imagine the connections between the virtuous carbon off-setter and the impact of the global aviation industry. The emissions of the affluent and the pollution of the poor are generally understood in quite different environmental imaginaries, become visible in different ways and to different degrees, and are addressed by different kinds of politics. Yet separating out these environmental subjects and environmental agendas belies the way that they overlap in space, and are productive of conflicts in segmented societies. Environmental class divisions stretch across extended geographies of consumption, production and emission, but also represent sites of contest within divided cities. Amita Baviskar (2002) has written of the tension – at times violently expressed – between the 'bourgeois environmentalism' of an expanding middle class in Delhi, and what might be called the 'grey' and 'brown' practices of the poor, with mobilizations and public interest litigations against polluting and irregular industries, and squatter settlements on public land, resulting in the closure of factories and the demolition of slums that employed or housed hundreds of thousands of urban workers and residents (see also Chatterjee 2004; Ghertner 2011, 2012). In a quite different context, but in a similar vein, Sarah Dooling (2009) describes the 'ecological gentrification' involved in civic initiatives to green the marginal spaces used by homeless residents in Seattle. The distinction between 'green' environmental politics and 'brown' and 'grey' agendas does not simply correspond to different stages of economic development along some linear path of ecological modernization, nor does it map neatly around a transnational geography of low-, middle- and high-income economies; rather, it captures tensions and divisions between the 'really real' environments in which different people live in the same cities. Nikolas Heynen and his colleagues (2006: 6) note how the complex 'web of socio-ecological relations that bring about highly uneven urban environments . . . have become pivotal terrains around which political action crystallizes and social mobilizations take place'; these include not only radical or resistant environmental politics, but aggressive, defensive or exclusionary politics of sustainability driven by those who perceive their quality of urban life as threatened by the pollutions of the poor.

Urban mobilities

A 'grow now, clean later' principle may refer primarily to processes of economic and industrial growth, but it has clear spatial implications. The forms of urban expansion and intensification that economic development entails are decisive for cities' capacity to 'clean now', or at least clean *soon*. Densification and sprawl – conventionally taken to represent distinct physical models of urban growth – in practice often go together in current processes of urbanization. The freeway, the ring-road and the fly-over have emerged as keynotes of an international style of infrastructural development, in part owing to the extended 'cultural footprint' of First World visions of a motorized city. Recent patterns of urban growth suggest that many developing cities are following an established model which sees car use increasing as the middle class expands (Banister 2011). Public transport, cycles and pedestrians are quite literally crowded out, as cars come to dominate urban environments which are not well adapted for them in terms of street layouts and urban fabric, road quality and coverage – cars are not only energy-hungry, after all, they are also hungry for *space*. As well as transforming older cities, in increasingly connected urban economies transport plays a major role in shaping new metropolitan forms: from the expressway urbanism and high-speed corridors emerging in India – linking Pune, Mumbai and Ahmedabad in the north, or Bangalore and Chennai in the south – to 'aerotropolises' centred on airports, such as Masdar in Abu Dhabi, Sungate in Windhoek, Namibia, or Songdo, near Incheon in South Korea.

Current patterns of economic and physical development in this way would seem to bear out Lewis Mumford's (1938: 235) baleful analysis of urban growth as a series of advances in 'the technical means of congestion'. As technical solutions to the concentration of large numbers, urban systems – of building, sanitation, infrastructure and transport – work only to compound the effects of congestion with further congestion. This problem is especially pronounced in the field of urban transport: Mumford (1938: 238) argues that the outcome 'of all these assiduous attempts mechanically to mobilize and disperse, night and morning, the inhabitants of the metropolis is nevertheless plain: one and all, they have intensified the pattern of congestion'. In this perverse equation, more roads leads to more cars and longer traffic-jams; expanded airport capacity means more planes circling overhead; extended rail networks induce more people to transit greater distances from home to work. Technology, design and behaviour – in this view – move in lock-step to bring about the unhappiest environmental outcome of all: congested sprawl. All of this exacts a psychological, physical and economic price – if Mumford had been a post-Brundtland man, he might have said it was socially, environmentally and economically unsustainable, but his language is more trenchant: 'Confusion: constriction: costiveness – these are the typical by-products of metropolitan congestion' (Mumford 1938: 2381).

Transport infrastructure is basic to cities' efficiency, but also to their environments and quality of life; moreover, decisions made in this realm impact on urban form from the scale of housing typology to urban block, to the design of streets to the wider transport network, to the city's spatial and ecological footprint. Transport planning, far from being a technical engineering exercise, exists at the meeting point for urban design, social welfare, political economy and environmental policy. In terms of thinking about the urban environment as a *distribution* problem, what Kevin Lynch (1965) called the 'movement system' is critical in bringing together the physical and social dimensions of this problem. Lynch emphasized the movement system as a key point 'of leverage for improving large-scale environmental quality', and the concept in itself is useful in integrating 'hard' elements – road networks and transport infrastructures and the way these make up urban form – with the 'soft' – the distributions and movement of people in the city. This last point is crucial: the technology–design–behaviour environmental equation is an especially important one in respect of urban transport. Part of the challenge in adapting urban movement systems to the threats of climate change, terminally declining oil production and environmental risk is a technological one: developing low- and no-carbon alternatives to the fossil-fuelled transport economy, and creating viable collective transport alternatives to the private car. Partly the challenge is one of design, orienting land use around compact, mixed developments that cluster different urban uses and thereby reduce travel distances in the

Prenzlauer Berg, Berlin, 2012.

city, substituting proximity for mobility. But a significant part of the
environmental challenge for urban transport is behavioural. Even in
robust regulatory contexts, social behaviour is the black box in the
movement system: by certain estimates, for instance, technological
innovation can achieve no more than half current European targets
for reductions in transport emissions – the balance therefore will need
to come from behavioural change (see Banister 2011: 1539).

Social behaviour around transport is steered by the 'hard' elements of the movement system. Embedded patterns of land use and levels of transit provision have a significant influence on individuals' patterns of mobility. There is a significant degree of path-dependency that can make an established hard–soft equation difficult to crack, of course, but individual and collective behaviour does change over time, and for a number of reasons. Transport choices are constrained by physical and economic factors, but also shaped by urban cultures. Again, the complexity of distribution problems in the city is crucial in this context: public transit ridership and car ownership, for example, do not always correlate with lower and higher income levels. Los Angeles, to take one instance, has invested in transit infrastructure in recent years, but any growth in transit usage has been almost entirely due to the city's immigrant population: Evelyn Blumenberg and Alexandra Norton (2010: 10) note that in California as a whole, 'immigrants comprise just over a quarter of the population (27 percent), but more than half of all transit commuters.' The authors contend that any decline in rates of immigration is therefore likely to mean declining rates of ridership. While there is a strong case to be made for public provision on equity grounds, there are also obvious drawbacks to public transit becoming a service of last resort: quite apart from questions around efficiency, how equitable is public provision if it *only* serves those who are worst off? This appears more a kind of compensatory provision than a matter of transit equity. The most viable systems operate where public transport is a mode of collective, rather than minority, consumption, used across income and ethnic divides. This is the case in large cities like London and New York, where public transport is the most efficient means of travel for the greatest number of people (even if it doesn't always *feel* so convenient – in the 1930s, Lewis Mumford [1938: 241] was already complaining about the 'tightly jammed subway train, rank with the odor of human bodies on a summer's evening'). It is also the case for smaller high-income cities well served by public networks – Swiss cities, and Zurich in particular, have among the highest rates of public transit ridership in the most developed economies. Other European cities – such as Berlin, Copenhagen and Vienna – have fairly even shares between walking and/or cycling, public transit and private cars, with Copenhagen a stand-out case for cycling: at over a one-third share, more journeys to work are made by bicycle than by any other single means. Among European cities with the highest GDP per capita – including Paris, Frankfurt, London, Stockholm, Vienna, Zurich – a clear majority of people walk, cycle or take public transport to work; only Hamburg and Utrecht buck the trend, with around half of all journeys to work in those cities by private car. In some other contexts, the shift to non-motorized transport is also one away from collective provision: travel patterns in British cities such as Edinburgh and Bristol, which have high proportions of people walking and cycling, suggest that the latter take people off public transport rather than out of private cars.

Simple assumptions about urbanization, economic growth and transport development are difficult to sustain in the face of a range of existing alternatives. If few rapidly growing cities are going to turn into Paris (where more than 80 per cent of all travel in the city itself is on foot or by public transport, and more than 50 per cent in the larger urban region – see Caenen et al. 2010), it's not clear that the future has to be Los Angeles. The largest cities in India and China have low but rapidly increasing rates of car use, and Indian megacities (Mumbai, Delhi, Kolkata) already have high public transport usage (see Pucher et al. 2005, 2007). In both contexts, economic growth and increasing transport demand have outstripped investment in transport infrastructure. Rui Mu and Martin de Jong (2012: 8) suggest that urban trips in China increased from 3.7 billion in 1995 to some 70 billion in 2009. While China moved early, and hard, on road-building – more than doubling the road network between 2001 and 2009 (Mu and de Jong 2012: 6) – urban governments more recently have undertaken more serious investment in heavy and light commuter rail and bus rapid transit systems, while urban expansion in different cities has followed different paths of motorization and transport alternatives (see, e.g., for Beijing, Zhao 2010; for Guangzhou, Zacharias 2012; and for Shanghai, Cervero and Day 2008). Similarly, patterns of public transit use vary in India, from the very high ridership levels in denser, more contained cities with sparse road networks, such as Chennai (over 80 per cent of trips on public transit, and 5 per cent of urban land used for roads) and Mumbai (over 60 per cent ridership and 11 per cent road coverage), to lower-density cities with more sprawling urban form and denser road coverage (both Chennai and Delhi have around 40 per cent share of trips by public transport; and more than 20 per cent of Delhi's land area is used for roads) (see Pucher et al. 2005). In recent years urban rail (including metro) networks have been built or extended in Delhi and Chennai, with bus rapid transit (BRT) systems built or planned for Ahmedabad, Bangalore, Chennai, Delhi, Kolkata, Mumbai, Pune and several other cities.

Investments in major public transport infrastructure, however, take much longer than increases in private car usage as cities and economies grow. The relationship between increasing per capita income and rates of car ownership is fairly incontrovertible, but Mark Kutzbach (2009, 2010) notes that this association differs according to the way in which economic growth is distributed. He postulates that the GDP/car link varies for economies with relatively higher and lower levels of income inequality. If wealth expands more quickly at the top, so car consumption will grow rapidly at that end of the income scale. A more equitable distribution of income growth, however, means that overall rates of car ownership will grow more slowly, given that a smaller proportion of the population will be able to afford them. While the richest will take to cars, a more slowly expanding middle class will – at least initially – continue to ride the bus. The policy trick, Kutzbach contends, is therefore to provide disincentives for car use and to expand and enhance public transit before middle incomes grow to a level where cars become afford-able: either by creating more extensive, efficient and attractive transit systems (as in Curitiba), or by taxing and regulating car use (as in Singapore, where – to be fair – high licence charges and conges-tion levies are more than off-set by the inducements of an extensive, efficient and high-performing urban transit network). In contrast, Tata's 2009 roll-out in India of the one-lakh car is likely to have the counter-effect (even if the same company has significant interests in urban BRT systems, and the Tata Nano was subject to fairly rapid price inflation).

Kutzbach's argument that governments should provide disincen-tives for car use and incentives for collective transport as urban economies grow is an important one, but one that runs counter to current trends. It seems fair to claim that the greater part of transport investment – both public and private – benefits the better-off urban classes rather than the poor; in particular, 'investment in major road projects does not meet the transport needs of poor people, especially women whose trips are primarily local and off road' (Woodcock et al. 2007: 1078; see also Banister 2011). It is not only through the allocation of capital but in the allocation of space that investments in a city's movement system show which uses, and which users, have priority. As former mayor of Bogotá Enrique Peñalosa (2007: 312) has argued, 'A protected bicycle lane in a developing world city is a powerful symbol, showing that a citizen on a US$30 bicycle is as important as one in a US$30,000 car. . . . Quality pavements and bicycle lanes show respect for human dignity, regardless of the level of economic development of a society.' Ordinary streets are a common urban resource. They perform different functions – of commerce, encounter and consumption as well as of transit – and they are flexible in use. Moreover, they support patterns of mobility that are not over-determined by the technical means of congestion, and that do not figure very highly in transport mappings or in measures of urban emissions. Their real 'cultural footprint' is large, even as their ecological footprint remains low.

A city's movement system is a 'distribution problem' in at least three senses. It concerns the distribution of built form and its relationship to un-built space both within and beyond the city. It also concerns the distribution of different functions – production and work, consumption and leisure, habitation and public life – and the patterns of integration, connectivity and access between these. And it concerns the distribution of people, not only according to official transit routes, but through less fixed routes and variable relations of mobility and proximity (see Jaffe et al. 2012; Knowles 2011). The way in which these 'hard' and 'soft' factors interact is shaped by the distribution of other resources – money, information, power, opportunity – and in turn reinforces these distributive effects through the routine organization of urban space. AbdouMaliq Simone (2011: 357) contends that places are

> always transformed by what people, materials, technical and discursive instruments do in the passing. This doesn't mean that people are always mobile, adaptable and flexible; it doesn't mean that some people are not incessantly cornered or enclaved. These processes, too, are aspects of urbanization, part of the trajectory of oscillating movement through which a wide range of economic mobilities are hedged through the cordoning off of others. So as physical and political infrastructures stratify movement into different interactional possibilities, and steer people into specific densities and speeds, as well as open up weakly controlled reverberations, urban life makes itself known in various ways.

Simone refers to these processes as the 'surfacing of urban life' – the ways in which physical infrastructures, political and economic geographies of entry, access and exclusion, and more protean patterns of everyday movement produce the urban environment as a 'textured surface' of mobility and immobility. A city's movement system is composed out of these interactions between physical, socio-economic, behavioural, legal and political forms. The soft stuff of social behaviour is not entirely ordered by the hard stuff of infrastructure and technology, and not wholly legible as an object of urban design, but it remains key to the social vitality and economic efficiency of cities, as well as to their environmental performance. The environmental benefits of effective mass transit, and of non-motorized transport as a mobility choice rather than practical necessity or marker of poverty, may be foremost in current arguments for these kinds of transport strategies. However, the case to be made for such movement systems on the grounds of social equity and economic efficiency may be just as compelling, even if harder to measure.

Conclusion: the unsustainable and the insupportable

Almost a century ago, the Chicago School sociologist Ernest Burgess (1925: 47) argued that a sociological analysis of 'the growth of the city' should focus on the issues of *expansion, metabolism* and *mobility*. In the present-day context of urban growth, these issues reappear as critical points of engagement. Does continuing urbanization consti-tute an environmental threat or an eco-technical solution to problems of resource depletion, over-consumption and climate risk? How can urban forms be understood as part of a socio-natural metabo-lism composed of complex flows of materials, resources, people, commodities, information and energy? And how do the movement systems of cities – composed of both 'hard' infrastructure and 'soft' bodies in motion – shape urban environments not only as physical forms but also as networks of human behavior?

Cities, like other social systems, distribute resources and risks across populations and territory. As complex ecologies, they config-ure both economies of scale and economies of harm. The mechanisms that allocate these resources and risks are as much socio-economic as they are biophysical. In both respects, I have proposed, the urban environment is a distribution problem. Across different spatial scales, this environmental economy is characterized by the inequitable dis-tribution of goods – natural resources, land, ecosystem services – and perverse distributions of bads, as populations that contribute least to environmental harm may be most vulnerable to its effects. In this sense it can be argued that 'there is no such thing as an unsustainable city in general, but rather there are a series of urban and environmen-tal processes that negatively affect some social groups while benefit-ing others' (Swyngedouw 2006: 115).

The language of urban 'sustainability' is an easy target for criticism, but it can be an oddly anodyne term for what is a highly conflictual field of distribution. The discourse of urban sustainability is neces-sarily one that is oriented to the future, but it is troubled by conflicts and contradictions over *present* needs: both the over-production of

needs for middle- and high-income groups, and the under-supply of
the basic needs of the urban poor. Understanding the social production of urban environments as a problem of distribution is a way of
re-posing the question of 'who is getting how much' of the gains and
the costs of urban settlement (Lynch 1981: 118). These problems
of distribution are redoubled by the boundary problem in thinking
about urban environments, the difficulty not only of determining the
limits of any city in an extended geography of interdependency and
impact, but also of territorializing the resource demands and emissions share of a specific urban population. Environmental effects are
part of an international export economy ordered around the out-
sourcing of their production and the off-shoring of their impacts.
Insofar as environmental inequalities are market outcomes, they are
produced within systems of allocation marked by the concentration
of comforts and the maldistribution of risks. Natural hazards, climate
events and changing environments may be impervious to social distinctions of class, gender or race, but the social production of nature
around uneven geographies of vulnerability means various groups are
positioned quite differently in terms of their exposure, resistance and
resilience to crisis. Environmental emergencies highlight in very stark
ways the more routine geographies of inequality that produce and
reproduce urban environments as uneven territories of benefit
and harm.

Whether urban growth is an environmental problem or an environmental solution ultimately is neither a biophysical nor a technical
question. But it is a *design* problem in the fullest sense, bearing on
the design not only of buildings, infrastructure and spaces, but also
of planning policy, legal regulations, service provision and systems
of social support. Kevin Lynch (1995a [1968]: 205) once wrote that
'[e]nvironmental quality may appear secondary among the pressing
issues of urbanization in a developing country.' He rejected such an
assumption, given the ways in which 'environmental form and social
function are repeatedly linked together' in any city. The environmental life of urban form is conditioned not just by materials, energy
and transport systems, ecologies of waste and recycling, but also by
the way in which such structures give shape to uneven geographies
of over-consumption and chronic vulnerability. These geographies
'surface' in distorted ways, from the distended and fragmented
footprints of the polluting classes, to the perverse distributions of
environmental risk and harms across distant spaces, but also within
cities. The relationships between design, technology and behaviour
are formative of urban environments in more or less efficient, more

or less sustainable, and more or less defensible ways. The design of urban forms – how urban land is developed and utilized; how populations are settled; how buildings are configured, constructed and used; patternings of built and open space; integration between different places and functions – is powerfully shaped by systems of technology. These include the engineering of production, resource, transport and waste infrastructures; building technologies for construction, performance and conversion; transport technologies for the movement of people, information and goods; and everyday technologies of habitation and use. Such large and often highly technical systems in turn intersect with modes of collective and individual behaviour which they do not simply over-determine: the many large and small designs of human settlement, interaction and movement that compose the city as a socio-technical environment around fixed forms, complex flows and innumerable moving parts.

6

Infrastructure as 'Design Politics'

It's to objects that we must now turn if we want to understand what, day after day, keeps life in the big city together.

Latour and Hermant 1998: 63

Beneath the visible city an invisible city grows apace: a buried city of water pipes and sewers and gas mains and electric cables and steam pipes and telephone wires and vast cellars where heat and electricity are produced for the buildings above: a cities of ramifying subways and ominous tunnels in which the entire population spends no inconsiderable part of the day.

Mumford 1938: 239

'The most characteristic technical achievements of the big city,' Lewis Mumford declared (1938: 235), 'are those that further congestion.' As city governments sought technological solutions to the problems created by urban density, they succeeded only in compounding its effects. For Mumford, the canalization of water was the first of the city's technical 'means of congestion'; he remarked the way that a technical and ramified water supply helped ease the pains of urban congestion but also reinforced it, as the technics of urban hydrology – from the reservoir to the pumping station to the private bathroom – took up ever greater resource and more and more room, increasing density, building costs and land-grab. And piped water was only the start of it, as different urban infrastructures were layered over each other, enhanced supply sparking new demand and further congestion as an 'effect of all these new utilities as they cross and criss-cross, through and over and under the city' (Mumford 1938: 239).

If urban form is the bone structure of the city, then infrastructure is its arteries. Like Mumford before him, although in less lugubrious

vein, Matthew Gandy (2008: 108) hits on the complicated relationship between what we see in the city and what it submerges when he
speaks of the 'tension between the idea of the modern city as a visible
manifestation of conscious design and the complex array of unseen
networks extending beneath the city streets'. A key part of the conscious design of the modern city, of course, is that you don't see its
workings. Infrastructure breaks the surface at the subway entrance,
in the electricity pylon and the stand-pipe – as Mumford's 'buried
city' is suggested more or less evocatively by man-hole covers, the
miasma emitted from subway vents or drains. This 'underground
city' (Gandy 1999) or '*ville invisible*' (Latour and Hermant 1998;
see also Greenberg 1998) is ramified into more visible, if often less
coherent, networks of infrastructure and the expressed forms of what
might be called 'exostructure', which carry, connect and serve these
systems.

The discussion that follows is concerned with critical aspects
of the 'design politics' of urban infrastructure (see Vale 2013).
Infrastructure is considered as an object not only of technical design
but also of political and economic design; an important means of
constituting the city as a political space of incorporation and the
urban public as a *body social*. The political economy of infrastructure
might be taken as a primer for the shifting relations between public
and private forms of governance, regulation and provision over the
last century or more, as infrastructure systems are variously produced
as demonstration projects for the socialist city, the corporatist city
or the privatist city – or, more usually, in terms of hybrid forms that
mediate and re-combine 'state' and 'market' forms. The chapter goes
on to consider the infrastructural inequalities that map onto, and
help to produce, social and economic disparities in contemporary
cities. These cracks in the body social open up around gaps in the
infrastructural network, in the dark, dry parts of the city which lie off
the grid or at the end of the pipe. The splintering of infrastructural
systems, however, is not just an issue of infrastructure poverty. As
we have seen in chapter 3, the production of urban inequalities is
not simply a matter of cities' concentrations of poor residents. In the
context of infrastructure, as more generally, current geographies of
urban inequality are shaped by the concentrations and segregations
of the rich. Infrastructure secession may be seen as a further means
of elite withdrawal in and from the city, as securing infrastructure
becomes a key element of the larger security complex for the affluent
and the anxious. Finally, the discussion turns to the contrasting scene
of informal and auto-infrastructures. It may be conventional to think

about infrastructure in terms of 'technical means of congestion' and organization, but a great deal of the work of urban infrastructure is provided by low-tech and no-tech solutions; forms of infrastructure that are not engineered by experts but embodied by everyday social actors. These ordinary infrastructures in the city provide human pipelines for water and fuel, extensive and flexible transport net-works, often complex logistical systems for the distribution of goods, food and information. As a primary mode of ordinary urbanism, these embodied infrastructures are the designs of resourceful actors, at least as resilient and often as invisible as the submerged networks of the technical city. They underline the extent to which human resource remains the most basic and the most crucial element of the resource economy of a city.

Infrastructure as urbanism

Thinking about infrastructure as urbanism involves a couple of moves. It means thinking beyond its technical qualities to consider its social and political life. The technical specification and functional role of infrastructure, that is, must be understood in terms of its polit-ical formulation and its social effects. It also means looking beyond its habitual reticence, foregrounding what is meant to be behind the scenes. It is a commonplace that we notice infrastructure only when it fails, but this raises the question of how we routinely manage *not* to see the functional stuff that surrounds us, the concrete reasons why our cities don't (and sometimes do) fall down. This conception of stolid, silent structure also overlooks the improvised and intermittent nature of much urban infrastructure around the world, where failure is normal and 'systems' are only weakly patched together.

Infrastructure may conventionally be understood in terms of mundane workings, but its imagination is a poetic game. Mumford (1938: 237) saw canalization and sewage systems in terms of a 'flood of water [that] cleanses the Augean metropolitan stable'. More broadly, 'urban infrastructure', Gandy writes (2005b: 28), 'can be conceptualized as a series of interconnecting life-support systems. The modern home, for example, has become a complex exoskeleton for the human body with its provision of water, warmth, light and other essential needs.' The domestication of energy is a key element of the urbanization of nature, as the development of networks of infra-structures pacifies, organizes and orders the city as an eco-technical environment. The integrated ideal of urban infrastructure, however, is rarely reflective of the workings – and failures – of infrastructure in practice, which very often is characterized by fragmentation, by the expression and reproduction of patterns of urban inequality, and by crisis as a *normal* mode of operation (see McFarlane and Rutherford 2008).

Susan Leigh-Star provides one of the most celebrated arguments for thinking about infrastructure in a social frame in her 1999 paper on 'the ethnography of infrastructure'. She is writing about information networks, but her characterization of infrastructure translates into more concrete urban forms in instructive ways. Leigh-Star (1999: 381–2) gives us nine means of recognizing infrastructure when we (don't) see it. Infrastructure is typified, firstly, by its embeddedness – it is 'sunk into and inside of other structures' (1999: 381) – and, secondly, by its 'transparency', by which she means that it does not require reinvention or assembly every time someone wants to use it. Infrastructure, thirdly, has a necessary degree of 'reach or scope'. Its use is 'learned', fourthly, by its users – one doesn't accidentally or unknowingly operate an IT system or catch a connecting bus. It follows, fifthly, that infrastructure is shaped by 'conventions of practice' around its deployment, whether by technicians or everyday users. Infrastructure, sixthly, embodies standards that allow for interconnection between systems and allow for augmentation. It is 'built on an installed base', and usually in 'modular increments'. Finally, in a wonderful and much-cited phrase, infrastructure 'becomes visible on breakdown' (see also Graham and Thrift 2007).

This is an excellent definition – except for all those ways in which it is *not* true of urban infrastructure. What Leigh-Star gives us may be less a characterization than an ideal-type that allows us to see how often 'real' infrastructure fails to conform to type. Her article also contains a much simpler take on infrastructure, which might be a guide for thinking about it in its urban contexts. Infrastructure, very simply, is both *relational* and *ecological*. Forms of infrastructure facilitate and mediate interaction – between people, between things, between people and things – and also shape an environment that 'holds' these interactions. These are objects, quite materially, that 'keep life in the big city together', as Bruno Latour and Émilie Hermant put it in our opening epigraph. The relational and ecological understanding of infrastructure holds for those instances where bits of infrastructure fail to conform to Leigh-Star's ideal-type – where things (taps, siphons, feeders) must be frequently re-assembled and re-connected; where everyday infrastructure (generators, water-trucks) is mobile; where failure is normal (see Trentmann 2009), and power or water systems are more noticeable when they *do* work.

Thinking about infrastructure as relational and ecological goes beyond its functional and technical qualities. The relationships and ecologies shaped by and shaping infrastructure are social as much as they are material. This is most evident in the degree to which the 'reach or scope' of an urban infrastructure system is less extensive than the inhabited territory of the city itself; where train lines, sealed roads, power cables, water and sewerage pipes fail to reach certain urban populations; where 'conventions of practice' include those of monopoly, preference and exclusion; where infrastructure breakdown is more frequent, more sustained and less soluble for some parts of the city than for others. The uneven geographies of infrastructure, as well as the rational dream of the total urban 'life support-system', underline the design politics of these material ecologies. Latour and Hermant ask us to think about and look at the things that 'keep life in the big city together'. In thinking about and looking at urban infrastructure, this means 'life' in its most basic sense – water, heat, sanitation. The conscious and unconscious design of urban infrastructure reflects, reinforces and re-makes lines of power and exclusion in the city. To paraphrase, slightly, Leigh-Star (1999: 379): '[W]hat values and ethical principles do we inscribe in the inner depths of the built . . . environment'?

Infrastructure as urbanism in this sense is not simply about keeping 'life in the big city together', but also about how things help to keep spaces and people in the city apart. Infrastructure networks (and not-works) are the exemplary expression of a 'splintering urbanism' (Graham and Marvin 2001) that dis-integrates cities and urban regions into uneven surfaces of connection and control, which both link urban interiors to distant exteriors and disembed them from their hinterlands. In a broader sense, infrastructure might be taken as the model morphology for a 'network' society (Castells 2000) in which connection does not require contiguity, and adjacency does not always mean association.

The political economy of infrastructure

Infrastructure systems exemplify not only the planned but also the socialized city. Municipal rail, ferries and metro, public roads and bridges, metropolitan water companies, port authorities and coal boards produced the modern city as a domain of collective provision and consumption. Public infrastructure has been the most basic element of the socialized city, and its creeping (or galloping) commodification is also exemplary of the privatized city. The political economy of infrastructure involves a highly variable mix of public and private capital, ownership and delivery structures, regulation and its absence. It offers both an historical model of state control – with all its fragmentations and devolutions – and a contemporary model of the vagaries of 'privatization' – the various investment streams and financing mechanisms, governance arrangements and regulatory fixes that the term covers, and oftentimes obscures.

The conversion of investment capital into physical forms, and the materialization of political authority in the built environment of infrastructure, makes real certain conceptions of the city as a common good (or shared evil), and of the urban denizen as citizen. The engineering of infrastructure – in both its technical and organizational senses – is a pre-eminent field of 'design politics': a physical ordering of the city that at the same time makes a public of its inhabitants. Lawrence Vale (2013) develops the concept of design politics to capture the way that architecture, planning and urbanism are implicated in political rationalities and policy designs. The map of its underground railway marks out a city as a territory as surely as, and in certain ways more meaningfully – more experientially, more empirically, more *really* – than, a mapping of electoral boundaries. The pipe that runs under my building and connects to the sewer main in the street is a line of civic membership activated far more frequently than my intermittent trips to the polling booth. This is a material configuration of the 'body social', rather than formalized constitution of the 'body politic' (see Isin 2007). Moreover, these are bases of belonging within a collective urban body that do not rely on official or legal membership; infrastructure in its relational and ecological modes incorporates the urban citizen without ever asking to see his or her papers. Infrastructure collapse, what is more, may as likely be an index of the failure of a social system as of technical breakdown: when water and oil supplies dried up in Libya in the revolutionary moment of summer 2011, it was not because the technical systems failed, but because the social and political system that secured these supplies had collapsed.

Urban infrastructure can be understood in this way as 'congealed social interests' (Graham and Marvin 2001: 11) – interests congealed not only as sunk capital investment but also as political designs on the physical and the social environment of the city. Edward Glaeser (2004) stresses that infrastructure developments over the nineteenth and twentieth centuries had as much to do with advances in government as they did with technical innovations. The ways in which various economic and political interests congeal in urban infrastructure offer a primer for the study of urban governance, especially in disrupting generalized conceptions of 'public' and 'private' forms of regulation. The socialized modern city exemplified by London, Paris, Berlin or New York in the late nineteenth century and most of the twentieth rarely equated to a uniformly or straightforwardly 'public' model of infrastructure investment, delivery and management. The composite nature of the modern state was typified by the amalgam of municipal boards, private companies and public benefit corporations that owned and operated systems of water, transport, energy and communications; the fragmentary character of governance by the range of city commissioners, government inspectors and controllers with oversight of their provision, upkeep and management. A unitary notion of the state unpacks into the complex agencies of the chief engineer, prefect, parks commissioners and their army of subordinates. The archetypal city-makers of the nineteenth and twentieth centuries were engineers, officials and architects such as Joseph Bazalgette, Baron Haussmann, Frederick Law Olmsted and Robert Moses, rather than any elected politician or unelected statesman. Indeed, the politics of infrastructure might be seen as the basis for the modern idea of urban government, exemplified by London's 1856 formation of a Metropolitan Board of Works, which would in 1889 be succeeded by the London County Council. Under the city hall, the *hôtel de ville* and the *Rathaus* lies the sewer (see Osborne 1996).

If infrastructure unsettles a simple notion of the state in thinking about the organization of the modern city, it also disrupts crude notions of privatization as the keynote of twenty-first century urbanism. What works as a description of a broad – indeed pretty much universal – trend in the organization of urban ownership and governance resolves at local scales into diverse patterns of investment, authority and delivery. It is the case that the most powerful social interests that now 'congeal' in urban infrastructure are private interests, but these are sedimented in the built environment, and imbricated with public interests, in complicated ways. It is important to stress this point given the pronounced trends towards the privatization of urban environments that can be seen in both over-developed and developing contexts. These range from the complex financialization of infrastructural projects and products, to privatizations of transport and utilities infrastructure, to the kinds of effluent entrepreneurs that apply user-pays principles to ensure full 'cost recovery' in toilets in slum settlements (see Davis 2006; Graham and Marvin 2001; McFarlane 2008; Torrance 2008). In urban contexts where it seems anything can be commodified or capitalized, and in conditions of 'splintering urbanism' that fragment infrastructure supply and control across distributed and disaggregated systems, it is crucial to recognize the complex financing, ownership and control arrangements that lie behind the morphology of the network without simply collapsing this into unexamined categories of 'neoliberalism' or 'privatization'.

A key point of reference might be taken here from Karen Bakker's work on water. As Bakker (2007) notes, water exemplifies a common-pool resource from which it is difficult (practically and ethically) to exclude users, but where stocks are subject to depletion from over-use. Water is non-excludable and substitutable: that is, it is a common but rival good. The chief argument for forms of marketization in the supply of water is, simply, that water is a scarce resource and market mechanisms deal most efficiently with conditions of scarcity. Bakker (2007: 442) points out, however, that there are qualities of water itself, as well as aspects and implications of its use, which make it difficult to conceive water supply in market terms:

> [W]ater is a flow resource over which it is difficult to establish private property rights; it is characterized by a high degree of public health and environmental externalities – the costs of which are difficult to calculate and reflect in water prices; and it is a partially non-substitutable resource essential for life with important aesthetic, symbolic, spiritual and ecological functions which render some form of collective, public oversight inevitable.

These complex overlappings of the environmental, the social and the political mean that stewarding water involves the hybrid challenge of 'governing the relationship between the hydrological cycle, and socio-natural economies and polities' (Bakker 2007: 444; see also Johnston 2003). Arguments either for 'water democracy' or against 'water socialism' (Bakker 2007: 439) are complicated by the fact that urban water supplies are demonstrably subject to both state and market failure. Neither do these failures resolve themselves into easy characterizations of public waste, cost and disrepair, on one side, and market exclusions and externalities, on the other. As Bakker (2007: 444) argues, there are numerous cases in 'the global South, where "public" water supply systems often supply only wealthier neighbourhoods in urban areas, leaving poor and rural areas to self-organize through community cooperatives or informal, private,

Hooghly River, Kolkata, 2010.

for-profit provision by water vendors, often at volumetric rates much higher than those available through the public water supply system'.

On the other side, there appear real limits to the opportunities for large private interests to find profitable investments in water markets in under-served developing cities. Bakker again (2007: 440) notes 'the significant barriers to market expansion in the water supply sector in the South. . . . High-profile cancellations of water supply concession contracts – including Atlanta, Buenos Aires, Jakarta, La Paz, and Manila – seem to bear out the hypothesis that water presents difficult, and perhaps intractable problems for private sector management' – in both high- and low-income cities. If Big Water has been viewed as a clear and present threat by political movements against globalization and privatization, especially in respect of large dam and other infrastructure projects, privatization of the commons and degradation of local hydro-environments (Shiva 2002), the returns on investment have frequently appeared too uncertain, the sunk capital and transaction costs too high, for the market in water to prove really attractive to large private sector players. This would appear to be in important ways a problem of scale, as well as of the levels of regulatory compliance to which large private sector suppliers tend to be subject. The choice for urban water supply is rarely (if ever) simply one between a fully public system and a wholly privatized one. Public water utilities frequently rely on private financing, maintenance and management; market suppliers are subject to public oversight, targets and regulation. Semi-public companies routinely include large institutional investors. At a smaller scale, public officials operate in markets of influence, bribery and preference that in turn mean that private actors must work with and through public agencies in their profit-seeking activities. In the space between and below large public infrastructure and large private providers a complicated mixed economy in urban water infrastructure and supply emerges. The most lucrative market returns may be to those small to medium private actors who can organize illegal connections, broker relations with public officials or truck in water to urban areas where supply is limited, uncertain or non-existent.

The design of urban water infrastructure, then, includes the 'conscious design' of metropolitan sewer systems, cycles of clean and grey water pipes, reservoirs and outfalls. But water capture, collection and distribution also operate in less formal or systematic ways, via rainwater harvesting, tanks and butts; irregular and illegal wells, canalization, pipes, hoses, taps and cesspits; water tankers and jerrycans. These infrastructure designs are no less 'conscious', but harder to map, difficult to regulate and easy to destroy. They may indeed represent a type of infrastructure that is 'un-transparent', not only in the sense that it is not visible, but also in the sense that it must frequently be re-assembled. What is ready-at-hand may not always be ready-to-use. Such un-transparent systems of infrastructure are particularly subject to the political economy of stand-over, bribery, profiteering and exploitation, whether this takes the form of the corrupted state or the distorted market. But it also opens up potential for self-organization, communal provision and regulation, and forms of local enterprise that are not necessarily in the grip or the pay of public or private water mafia. Often this will involve the arduous and time-consuming labour of water collection and transportation – on foot, animal or bicycle. A draught of water can take all day.

Infrastructure and inequality

These uneven waterscapes of access and supply variously configure what Matthew Gandy (2008) calls 'hydrological dystopias' and systems of what Stephen Graham and his colleagues (2013) refer to as 'hydrological apartheid'. Edward Glaeser (2004) argues that, before the twentieth century, western cities were 'killing fields', depressing the life expectancy of their inhabitants by some five years on average, through the contagion of dirt and disease, such that 'public provision of clean water is surely the single biggest improvement in the quality of urban life in history.' But it is an uneven history. For Gandy (2008: 126), a dominant 'Western model of the "bacteriological city", with its universal water and sewerage systems, rests on the assumption that urban space is both relatively homogeneous and spatially coherent, which is at odds with the extreme forms of social polarization and spatial fragmentation experienced in the cities of the global South.' It should be noted, here, that homogeneity and coherence are not pre-existing qualities of urban spaces themselves, but conditions produced *through* the extension and integration of infrastructural systems. The underground city is key to both the visualization and the actualization of the city above-ground as a continuous surface.

Conversely, the fissures in the city above-ground become legible in the effective distribution of infrastructure – that is to say, urban inequalities are expressed in differential access to infrastructural systems and goods. Uneven and exclusionary flows of water and electricity highlight the often stark limits of an economy of 'flows' (Castells 2000), where urban populations and pockets remain off-grid, *hors service*, cut off. Infrastructural inequity is evident, moreover, not only in lack of access, but also in unwanted adjacencies – the siting of low-income and informal housing (as we have seen in chapters 4 and 5) up against arterial road and rail, next to bad neighbours such as dumps and sewage outlets, or amid the atmospheric noise of mobile phone masts, pumping stations and overhead power lines. The *overground* city of expressed infrastructure creates both desirable and unwanted forms of proximity: the differences, for instance, between living near a metro station or a bus stop, and living along a railway cutting or a highway. The tasks of city design entailed in these distributions of infrastructure involve both the physical design of *things* – bridges and tunnels, sewers and sub-stations – and the political design of *services* – transport, water, waste and fuel. Indeed, these are instances where the physical design of urban environments is inseparable from the design of urban publics.

The point is not only that inequalities and difference are distributed across urban spaces in ways that become legible for the slum tourist or the census bureau. The physical environment of the city gives material form to its uneven social geography. Edward Soja's (2010) account of the struggles over mass transit in Los Angeles speaks very clearly to this infrastructure of inequality in the city. The campaign against a light-rail system serving suburban areas, and for a decent bus network that might serve the city's overworked and underpaid (very many of them women, most of them non-white), underlines an urban condition in which the basic elements of collective consumption – transport and other infrastructure, open and green space in the city – increasingly are not *collective* at all, but offer either locational incentives for the more privileged classes, or services and spaces of last resort. In Los Angeles, the transport poor *mobilized* in the face of transit inequities. As with other forms of collectivity, and other forms of inequality, infrastructural inequities are potential sites of organization and conflict, as the 'interrelated web of socio-ecological relations that bring about highly uneven urban environments . . . become pivotal terrains around which political action crystallizes and social mobilizations take place' (Heynen et al. 2006: 6). The concept of 'resource wars' – over oil, gas and water – is well known in the study of international relations, but also bears on conflicts within and between cities; Stephen Graham and his colleagues (2013) write vividly of the 'water wars in Mumbai' that set residents of the city's *Zopadpatti* settlements in conflict with the police and other public authorities, private profiteers and other local populations. Such water wars in part are battled by marginal populations in the everyday struggle for access to basic goods, but are also waged by public agencies on behalf of privileged urban populations as part of a spatial 'war on the poor' in a perversely developing city. Most striking here, as Graham et al. note, is the city government's licensing of private swimming pools in new residential developments, as well as of water parks on the urban periphery, in a context of a 'parched city' unable or unwilling to meet its population's daily water needs.

Network secession and infrastructural elites

Infrastructure networks may be 'privatized' in various forms, but in principle they remain systems of collective consumption. Alongside modes of commodification and marketization, and the inequities in access and quality that often mark infrastructure provision, it is possible to identify more effective kinds of 'privatization' and more definitive patterns of exclusion in what might be termed *infrastructural secession*. Matthew Gandy remarks the fact that economic and urban growth does not necessarily bring improvements in quality of life, or of service provision, for significant urban populations. 'Many cities', he notes (Gandy 2008: 122), 'face a paradoxical combination of increasing wealth and deteriorating public health. . . . Severe disparities in public health can persist because of the array of technological, scientific, and architectural innovations that enable wealthy households to insulate themselves from the environmental conditions of the poor.' Some of this takes the form of privilege in real estate and housing markets, recourse to the private car as well as to the private hospital, but at an extreme it can operate through secession from forms of collective infrastructural consumption. If modern innovations in infrastructure – especially in respect of sanitation, water and fuel – helped to constitute the city around an ideal of the urban public, then the private city is in part typified by the fragmentation of infrastructure systems, and the capacity of certain actors to sequester themselves from the shared network.

Of course, it is not unusual for certain institutions and areas to seek to secure their own infrastructure against wider breakdown or crisis – whether the generators and heli-pads are in public hospitals or in elite hotels. Infrastructural autarky is often crucial to the military organization of space, epitomized by Baghdad's Green Zone following the 2003 invasion of Iraq: an infrastructural enclave in the hot, dark, dry city around it. However, this version of 'military urbanism' (Graham 2010) increasingly is generalized as a model for urban infrastructure – one is put in mind of the Goldman Sachs headquarters in lower Manhattan, the only illuminated building in that part of the city during the days of black-out following Hurricane Sandy in 2012. The crisis model of infrastructure has come to inform plans for housing and urban neighbourhoods, not just military bases, presidential palaces, expensive resorts or investment banks. One way of explaining the growth of ex-urban, enclave developments in emerging economies is in terms of an attempt to secure reliable infrastructure, whether private roads linking to highway access to cities and (especially) airports, or private energy and waste systems. The architect Rahul Mehotra has suggested that the attractions of new residential developments in the Pune-Mumbai region may have as much to do with a concern for infrastructure security as with concern over personal security in contexts where crime rates are low but basic services are uncertain. The model of the gated community taken from US, Latin American or South African cities, with their emphasis on crime, fear and personal security (Caldeira 1996, 2000; Jürgens and Gnad 2002; Landman 2004; Lipman and Harris 1999; Low 2001, 2003), may be a precedent but is not a simple analogue for the development of residential enclaves in relatively low-crime environments. Spatial distinction is certainly in play, but so too is infrastructural secession.

Alongside the 'gated communities' and 'security villages' of fearful and divided cities, infrastructure enclaves represent a further instance of the 'capsularization' of urban territory (see De Cauter 2005) – the retreat into protected, defended or even sealed units that insulate their users against loose, liminal or labile spaces. Gandy (2006b: 383) gives us a trenchant picture of these logics at work in Lagos:

> The intense social polarization and spatial fragmentation since the mid-1980s have led to a scenario in which many households – both rich and poor – attempt to provide their own water supply, power generation and security services. As night falls, the drone of traffic is gradually displaced by the roar of thousands of generators that enable the city to function after dark. Many roads in both rich and poor neighbourhoods become closed or subject to a plethora of ad hoc check-points and local security arrangements to protect people and property until the morning.

In certain contexts, as in Lagos, infrastructural autarky is a response to the unreliability or simple lack of collective infrastructure. In other settings, infrastructure enclaves secede from and substitute for existing, often public, municipal provision. This includes alternative urban projects in high-income cities framed in terms of environmental sustainability and self-sufficiency, where energy security is pursued through decentralization and self-organization. This is rather different from the 'moral minimalism' analysed by Setha Low (2003), where community conflicts in residential enclaves are managed through a culture of sameness and a homeowner politics of propriety. There are larger moral and political claims in self-build infrastructure and self-organized resource generation and recycling. At the same time, they offer another instance of the perverse analogues to be found in the 'lifestyles' of the urban rich and the urban poor – in this case, as dual models of off-grid, low-carbon living.

As forms of collective consumption – water, air, open space, power, transport, waste – become privatized, they become subject to the same kind of positional struggles as other kinds of commodities. On the other side, public infrastructures become residualized as networks of last resort. This is evident in the downgrading of public housing stocks and supplies in the United Kingdom, of public transport (especially buses) in numerous US cities and of water and power supplies in even more cities in developing contexts. Competition over notionally 'collective' infrastructures plays out in terms of the monopolization of public provision by urban middle classes and elites (as the work of Graham et al. [2013] on Mumbai's 'water wars' indicates), or conversely in secession from socialized provision in infrastructure 'security villages' and compounds. Infrastructure elites, that is, may be constituted through preferential access to public resources, or through capsular strategies for insulating infrastructure against wider systems shortages, breakdown or crisis.

Embodying infrastructure

The discussion to this point has focused on the infrastructure of *things*, the networks and not-works of pipe, cable, tarmac, rail, concrete; nodes within these networks (wells, reservoirs, dumps, stations, interchanges and exchanges); and the variable flows – of water, fuel, power, vehicles – through them. Such an understanding of infrastructure is conventional, and inflected by the modern understanding of infrastructure as an object of material and 'conscious design' in the city. Critical approaches to infrastructure as a less transparent and less complete kind of 'assemblage' consider the complex and often incoherent connections of socio-material elements – expressed and submerged infrastructural *stuff*, but also human actors, incidental materials, policies and plans, and information systems both virtual and social – that generate, distribute and appropriate basic services and resources in the city (see McFarlane 2011). Such an account does better at capturing the rigged-up 'systems' of infrastructure that serve autarkic elites but are also found in illegal electricity connections, oil-pipe piracy, groundwater drawdown, emergency and entrepreneurial water-tankers, improvised toilets and open sewers (see Graham et al. 2013).

Stephen Graham and Nigel Thrift (2007: 11) stress the prevalence of 'infrastructural improvisation' in cities of the global south, while Matthew Gandy (2006c: 508) writes of the way that 'cities such as Lagos, for example, are characterized by dilapidated networks of oil-financed urban infrastructures from the 1970s engulfed within the pyroclastic expansion of the informal city.' This 'post-productive' city, as Gandy puts it, overlays barely functional hulks of modern infrastructure with an explosive informality that both seeks to utilize and exhausts it. A more radical approach again shifts the focus beyond both hard infrastructure and incursions and improvisations in socio-technical networks to foreground 'people as infrastructure' (Simone 2004b). AbdouMaliq Simone uses this term to describe the way that regular and irregular patterns of transaction trace out networks of exchange in the city, but we can take this conception more broadly to think about the networks of *auto-infrastructure* through which diverse social actors provision, power and mobilize the city.

When Susan Leigh-Star (1999: 385) refers to the need to bring to the surface the 'invisible work' of infrastructure, she might as well be referring not to submerged or backgrounded technical networks but to the work of everyday communication, transport and distribution in the city that passes below the level of urban visibility. In light of various state and market failures, or more radical urban abandonment, human bodies themselves become infrastructural conduits, and micro-interactions are key points of exchange and distribution. Simone is especially concerned with the character of 'social infrastructure', the assembly and reproduction of urban social systems outside the frame of collective norms or formal organizations. He notes 'the way in which the apparently "ruined" spaces of inner city Johannesburg support a highly urbanized social infrastructure. This infrastructure is capable of facilitating the intersection of socialities so that expanded spaces of economic and cultural operation become available to residents of limited means' (Simone 2004b: 407). In this sense, 'the notion of *people as infrastructure* . . . emphasizes economic collaboration among residents seemingly marginalized from and immiserated by urban life' (Simone 2004b: 407; italics in original). This is to deploy the notion of infrastructure in a quite specific way, in terms of how 'complex combinations of objects, spaces, persons, and practices . . . become an infrastructure – a platform providing for and reproducing life in the city' (Simone 2004b: 408). Such an idea of infrastructure as a 'platform' for action and coordination departs from any simple notion of inert and engineered matter to engage with the ways that the conditions for urban social life rely on ongoing interaction organized across definite spaces. Excluded from formal modes of economic and often legal membership, marginal populations in the city produce their own 'platform' – sometimes unstable, often temporary – for economic action and livelihood strategies. In their reliance on clever and light-footed adaptation to the uncertainties and the insufficiencies of precarious urban life, these networks of social infrastructure are the *really* smart cities.

Simone is particularly interested in the 'infrastructures' configured by informal and illegal economies, but the notion of people as infrastructure extends more broadly to the networks of communication, supply and resource ramified around people in the city, in ways that re-connect with a more conventional understanding of urban infrastructure. Simone instances the illegal drug economy of transport, processing and distribution – one could also instance the hearsay and first-hand communications networks of urban in-groups; the rickshaw and cart pullers, *becak* and cyclos that make up a crucial transport infrastructure, especially in Asian cities; Mumbai's *dabbawala* network of tiffin couriers or the tea boys of Middle Eastern markets; the garbage pickers, manual scavengers, *cartoneros* and *Zabbaleen* who sort, remove and recycle waste; and the basic physical infrastructure that is women waiting for and carrying water, or gathering and carrying wood and other fuel. In these latter instances, human bodies become the primary form of infrastructure, as urban networks of communication, transport, food, waste, water and fuel are reproduced through the everyday work of walking, pedalling, waiting, talking, picking, gleaning, fetching and carrying.

Such mundane and often illicit networks are characterized at once by 'regularity and provisionality' (Simone 2004b: 408), with the embedding and re-embedding in space of informal associations and repeated interactions. With minimal or no fixed infrastructure, low technology and variable degrees of formal organization, these systems of 'people as infrastructure' may be relatively un-transparent, in Leigh-Star's sense – neither are they 'sunk into' other structures or 'built on an installed base'. Moreover, the geography of these networks can be difficult to track, and rarely resolves into the visual order of the fixed transport network or underground sewer system. While many of these systems of supply, communication, distribution and disposal rely on face-to-face or hand-to-hand interaction, they operate across or call up far more extended territories. Mumbai's *dabbawala* network distributes up to 200,000 lunch boxes across the city six days per week. Informal transport networks are basic to the movement systems of numerous cities, substituting for, competing with or augmenting absent, inadequate or expensive formal transport networks (see Cervero and Golub 2007). In an even more distributed sense, Simone (2004b: 425) sees African cities such as Johannesburg as 'a platform for people to engage with processes and territories that bear a marked sense of exteriority' – surfacing a range of connections that extend beyond the city to rural settlements, foreign cities and wider transnational networks.

Conclusion: the design politics of infrastructure

Interactions between people and infrastructure range from the conscious design and purposive engineering of the modern city; to ways in which the urban 'exoskeleton' of railway cuttings and highway flyovers, reservoirs and rubbish dumps create living spaces and economic opportunities for more or less marginal urban populations; again to the improvised and resourceful generation and appropriation of infrastructure resources; and on to the everyday labour in which people *embody* infrastructure. Similarly, the agents of infrastructure may be less the master-builders and engineers who epitomized the modernization of the nineteenth- and twentieth-century city than the fuel pirate, effluent entrepreneur or water-carriers of improvised urban infrastructures. Such infrastructures are products of conscious design, but also subject to more everyday design practices: the endless and more haphazard work of repair and maintenance (Graham and Thrift 2007), augmentation and re-tooling, diversion and cadging.

In these different ways, urban infrastructure is a critical domain for forms of design politics. Lewis Mumford (1938: 239) remarked on how hard it would be to maintain 'the existence of a rational collective organization of the physical means of life without the necessary organs of collective association and responsible social control'. If the model of the 'bacteriological' and integrated city provides only a poor fit for the diversity of urban materialities today, there is nevertheless an important model to be taken from 'the role of public works projects in the construction of a functional public realm' (Gandy 2006a: 14). The 'resilience' of urban infrastructures is not simply a question of technical robustness or precision engineering, but also one of the resilience of political and economic capacities. Infrastructure failures – those moments when submerged or backgrounded networks become visible as problems – are routinely political failures: in New Orleans or the United States' blacked-out eastern seaboard, in the

piles of uncollected garbage rotting on the pavements of Naples or
the constant traffic jam that is daily life in São Paulo. Some of this is a
matter of government and public authorities, but it also concerns the
building and underpinning of social infrastructures. Matthew Gandy
(2006b: 390) suggests that the 'potential role of infrastructural networks in forging social collectivities through the "binding of space"
holds implications for many cities facing similar problems of poverty,
social fragmentation and governmental failure.' AbdouMaliq Simone
(2011: 356), too, has a line on the infrastructural *binding* of space,
people and things that goes beyond built forms:

> Urbanization is not simply a context for the support or appropriation of
> specific lives as it is the plane upon which people – circling, touching,
> avoiding, attaching – come together, sometimes kicking and scream-
> ing, as an infrastructure. This is an infrastructure that meshes con-
> stantly changeable and sometimes expendable bodies. Urban existence,
> never pretty or efficient, rumbles onward as the provisionally stitched
> together, jigged up intersections of bodies and materials upon which
> things are both moved and caught . . . .

The 'infrastructure of everyday lives' (Gilroy and Booth 1999)
is rigged up around and through mundane exchanges and informal
support structures. It mediates between the uncertainties of public
provision and the exclusions of private resource. Against a bacteriological or palliative model of infrastructure, Ash Amin's vision of
'the good city' is grounded in a 'preventative and curative infrastructure' that secures the conditions of ordinary urbanism – 'a silent
republic of things' which underwrites the public character of the
body social (Amin 2006: 1015). This system of objects is one of the
reasons people know they live in the city as a collective space, but
it is made and re-made through many barely visible associations,
manouevres and connections, as well as through more substantial
and public interventions. Things mediate social relations and in turn
embed social relations in concrete forms. In the moment of flick-
ing a switch or turning a tap, a dense network of social action and
interaction is called up. In other contexts the ethnography of urban
infrastructure is more visible, in expressed materials and arduous
human labour, in improvisation and ingenuity, and in infrastructural
inequalities. As a key element of city design, infrastructure requires
us to work 'from the relation of people to things, as well as from
the relation of people to each other' (Lynch 1995c [1975]: 789).
The design politics of infrastructure is a blueprint of how the city

Regent's Canal, London, 2012.

is imagined and constituted as a collective surface, as a shared life-support system, or as a field of scarce and rival resources. The stuff of infrastructure keeps life together in the big city at the same time as it works to hold people, spaces and resources apart.

Jawaharlal Nehru Road, Kolkata, 2010.

7
Afterword: The Possible City

Most utopias fail to keep space and society simultaneously in mind.
Lynch 1995c [1975]: 789

We will either master this ominously complicated entity or perish under it. The common life for a noble end, of which Aristotle spoke, probably can, as human experience seems to show, be better lived in cities.
Wirth 1940: 755

The discussions in the preceding chapters have considered the diverse ways in which contemporary urban forms are shaped by the designs of social actors. Such designs are more or less purposive and more or less conscious. The concept of 'design', in this sense, enfolds elements of desire and deprivation, deliberation and disadvantage, intended and incidental outcomes. Understood in terms of the 'inter-relations between urban forms and human objectives' (Lynch and Rodwin 1958: 201), the design of cities routinely results in patterns of unequalization, injustice and maldistribution. However, an argument that cities are made through ordinary practices of urbanism, and by many different agents, can hardly sit easily with a conclusion that these social processes – and these everyday experts in the design of cities – merely reproduce structures and spaces of inequity, injury and exclusion. If a central aim of this text has been to extend the creative, logistical and political design of cities beyond the realm of the qualified and the credentialled, then it's not clear that the ordinary practitioners are doing so much better than the professionals and the politicos. Neither should the aim be, however, to underplay the inequity and the unsustainability that characterize much of contemporary urbanism in order to make pious gestures towards the pocket park and the slum start-up. It is perhaps a side-effect of my own convictions about cities – their capacity to hold together difference, to allow space for people to make their lives and their livelihoods, to afford human freedoms as well as to support solidarities, to generate everyday intensities – that I have been so concerned with the counter-narratives of segregration, abandonment, disconnection and homogenization. Kevin Lynch's epigraph underlines how hard it can be to integrate progressive social objectives with good spatial designs: the virtuous orthodoxies of the mixed-use development, the linear park, the post-industrial atelier, the pop-up, the urban allotment and the un-programmed public space remind us that the 'spatial proposals' of social utopians can become 'as banal and conventional as are the architects' thoughts of society' (Lynch 1995c [1975]: 789). 'In contrast,' Lynch goes on (1995c [1975]: 789), 'we find strong descriptions of place in most anti-utopias, where physical oppression abets social oppression in a very direct and circumstantial way.' The devil, it seems, gets all the best designs.

In contemporary conditions of rapid and largely unplanned urban growth in many developing contexts, continuing sprawl and super-sized housing on the edges of many rich and middle-income cities, and the kinds of 'giantism and loss of control' identified by Allan Jacobs and Donald Appleyard (1987) in cities across the global income divide, the will to design can seem inadequate, even quixotic. Between the persistent and pervasive urbanism of informality, at one end, and the spatial presumptions of large developers and public–private agencies, at the other, the space available for urban interventions that mediate informality or mitigate giantism can seem very tight indeed. Lynch remained convinced, however, that there were 'grounds for utopia' in thinking about the design of cities. These were to be found less in any blueprint for an urban ideal than in skilful reworking of existing urban forms. Lynch was especially concerned with sites that were dormant, degraded or disused. The arguments he sets out in his reflections on 'the possible city' have since become more standard gestures in approaches to urban design, but they do not lose their force in thinking against some of the assumptions and arrogations of urban business as usual. In particular, Lynch (1995b [1968]: 780) wanted to aim off 'the protected and expensive, committed environment' – over-designed, over-valorized, and over-programmed – so as to focus on the uncommitted places that allow for greater autonomy and creativity in the making of space. He was an early advocate of what is now called urban 'retro-fitting', proposing that one critical strategy for dealing with the existing city is the search for underused space and time, and its readaptation for a desired activity. We can explore the use of streets as play areas, or the possibilities for using roof tops, empty stores, abandoned buildings, waste lots, odd bits of land, or the large areas presently sterilized by such mono-cultures as parking lots, expressways, railroad yards, and airports. (Lynch 1995b [1968]: 776)

Re-making space *in time* – such that streets at times hold activity in place rather than simply routing transport flows – works in tandem with more substantive adaptations of latent or empty space, as well as of those large tracts given over to transport technologies to the detriment of ordinary mobilities: what Marc Augé (1995) would later describe as the 'non-places' characteristic of *supermodern* travel. This is one element of a more general project to recalibrate the city around alternative uses of space and measures of value. The grounds for utopia, that is, were to be found not in some ideal version of urban space, but in the re-making of existing sites whose capacities are unrealized and whose sources of value are overlooked. It is an urban utopianism grounded in present conditions rather than speculative projections, and may prove an urbanism that is better suited to lean times and modest means – as well as to over-built or rapidly developing environments – than more ambitious programmes of city-making.

How can we make out the contours of the 'possible city' from the discussions that have developed in preceding chapters? In respect of each of the key aspects of urban form and process considered so far – density, diversity, informality, environment, infrastructure – certain propositions might be drawn for the ways in which urbanists (both credentialled and 'non-qualified', official and unofficial) may shape their cities as built forms, socio-economic systems, environments and surfaces of common life.

Density

Density is one of the defining characteristics of cities as a mode of human settlement, and it has come to be seen as key not only to the economic benefits derived from urban agglomeration, but also to the environmental sustainability of urban forms. Urban densities support thick labour and consumer markets that increase competition and choice; are consistently linked to higher output and income levels; reduce transport costs for materials, goods and workers within urban economies; and lower the per capita costs of such public service provision as capital works, roads, police services and education. In contemporary economies, urban densities are seen as especially beneficial in promoting innovation and enskilling, creativity and information spill-overs in the knowledge-based industries that are leading urban growth. In environmental terms, higher urban densities make collective and non-motorized transport alternatives more viable and efficient; draw down less land from peri-urban borders; support economies of scale for combined and alternative energy sources; and promote collective provision of green space, waste and recycling services, and resource and transport infrastructures. The social benefits of urban density tend to be more contentious, but the positive case to be made here includes important equities of scale and access around public transport and urban amenities; routine potential for social interaction, exposure and tolerance across class, ethnic and cultural differences; greater choice of cultural and consumer services for different population segments; and thicker geographies of opportunity in employment and housing markets for economically and culturally diverse populations.

Given that density is something that cities *do* as an effect of economic intensification and population growth, the challenge for urban planning and design is how to steer urban densities in more efficient, sustainable and liveable ways. Approaches to urban density must also respond to powerful counter-logics of sprawl and de-densification variously associated with the locational lure of lower land values for industries and employers, with growing affluence and prevailing cultures of residential preference, and with peri-urban land settlements by incoming and often informal urban populations. In different urban contexts, movements out from the centre by businesses and suburbanizing households, and movements into the periphery by rural–urban migrants, produce various patterns of sub-division, land invasion and urbanizing hinterlands that increase the spatial take of cities and intensify the pressure on urban resources and infrastructure.

Density and compactness may have become new orthodoxies of good urban design – and may mark a clear divergence between the views of urban experts and the expressed preferences of those ordinary urbanites who are sufficiently enriched and empowered to make residential choices – but these are not simply ends in themselves. The point of urban density as a planning and design strategy is just what you want to achieve with it, and the ways in which these objectives are to be achieved spatially. There are different things that different urban interests might want to do with density: increasing or lowering land, property and rental values; adding housing supply or enhancing space standards and housing quality; decreasing environmental costs or relieving congestion; promoting urban dynamism or decompressing social environments. These deliberations over the organization of space also imply designs on human behaviour around transport choices, resource use, waste and recycling, housing preferences, individual and collective consumption, and social attitudes. An empirical category that is measured as numerical ratios of mass or volume to area unpacks into a series of designs on social life as much as on urban space.

The question of which objectives strategies for density are designed to achieve is crucial for the spatial forms in which they are realized. Patterns of land use and degrees of integration between different functions, levels and compositions of mixed use, the connectivity and accessibility of transport systems, the design of built forms and their relationships to open spaces, including street, squares, yards and parks: these elements shape the distribution of densities across an urban area, and powerfully affect the perceived or affective densities of urban inhabitants. An extended approach to density, moreover, will take in not only residential or employment densities but also the more variable intensities of movement, interaction and occupation in different places over different time-frames – hence the benefits or the costs of urban densities also derive from the design and management of temporary events and seasonal rhythms, as well as the everyday pulse of the city.

The design and management of density operates at nested spatial scales, such that the raw density measure for a city as a whole is mediated by the organization and integration of different urban functions; the routing of transport networks and the clustering of uses around transport nodes; patterns of mixed use at different urban scales; neighbourhood forms and urban blocks; street design and layouts; the patterning of open spaces; typologies of built form; relations between buildings and streets; transitions between public and private space; common areas in buildings; space standards and interior layouts. It follows that both designs on, and behaviour around, density work up from the individual to the metropolitan dimension, and what happens at each level has implications running up and down the scale. 'Right' levels of density will vary in different urban contexts as well as across different cities, but various tipping points might be reached when the positive claims to be made for density – competition and innovation, efficiency and collectivity, interaction and diversity – become dysfunctional or counter-productive, giving over into market and information saturations; cut-throat competition; inflated time and money costs; congestion, overcrowding and collective over-consumption; social tension, mistrust and conflict. At dysfunctional levels of density, moreover, there may be little room for urban adjustments and incremental change outside of scorched earth policies of demolition, clearance and re-building, on one hand, or sprawl, on the other.

Diversity

Just as cities will *do* density independently of the interventions of politicians and planners, so diversity is a characteristic feature of urbanism as a way of life that strategies for city design and management respond to in various ways. There are important claims to be made for diversity as a principle and objective of urban design and planning, understood in both functional and social terms. Economic diversity is a critical factor in contemporary urban economies, distributing the economic weight – and the economic risk – across different industrial and employment sectors. A mix of people and skills helps sustain more dynamic and competitive labour, supplier, consumer and housing markets; helps to hold down wage and price inflation within different market segments; encourages innovation, enterprise and new market entries. The benefits of diversity are seen to work across income scales: urban mix can be good for lower-income, new migrant and minority groups in providing access to more diverse labour and housing market as well as opportunities for socio-economic mobility, while social and cultural diversity is seen as a pull factor for high-skilled workers in advanced and creative sectors of contemporary economies.

There are significant environmental benefits, too, to be had from the mix of functions and uses that underpins urban diversity. The functional integration of residential, commercial, institutional and leisure uses makes access in the city a matter of proximity rather than a question of mobility, promoting walking and cycling as well as collective modes of transport. It reduces travel time and costs, lowers emissions from transport and offers environmental cost-efficiencies in well-used buildings, blocks and streets that support a mix of different uses and users over time. In social terms, urban diversity allows many different kinds of people to find their place in the city, supporting cultural and sub-cultural solidarities and affording diverse spaces of gathering, interaction and amenity. Social diversity may create more acute challenges for urban cohesion and conflict than more homogeneous settlements tend to face (although the latter will have their own lines of tension and points of conflict), but also fosters cultures of tolerance, spaces of refuge and safety, and routine sites of interaction, exchange and learning. A quality of urbanity (or 'cityness', as Sassen [2005b] puts it) may be harder to measure than the spatial footprint of a city or its gross density, but is deeply tied to the experience of difference as a spatial and social condition; it is one of the rationales for living in or moving to a city that – while it may be less instrumental – is no less important than the economic opportunities afforded by urban life.

Urban diversity is a positive objective for city design in creating more vibrant places, leveraging economic advantages and promoting social equity and environmental sustainability (see Talen 2006). A mix of functions supports more 'vital' urban spaces that are better used by a range of users, and open up opportunities for social encounter and interaction. City diversity encourages enterprise development in different sectors and at different scales, sustains more diverse labour and consumer markets, promotes economic innovation, knowledge transfer and the 'Jacobs externalities' derived from exchanges between different industries and skills. In equity terms it enhances access to urban services, resources and amenities for people with different needs, capacities and incomes. And urban diversity creates efficiencies in land and resource use through the integration of functions and the shrinking of transport distances. Designing for diversity therefore gives priority to an integrated balance of different functions – whether through strategies of mixed use at building, block and street scales, or through accessible adjacencies at larger neighbourhood, district and city scales. At the level of the building and the block, the use of variable and adaptable typologies helps to de-homogenize living and working environments while also allowing for changes in residential and work patterns across individuals' and households' lives. Designing for diversity includes the design of urban services and amenities for a range of populations with different needs and preferences, and of non-exclusionary shared spaces and services that might be used in common (if not in exactly the same ways) across lines of cultural, class and generational difference.

Such strategies of designing for diversity are well recognized in professional and policy contexts, but an emphasis on the virtues of mix can obscure the benefits of degrees of sameness and separation in the city. Ethnic neighbourhoods and low-income areas have become targets for diversification and de-concentration in a number of urban settings, but such areas provide resources, opportunities and services that tend to come under threat from both market- and policy-led processes of urban mixing. Ethnic enclaves, in particular, generate resources for livelihoods, social needs and cultural preferences that often fall outside the range, capacity or planning foresight of urban governments. Local businesses, religious and cultural associations, civic and political institutions, welfare services, shops, schools and restaurants represent forms of everyday urbanism that serve crucial functions for migrant and minority populations whose needs may otherwise be under-served by planning and design (whether public or private) for the 'majority' city. In a similar manner, lines of socio-economic separation in the city mark out lower-rent areas that offer cheaper entry to housing and other markets for poorer populations. Low-income neighbourhoods provide substantive welfare functions in the forms of housing affordability, cheaper retail and other services, and opportunities for enterprise and employment; they may also generate social solidarities and a greater sense of belonging in and control over local spaces.

If forms of ethnic, racial or class segregation represent 'one of the key methods of accommodating difference' in the city (Peach 1996: 379), and – as Loretta Lees (2010: 2307) more recently has argued – a central principle of 'planning for urbanity' should be the affordance of '"visible" spaces for the poor, socially marginal, and/or deviant', then there is a significant risk that attempts to desegregate and diversify the city work to the detriment of the least advantaged. Processes of housing market gentrification as well as policy strategies for social mixing tend to carry a 'diversity premium' that proves most attractive to and most lucrative for more affluent incomers and homeowners, such that efforts to design in density frequently work to 'undiversify' urban areas through patterns of displacement or processes of local colonization and incubation by higher-income groups. As in the case of urban density, the critical question will be what politicians, planners or developers are seeking to achieve in the pursuit of urban diversity, and at what point these objectives tip over into high-end homogeneity or micro-segregations in space.

Diversity is a crucial but complicated urban value, and the moral charge it carries in much recent urban policy may obscure more practical arguments for income and tenure diversity at the local grain of urban neighbourhoods. It is not possible to legislate or plan for social interaction or encounter, or to engineer resources of social trust – and these qualitative benefits of urban mixing are both difficult to measure and may be less desirable for urban residents than they appear to well-intentioned politicians or planners. The deconcentration of poverty areas and supply of affordable housing stock in central cities are more straightforward but also more politicized planning objectives. A rhetoric of 'social mix' or 'mixed communities' provides a moralized gloss for pragmatic interventions in housing markets to ensure that a share of lower-income households and lower-income workers is retained in core cities with inflated real estate sectors – whether the political rationale is based on equity grounds or on arguments for economic efficiency (or, as is more likely, some combination of the two). Housing subsidies, household relocations, mixed-tenure developments and estate renewals, affordable housing targets, shared-ownership schemes and other quasi-market tenure strategies act as partial substitutes for public housing in contexts of state roll-back and housing inflation. The key question, as for densification strategies, is at what point engineered diversity produces counter-effects – of gentrification, displacement, local segregations. One set of responses to this problem is geared less to new developments or market incentives for incomers than to protections for existing populations who are especially vulnerable to the indirect displacements of local upscaling: rent controls for residential and commercial uses, as well as income ceilings for social housing tenants, can help to secure the cheap end of the 'mix' against the inflationary effects of housing market renewal.

Designing *for* diversity may be the wrong way to think about strategies for promoting or protecting urban mix. Diversity is something that big cities *do*, in accommodating critical masses of different populations and affording diverse spaces of settlement, solidarity, enterprise and exchange, but also in sorting by socio-economic difference around segmented housing, consumer and labour markets. These processes are reinforced in various ways by legal segregations and public allocations. It could be that the better objective for policy, planning and design in contemporary cities is not to engineer diversity but to design *against* segregation, in securing equities of access to decent transport, services, open space and other urban amenities across city neighbourhoods; providing minimal protections through tenure security and rent controls for lower-income residential and commercial populations in 'diversifying' areas; maintaining a mix of building typologies in local commercial districts including a fine grain of smaller units to accommodate small businesses and traders; and designing non-exclusionary public spaces and services that support equitable access and common use for urban populations that are defined by difference, from parks and community spaces to pavements and pedestrian routes. These design strategies take in legal and policy designs to protect and shore up the ways in which cities do diversity, as much as they involve physical design for mixed-use developments and streets or for shared spaces of public use.

Informality

The notion of planning or design for informality seems, on the face of it, contradictory. Informality in cities – from slum settlements in majority poor cities to creative or illicit occupations in rich-world cities or the extra-legal prerogatives of urban elites – is a primary mode of everyday urbanism: the ways in which cities are made beyond the purview of the plan, the designs of policy or the gaze of the law. A conception of informality as counter-posed to formal processes, as characteristic of the 'organic' rather than the 'planned' city, belies the ways in which informality and formality are co-produced in the city; the fact, as Kim Dovey (2011: 351) put it, that 'all cities embody a mix of informality/formality and urbanity requires informality.' It also tends to assume that informality is a problem for urban planning and design – which, of course, it sometimes is – rather than a resource for more flexible, more responsive and more pragmatic city-making, which it also can be. Getting the informality/formality mix 'right' is a challenge for cities in different situations, whether in allowing spaces for informal occupation and enterprise in the tightly stitched cities of the over-developed world, or in integrating sites and practices of informality into the over-stretched cities of the developing world. In certain settings, the response from a legal, policy and planning standpoint might be to encourage *more* informality through permissive planning measures, improvised uses and temporary occupations, and relaxed licensing rules; in most urban contexts, however, the strategy will be towards formalization, through the legitimization of non-conforming tenures and unconventional trades, the extension of social and infrastructure services to undocumented citizens and unplanned settlements, or the recognition of the right of squatters and others to participate in local deliberations and decision-making.

Such strategies of 'planning for informality' begin not with the blank slate or the cleared land but with existing urban conditions; making visible the 'blind' topography of the informal city and working from it (see Gandy 2006b: 389). Much of the work of design in this context will concern the underpinning designs of law and infrastructure. It includes basic provision of bulk infrastructure to informal settlements – integrated, where possible, to mains networks – to ensure collective access to clean water, durable roads and paths, effective sewerage and safe energy. These measures involve some cost, and require the greatest capacity on the part of government agencies or non-governmental organizations, but are likely to prove less costly by all measures than programmes of eviction, clearance and relocation. Where city agencies are unable to provide decent alternative land or housing for informal settlers, the minimal formalization of squatter sites secures the basic necessities of collective life and in doing so supports the auto-upgrading that is characteristic of informal neighbourhoods given the least degree of security and amenity. Even where public authorities are able to provide land and housing alternatives, the better solution is often to consolidate the urban settlements that already exist, including the employment, commercial, institutional and cultural networks and resources embedded in them. There are of course real points of political tension here: where informal settlements occupy public or common land in or around cities, this represents a form of 'privatization' that renders these sites largely inaccessible to others and unavailable for alternative (including public) uses. At the same time, the underlying legal status of the land makes settlers vulnerable to eviction, intrusion and invasion. There are different versions of the urban public in play – and differential 'rights' to urban spaces – that policy-makers, social and political organizations, resident and citizen groups can only determine in agonistic ways. Advocates of squatters' rights – in supporting the recognition and legalization of informal occupations – may have to stand by a claim that some effective privatizations of urban space are more equitable and more desirable than conventional debates would generally have it.

Legal designs are central to modes of planning for informality: whether in the 'positive' design of temporary, intermediate or irregular forms of tenure and licensing, or in the 'negative' mode of discretionary waivers of legal regulations and requirements. Institutional designs are also critical – including the promotion and protection of alternative systems of credit and saving, or the recognition of self-help groups, undocumented citizens, informal local representatives and especially women in processes of consultation, planning and decision-making. Again, the question for urban design, planning and governance is how much informality is too much. The other side of arguments against the deadening effects of red tape, bureaucracy and planning rigidities in conditions of over-formality that allow little room for improvisation, inventiveness or enterprise is the problem of dysfunctional informality. Given that informal settlement is a normal part of everyday urbanism in very many cities, integrated into the broader urban fabric through insertions and attachments into existing morphologies and supported by various economic interdependencies, at what degree do informal settlements become segregated, defended, marginalized or dangerous to their inhabitants as well as to unwary incomers? At what point does a permissive regulatory attitude to unconventional businesses reinforce the exploitation of workers rather than foster small-scale enterprise and economic self-sufficiency? Under what conditions does the 'social order of the slum' (Suttles 1968) shade into stand-over control by local mafia or strongmen, and reinforce the domination of women and children? And when do the extra-legal arrogations of the powerful produce spatial exclusions and social injustices for those more routinely subject to the rule of law and the rulings of planning? These are all contextual issues, not easily answered in terms of fixed definitions or simple oppositions of formality and informality.

The responses, too, will not always be legal or official. If the distinction between formality and informality is not particularly meaningful under a sociological understanding in which all forms of human organization and settlement are productive of social order, of rules and norms that are codified to different extents and with various degrees of force, then this is consistent with urban realities in which physical forms and social arrangements are designed and managed by a range of actors who are generally less rather than more official: from traders and householders to family and kin networks, local civic and welfare institutions, voluntary and communal organizations, business associations and social entrepreneurs, gangs and criminal networks, political parties and fixers, religious and cultural leaders, guerrilla designers and self-builders, planners and developers, utility companies, financial institutions, makers of law and policy, elected or unelected politicians. The categorical distinctions that exist – more or less clearly – in law or in planning come apart in urban contexts in which formality and informality are co-produced and interdependent; neighbourhoods get built out in orderly but 'unplanned' ways; design emerges as an effect of making space, rather than as a precondition for it; occupations and inhabitations run ahead of entitlements; and various shadow states are often more powerful than official ones.

Environment

Cities figure prominently in current debates over environmental sustainability and climate change mitigation. Urbanization is a resource-intensive process, consumes and frequently degrades land, produces heat and emissions, draws down resources from peri-urban hinterlands and places pressure on wider ecosystems. The business of keeping a city running is emissions-heavy, with urban buildings and transport taking a significant share of overall emissions from human settlement activities. At the same time, urbanization offers environmental economies of scale by concentrating users of resources, energy, transport and built structures, making collective form of provision, consumption and recycling more viable and cost-efficient, and potentially reducing transport distances for people and goods and reducing land use per capita. How these contrary logics are resolved is a critical challenge for the design and management at cities from individual and household levels to the metropolitan and city-regional scale.

The management of urban environments turns around the intersections between design, technology and behaviour. Compact, low-carbon and resource-efficient urban forms set problems for infrastructure planning and building design, as well as for urban technologies from the household to the city grid and beyond. Individual and collective behaviour is shaped by these design and technical solutions, but can be hard to shift or to 'nudge', given the ways in which social practice is embedded in built environments as much as in collective psychologies. Behavioural patterns may be the hardest part of the urban environmental puzzle to crack, but urban populations may also be particularly amenable to behavioural change, given their access to information, capacities for adaptation acquired in urban environments in which change is normal, and the density of urban demonstration effects that allow opportunities for social learning.

The dynamic interactions between cities as built forms and as behavioural bundles are both productive of environmental bads and a source of potential efficiencies. There are basic environmental economies to be had from collective provision and processing of transport, energy and waste, denser and more compact built environments, and functional integration between different land uses. Urban populations constitute critical masses for behavioural adaptation and environmental action. City governments, meanwhile, have significant capacity to steward environmental solutions and regulations, working at a scale that combines relative flexibility and responsiveness with sufficient authority and reach to have a substantive impact. With varying degrees of leverage over land use planning, transport planning and provision, capital estates and building controls, public realm and external lighting, food standards and urban agriculture, water and energy, waste and recycling, city governments exercise considerable power over major urban emissions sources and potential environmental strategies.

The environmental take and the emissions share of urban settlements vary not only between different cities but within urban populations. The cities (and bits of cities) of the urban poor have a profoundly different environmental and emissions profile from the urbanisms of the rich, as well as deeply uneven vulnerabilities to environmental risk. City governments, too, have quite different capabilities and authorities in respect of environmental regulation, innovation and mitigation. However, there are a number of principles of design, planning and management for more sustainable urban development that are relevant to cities and governments with variable economic and political capacities (see Kenworthy 2006). These include compact urban forms integrated around mixed uses to ensure more efficient land use and the protection of urban hinterlands; movement systems centred on mass transit, in which non-motorized alternatives are viable and encouraged, and road infrastructures and private motor use are 'de-emphasized' (Kenworthy 2006: 68); water, energy and waste management operated as 'closed-loop' systems that maximize synergies, reduce external dependency and limit externalities; maintenance of the public realm as a space of public culture, supporting equitable access, and including the transport system and infrastructures; and the design of public and other environments at human scale. Such strategies suggest it is not the case that 'only when we are sufficiently rich can we afford the relative luxury of caring about the environment' (Lomborg 2001: 33): integrated systems of resourcing and recycling, de-emphasized road coverage and the stewardship of urban biodiversity are not simply elective privileges enjoyed by rich-world cities, but urban environmental strategies in which the demonstration effect tends to run in the other direction – indeed, Jeffrey Kenworthy (2006: 67) sees the 'highly auto-dependent, resource-consuming cities of North America and Australia' as particularly in need of 'remedial action on an unprecedented scale'. Moreover, the clincher for Kenworthy is not any kind of technological fix, but an extended and inclusive planning process based on principles of 'debate and decide' rather than a mechanics of 'predict and provide'.

Infrastructure

Infrastructure networks integrate cities as shared spaces of common life, but also splinter urban territories into zones of differential access and exclusion. Often taken to exemplify the designs of public power and formal planning, the realities of urban infrastructure more usually involve unsteady integrations of public, private and informal infrastructures. This is an infrastructural patchwork as much as a network, which extends from metropolitan sewerage systems and power stations, corporate water and financialized energy, to off-grid septic tanks and generators, and communal latrines or pirated electricity. The design politics of how infrastructures are developed, governed and integrated is core to the ways that the common life of cities to which Louis Wirth (1940: 755) refers is conceived and realized. Ash Amin (2006: 1015) makes a compelling argument for a version of 'the good city' that is grounded in 'preventative and curative infrastructure'. This 'silent republic of things' underpins the collective life of the city, and the basic rights of urban citizens. Such a conception of the urban good is visible in the municipal services and systems of the socialized modern city, but also in strategies to provide bulk infrastructure to informal settlements in unplanned urban consolidations – a civics of the stand-pipe and the sewer that extends substantive rights of urban citizenship absent legal property titles or formal enrolments.

The 'infrastructure of everyday lives' (Gilroy and Booth 1999) is rigged together from public provisions, private concessions and informal improvisations. It mediates the contingencies of public provision and the exclusions of private resource. This is an infrastructure made up around objects and networks, but also around human associations, labour and interactions – an embodied urbanism involving auto-infrastructures of transport and energy, waste and water, processing, communication and distribution. Infrastructure is an exemplary instance of how an urban order emerges 'from the relation of people to things, as well as from the relation of people to each other' (Lynch 1995c [1975]: 789). Formal and informal systems, technical and auto-infrastructures, public, private and communal provisions, compose the common life of the city in variously composing collective life-support systems, fragmented networks or uneven terrains of scarce and rival resources.

In this context as in others, the question of 'who is getting how much of it' remains basic to the design of urban forms and the management of urban processes. In thinking about the shape of the 'possible city', Lynch was concerned not only with the re-ordering of time and the re-centring of space but also with the reappraisal of value: 'As a prerequisite for unlocking this process of change,' Lynch (1995b [1968]: 775) asserts, 'its costs must be openly accounted for and justly allocated. The burden now falls on deprived and power-less people.' In the preceding pages we have seen a number of urban issues – environment, infrastructure, services, access – where skewed economic distributions are reflected in and reproduced by perverse spatial distributions. Shifting the burden of such maldistributions involves making claims for the 'deprived and the powerless' as agents as well as objects of design politics. It is in this same spirit that Ash Amin (2006: 1015) argues that an 'equivalence of right has to be assumed between those in the mainstream and those on the margins': including commensurable rights to occupy and appropriate space. These are claims for the social and spatial rights of urban citizenship that go beyond petitions for formal representation, private entitle-ments or access to services, to demand a part in the production of urban space (see Lefebvre 1996 [1968]). David Harvey (2008: 23) argues eloquently for this 'right to change ourselves by changing the city'; such a right is necessarily common or collective in nature, given that it 'inevitably depends upon the exercise of a collective power to reshape the processes of urbanization'.

Urban common life

This afterword began with Louis Wirth's reflection on the possibili-ties for 'common life' in the city. Cities provide contexts for forms of common life and the exercise of collective power that are not well captured by abstract notions of citizenship, and which do not conform easily to standard notions of what it means to be part of a public (see Sarkis 1997). Citizenship is conventionally understood within the frame of the nation, but while 'one of the essential pro-jects of nation-building has been to dismantle the historic primacy of urban citizenship and to replace it with the national, cities remain the strategic arena for the development of citizenship' (Holston and Appadurai 1996: 188). The fracturing of the nation-state as a domain of political authority and a space of belonging has forced a critical re-thinking of the equation of citizenship with the nation. Too often, however, contemporary problems of citizenship are understood via a tension between the national and the global, further abstracting what it might mean to be a citizen in the substantive territories of everyday life. Thinking about citizenship beyond the nation-state does not simply mean displacing the concept to a larger – transnational or global – scale. Cities provide spaces for the enactment of both the formal and substantive rights of citizens, for the constitution of the 'body politic' as well as the 'body social'. Moreover, cities are experienced as 'virtual' or imagined spaces of membership, but also and primarily as 'actual' spaces of inhabitation and agency, lived in terms of an immediacy and a materiality that is quite distinct from the abstract belongings or the legal inscriptions of the nation-state (see Isin 2007; see also Hall 2012).

The common life of the city to which Wirth referred is one that is founded in difference. If the nation-state has failed 'to produce convincing fantasies of the commensurability of its citizens' (Holston and Appadurai 1996: 202), cities render their citizens commensurable in the very fact of difference. Henri Lefebvre (1996 [1968]), as is well known, saw the right to difference as a crucial element of any broader right to the city as a meaningful as well as a material space. If cities provide spaces for the agonistic 'dramas of citizenship' (Holston and Appadurai 1996: 200), these are spaces that are differentiated in terms of property and legal status, and which produce different legalities of citizenship. It follows that if one is to defend a notion of meaningful, substantive citizenship, then one must also secure and defend the spaces in which it becomes possible. The emphasis in much urban theory is on public spaces in this connection, but it can be important to defend the 'integrity of urban experience across property boundaries' (Sternberg 2000: 268), and in particular the role of urban form and urban space that is not simply residual and is ultimately 'uncommodifiable'. This opens up a further critical line of argument regarding the possible city, which has to do with the way 'uncommitted' spaces unsettle established demarcations of property and authority. In the face of the creeping 'propertization of public space' (Blomley 2004: 623), and the spreading incarcerations of the private, the ideal and actuality of spaces that can be made commonable – in practice, if not always under the law – can be a powerful way of enacting certain rights to the city. As urban environments are marked up by delineations of public and private, so social actors are constituted through partial and conflicting rights to space that splinter urban citizenship into various categories of rentier and squatter, consumer and loiterer, bystander and protester, householder or trespasser. Cities stage these conflicting rights as contests over space, in the politics of enclosure and foreclosure, entry and exclusion, development and displacement. As produced in practice, sites of commonalty subvert both the exclusions of private property and the prescriptions of the state, opening spaces in which we can 'make and remake our cities and ourselves' (Harvey 2008: 23).

These strategies for re-making the urban run counter to powerful logics of development and regulation in contemporary cities. New forms of enclosure are a keynote of recent processes of urbanization: whether in privatizations of common or public space, collective provision and services; or in the criminalization, clearance and harassment of various acts of 'commoning' – squatting, occupations and assemblies, informal settlements and common-pool resourcing of ecosystem services, including water, agriculture and fuel (see Hodkinson 2012; Jeffrey et al. 2012). It follows that it is neither property law nor public policy but situated social action that will extend the range of land, things and resources that may be made commonable at different times and places; through collective occupations of space, shared access to goods or de-privatizations of information, resources and energy. These may not map onto stable or coherent spaces, but are instantiated through actions, exchanges and inhabitations that can be temporary, mobile or distributed. The idea of the urban common, Paul Chatteron (2010: 626) contends, is 'relational': as an effect of practice, it is 'as much a verb as a noun'. Moreover, the work of commoning runs through often very minor practices – as Judith Revel and Toni Negri (2007: 9) put it: making, producing, participating, moving, sharing, spreading, enhancing, inventing, rekindling. Such acts of commoning constitute many small designs on the city, whether in the appropriation of physical spaces (gardens, greens and allotments, along riverbanks, in the uncommitted spaces carved out by infrastructure, in spaces of abandonment, vacancy or dereliction, in re-toolings of redundant space, in shared spaces of meeting and exchange, informal markets and other places of exchange, or in occupations and encroachments of proscribed spaces) or the distribution of urban resources (food and produce, goods and materials, fuel and water, but also care and social support, labour, information and know-how). These spaces and practices can recede behind the exigencies of private and the standard scripts of public life, but they form an infrastructure of common life that provides sites of autonomy, creativity and collectivity in the making and re-making of cities and subjects.

While these social practices of commoning are often mundane, small-scale and informal, there are city-level strategies for planning and design that may work to protect and extend the urban commons in a broader sense (see UN-Habitat 2012a). The economic benefits that derive from urban agglomeration are difficult to monopolize or commodify, and city governments can steward the conditions for innovation, skills synergies and information exchange, not least through the steering of integrated uses which support 'Jacobs externalities'. Beyond the blunt distinctions of public and private, urban infrastructures are the basis for the common life of a city, and whatever the nature of provision or ownership, connectivity between systems will be enhanced by strategic planning. Non-technical infrastructures of common life – climate, air and water quality – require coordination at neighbourhood, city and city-regional scales, with different agencies and different kinds of authority required at different levels. Urban authorities may be required to secure freedom of movement and access within the city as a common environment that is too often striated by informal as well as legal exclusions. And in the most classic sense of the term, the environmental commons requires stewardship to protect resources of clean air and water, to preserve and restore biodiversity, and to adapt to and mitigate environmental and climate change. Many of these tasks for the protection and promotion of the urban commons will require public forms of planning and management, but the work of coordination is not confined to state agencies so long as the urban commons remains a matter of inventive practice and improvised spaces.

Cities, finally, are among the clearest of cases that design is never simply a technical process – if by that we mean one governed by matters and measures of fact in some de-politicized zone of expertise and evaluation. In designing cities, social actors are making the conditions of their own lives and of their relations with others. Too often they do so in ways that reproduce and entrench inequality, such that urban environments congeal differentials in socio-spatial privilege as material facts. But cities are also exemplary sites for innovation, for invention, for derailments and diversities. The demotics of design intersects with formal languages of planning and development in contingent ways. Rem Koolhaas (1995: 971) ended his lament for urbanism by noting that, increasingly, 'the city is all we have.' In truth, the city does not yet – and never will – exhaust the ingenuities or the inhabitations of human settlement. But the possible city is grounded in the lineaments of the existing city. 'The guerrillas of the future', after all, 'will need a base of operations' (Lynch 1995b [1968]: 780).

References

Abrams, C. (1964) *Man's Struggle for Shelter in an Urbanizing World.* Cambridge, MA: MIT Press.

Agamben, G. (1998) *Homo Sacer: Sovereign Power and Bare Life* (trans. D. Heller-Roazen). Stanford, CA: Stanford University Press.

AlSayyad, N. (2004) 'Urban informality as a "new" way of life', in A. Roy and N. AlSayyad (eds) *Urban Informality: Transnational Perspectives from the Middle East, Latin America, and South Asia.* Lanham, MD: Lexington Books, 7–30.

Altvater, E. (2005) 'Globalization and the informalization of urban space', in A. Brillembourg, K. Feiress and H. Klumper (eds) *Informal City: Caracas Case.* Munich: Prestel Verlag, 51–5.

Amin, A. (2006) 'The good city', *Urban Studies* 43/5–6: 1009–23.

Amin, A. (2012) 'Telescopic urbanism and the poor'. Paper presented to the 40th World Congress of the International Institute of Sociology (IIS), Delhi, 19 February.

Amin, A. and Graham, S. (1997) 'The ordinary city', *Transactions of the Institute of British Geographers* 22/4: 411–29.

Amin, A. and Thrift, N. (2002) *Cities: Reimagining the Urban.* Cambridge: Polity.

Anand, N. and Rademacher, A. (2011) 'Housing in the Urban Age: inequality and aspiration in Mumbai', *Antipode* 43/5: 1748–72.

Andersson, F., Burgess, S. and Lane, J. (2007) 'Cities, matching and the productivity gains of agglomeration', *Journal of Urban Economics* 61/1: 112–18.

Appadurai, A. (2000) 'Spectral housing and urban cleansing: notes on millennial Mumbai', *Public Culture* 12: 627–51.

Appadurai, A. (2002) 'Deep democracy: urban governmentality and the horizon of politics', *Public Culture* 14/1: 21–47.

Arabindoo, P. (2011) 'Rhetoric of the "slum"', *City* 15/6: 636–46.

Arputham, J. and Patel, S. (2007) 'An offer of partnership or a promise of conflict in Dharavi, Mumbai?' *Environment and Urbanization* 19/2: 501–8.

Arputham, J. and Patel, S. (2008) 'Plans for Dharavi: negotiating a reconciliation between a state-driven market redevelopment and residents' aspirations', *Environment and Urbanization* 20/1: 243–54.

Arputham, J. and Patel, S. (2010) 'Recent developments in plans for Dharavi and for the airport slums in Mumbai', *Environment and Urbanization* 22/2: 501–4.

Arthurson, K. (2002) 'Creating inclusive communities through balancing social mix: a critical relationship or tenuous link?' *Urban Policy and Research* 20/3: 245–61.

Arunachalam, J. and Landwehr, B. (eds) (2003) *Structuring a Movement and Spreading It On: History and Growth of the Working Women's Forum (India), 1978–2003*. Frankfurt am Main: IKO, Verlag für Interkulturelle Kommunikation.

Arup and C40 Cities (2011) *Climate Action in Megacities: C40 Cities Baseline and Opportunities*. Version 1.0, June 2011. http://www.c40cities.org/media/research (accessed 6 June 2013).

Atkinson, R. (2006) 'Padding the bunker: strategies of middle-class disaffiliation and colonization in the city', *Urban Studies* 43/4: 819–32.

Atkinson, R. and Blandy, S. (2005) 'Introduction: international perspectives on the new enclavism and the rise of gated communities', *Housing Studies* 20/2: 177–86.

Atkinson, R. and Bridge, G. (eds) (2005) *Gentrification in a Global Context: The New Urban Colonialism*. London: Routledge.

Atkinson, R. and Flint, J. (2004) 'Fortress UK? Gated communities, the spatial revolt of the elites and time-space trajectories of segregation', *Housing Studies* 19/6: 875–92.

Augé, M. (1995) *Non-Places: Introduction to an Anthropology of Supermodernity* (trans. J. Howe). London: Verso.

Badyina, A. and Golubchikov, O. (2005) 'Gentrification in central Moscow – a market process or a deliberate policy? Money, power and people in housing regeneration in Ostozhenka', *Geografiska Annaler B* 87/1: 113–29.

Bakker, K. (2005) 'Katrina: the public transcript of "disaster"', *Environment and Planning D* 23/6: 795–802.

Bakker, K. (2007) 'The commons versus the commodity: "alter"-globalization, privatization, and the human right to water in the global South', *Antipode* 39/3: 430–55.

Banister, D. (2011) 'Cities, mobility and climate change', *Journal of Transport Geography* 19/6: 1538–46.

Bapat, M. and Agarwal, I. (2003) 'Our needs, our priorities; women and men from the slums in Mumbai and Pune talk about their needs for water and sanitation', *Environment and Urbanization* 15/2: 71–86.

Bauman, Z. (2003) 'City of fears, city of hopes', *CUCR Occasional Paper*.

London: Centre for Urban and Community Research, Goldsmiths College.

Baviskar, A. (2002) 'The politics of the city', *Seminar* 156. http://www.india-seminar.com/2002/516/516%20amita%20baviskar.htm (accessed 6 June 2013).

Bayat, A. (1997) 'Un-civil society: the politics of the "informal people"', *Third World Quarterly* 18/1: 53–72.

Bayat, A. (2000) 'From "dangerous classes" to "quiet rebels": politics of the urban subaltern in the global South', *International Sociology* 15/3: 533–57.

Bayat, A. and Biekart, K. (2009) 'Cities of extremes', *Development and Change* 40/5: 815–25.

Beall, J. and Fox, S. (2009) *Cities and Development.* London: Routledge.

Beauregard, R.A. (2010) 'Radical uniqueness and the flight from urban theory', in D.R.Judd and D.Simpson (eds) *The City, Revisited: Urban Theory from Chicago, Los Angeles and New York.* Minneapolis: University of Minnesota Press, 186–204.

Belmont, S. (2002) *Cities in Full: Recognizing and Realizing the Great Potential of Urban America.* Chicago American Planning Association.

Berube, A. (2005) *Mixed Communities in England: A US perspective on Evidence and Policy Prospects.* York: Joseph Rowntree Foundation.

Bickerstaff, K., Bulkeley, H. and Painter, J. (2009) 'Justice, nature and the city', *International Journal of Urban and Regional Research* 33/3: 591–600.

Biddulph, M. (2012) 'The problem with thinking about or for urban design', *Journal of Urban Design* 17/1: 1–20.

Blomley, N. (2004) 'Un-real estate: proprietary space and public gardening', *Antipode* 36/4: 614–41.

Blomley, N. (2008) 'Enclosure, common right and the property of the poor', *Social and Legal Studies* 17:3: 311–31.

Blomley, N. (2009) 'Homelessness, rights and the delusions of property', *Urban Geography* 30/6: 577–90.

Blumenberg, E. and Norton, A. (2010) 'Falling immigration rates means falling transit ridership', *Access* 37/Fall: 10–16.

Boarnet, M. and Crane, R. (2001) *Travel by Design: The Influence of Urban Form on Travel.* New York: Oxford University Press.

Bramley, G. and Power, S. (2009) 'Urban form and social sustainability: the role of density and housing type', *Environment and Planning B* 36/1: 30–48.

Brand, S. (2010) 'How slums can save the planet', *Prospect* February: 39–41.

Breheny, M. (1995) 'The compact city and transport energy consumption', *Transactions of the Institute of British Geographers* 20/1: 81–101.

Breheny, M. (1997) 'Urban compaction: feasible and acceptable?' *Cities* 14/4: 209–17.

Brenner, N. (2000) 'The urban question as a scale question: reflections on Henri Lefebvre, urban theory and the politics of scale', *International Journal of Urban and Regional Research* 24/2: 361–78.

Brenner, N. (2013) 'Theses on urbanization', *Public Culture* 25/1: 85–114.

Brewer, M., Sibieta, L. and Wren-Lewis, L. (2008) 'Racing away? Income inequality and the evolution of high incomes', *IFS Briefing Note No. 76.* London: Institute of Fiscal Studies.

Bridge, G. (2006) 'It's not just a question of taste: gentrification, the neighbourhood, and cultural capital', *Environment and Planning A* 38/10: 1965–78.

Bridge, G., Lees, L. and Butler, T. (eds) (2011) *Mixed Communities: Gentrification by Stealth?* Bristol: The Policy Press.

Bruegmann, R. (2005) *Sprawl: A Compact History.* Chicago: University of Chicago Press.

Brunner, P.H. (2007) 'Reshaping urban metabolism', *Journal of Industrial Ecology* 11/1: 11–13.

Buehler, R. and Pucher, J. (2012) 'Walking and cycling in Western Europe and the United States: trends, policies and lessons', *Transport Research News* 280/May–June: 34–42.

Burch, W.R. (1971) *Daydreams and Nightmares: A Sociological Essay on the American Environment.* New York: Harper & Row.

Burch, W.R., Cheek, N.H. and Taylor, L. (eds) (1972) *Social behavior, Natural Resources, and the Environment.* New York: Harper & Row.

Burdett, R., Travers, T., Czischke, D., Rode, P. and Moser, B. (2005) *Density and Urban Neighbourhoods in London.* London: Enterprise LSE Cities.

Burgess, E.W. (1925) 'The growth of the city: an introduction to a research project', in R.E. Park, E.W. Burgess and R.D. McKenzie (eds) *The City: Suggestions for Investigations of Human Behavior in the Urban Environment.* Chicago: University of Chicago Press, 47–62.

Burton, E. (2000) 'The compact city: just or just compact? A preliminary analysis', *Urban Studies* 37/11: 1969–2001.

Butler, J.S. (2005) *Entrepreneurship and Self-Help among Black Americans: A Reconsideration of Race and Economics.* Albany, NY: SUNY Press.

Butler, T. (2003) 'Living in the bubble: gentrification and its "others" in North London', *Urban Studies* 40/12: 2469–86.

Butler, T. (2007) 'For gentrification?' *Environment and Planning A* 39/1: 162–81.

Butler, T. and Hamnett, C. (2010) '"You take what you are given": the limits to parental choice in education in East London', *Environment and Planning A* 42/10: 2431–50.

C40 Cities (2012) *Quantifying the Emissions Benefit of Climate Action in C40 Cities.* 19 June. http://www.c40cities.org/media/research (accessed 6 June 2013).

Caenen, Y., Couderc, C., Courel, J., Paolo, C. and Siméon, T. (2010) 'Les Franciliens consacrent 1 h 20 par jour à leurs déplacements', *Ile-de-France à la page: Population* 331/April. http://www.insee.fr/fr/themes/document. asp?reg_id=20&ref_id=16023#un (accessed 6 March 2013).

Caldeira, T. (1996) 'Fortified enclaves: the new urban segregation', *Public Culture* 8/2: 303–28.

Caldeira, T. (2000) *City of Walls: Crime, Segregation, and Citizenship in São Paulo*. Berkeley: University of California Press.

Caldeira, T. (2011) 'World set apart', in R. Burdett and D. Sudjic (eds) (2011) *Living in the Endless City*. London: Phaidon, 168–75.

Carlino, G., Chaterjee, S. and Hunt, R. (2007) 'Urban density and the rate of invention', *Journal of Urban Economics* 61/3: 389–419.

Carruthers, J.I. and Ulfarsson, G.F. (2003) 'Urban sprawl and the cost of public services', *Environment and Planning B* 30/4: 503–22.

Carter, S., Dodsworth, F., Ruppert, E. and Watson, S. (2011) 'Thinking cities through objects', *CRESC Working Paper No. 96*. http://www.cresc. ac.uk/publications/thinking-cities-through-objects (accessed 6 June 2013).

Castells, M. (1998) 'Why the mega-cities focus? Megacities in the new world disorder'. The Mega-Cities Project Publication MCP-018. http://www. megacitiesproject.org/pdf/publications_pdf_mcp018intro.pdf (accessed 6 June 2013).

Castells, M. (2000) *The Rise of The Network Society* (second edition). Oxford: Blackwell.

Cervero, R. (2001) 'Efficient urbanisation: economic performance and the shape of the metropolis', *Urban Studies* 38/10: 1651–71.

Cervero, R. (2003) 'Growing smart by linking transportation and land use: perspectives from California', *Built Environment* 29/1: 66–78.

Cervero, R. and Day, J. (2008) 'Suburbanization and transit-oriented development in China', *Transport Policy* 15/5: 315–23.

Cervero, R. and Golub, A. (2007) 'Informal transport: a global perspective', *Transport Policy* 14/4: 445–57.

Chase, J., Crawford, M. and Kaliski, J. (1999) *Everyday Urbanism*. New York: Monacelli Press.

Chaskin, R. and Joseph, M. (2013) '"Positive" gentrification, social control and the "right to the city" in mixed-income communities: uses and expectations of space and place', *International Journal of Urban and Regional Research* 37/2: 480–502.

Chatterjee, P. (2004) *The Politics of the Governed: Reflections on Popular Politics in Most of the World*. New York: Columbia University Press.

Chatterton, P. (2010) 'Seeking the urban common: furthering the debate on spatial justice', *City* 14/6: 625–8.

Cheshire, P. (2007) *Segregated Neighbourhoods and Mixed Communities: A Critical Analysis*. York: Joseph Rowntree Foundation.

Churchman, A. (1999) 'Disentangling the concept of density', *Journal of Planning Literature* 13/4: 389–411.

Ciccone, A. and Hall, R.E. (1996) 'Productivity and the density of economic activity', *American Economic Review* 86/1: 54–70.

Cohen, B. (2006) 'Urbanization in developing countries: current trends, future projections, and key challenges for sustainability', *Technology in Society* 28/1–2: 63–80.

Colomb, C. (2012) 'Pushing the urban frontier: temporary uses of space, city marketing, and the creative city discourse in 2000s Berlin,' *Journal of Urban Affairs* 34/2: 131–52.

Coupland, A. (ed.) (1997) *Reclaiming the City: Mixed Use Development.* London: E & FN Spon.

Cruz, T. (2008) 'Trans-border flows: an urbanism beyond the property line', in I. Ruby and A. Ruby (eds) *Urban Transformations*. Berlin: Ruby Press, 226–39.

Cullen, G. (1961) *Townscape*. London: Architectural Press.

Cutter, S.L. and Finch, C. (2008) 'Temporal and spatial changes in social vulnerability to natural hazards', *Proceedings of the National Academy of Sciences* 105/7: 2301–6.

Cutter, S.L. and Smith, M.M. (2009) 'Fleeing from the hurricane's wrath: evacuation and the two Americas', *Environment* 51/2: 26–36.

Dai, E. (2005) 'Income inequality in urban China: a case study of Beijing', *Working Paper Series* Vol. 2005-04 (June). Kitakyushu, Japan: The International Centre for the Study of East Asian Development. http://file.icsead.or.jp/user03/832_220_20110622111711.pdf (accessed 6 June 2013).

Dave, S. (2010) 'High urban densities in developing countries: a sustainable solution?' *Built Environment* 36/1: 9–27.

Dave, S. (2011) 'Neighbourhood density and social sustainability in cities of developing countries', *Sustainable Development* 19/3: 189–205.

Davidson, M. (2008) 'Spoiled mixture? Where does state-led "positive" gentrification end?' *Urban Studies* 45/12: 2385–405.

Davidson, M. (2010) 'Love thy neighbour? Social mixing in London's gentrification frontiers', *Environment and Planning A* 42/3: 524–44.

Davis, M. (1990) *City of Quartz: Excavating the Future in Los Angeles.* London: Verso.

Davis, M. (2006) *Planet of Slums*. London: Verso.

De Cauter, L. (2005) *The Capsular Civilization: On the City in the Age of Fear.* Rotterdam: NAi Publishers.

de Soto, H. (2001) *The Mystery of Capital*. London: Black Swan.

Dempsey, N., Bramley, G., Power, S. and Brown, C. (2011) 'The social dimension of sustainable development: defining urban social sustainability', *Sustainable Development* 19/5: 289–300.

Dempsey, N., Brown, C. and Bramley, G. (2012) 'The key to sustainable urban development in UK cities? The influence of density on social sustainability', *Progress in Planning* 77/3: 89–141.

Denisova, I. (2012) 'Income distribution and poverty in Russia', *OECD Social, Employment and Migration Working Papers* No. 132. Paris: OECD Publishing. http://dx.doi.org/10.1787/5k9csf9zcz7c-en (accessed 6 June 2013).

Dicken, P. (2007) *Global Shift* (fifth edition). London: Sage.

Dodman, D. (2009) 'Blaming cities for climate change? An analysis of urban greenhouse gas emissions inventories', *Environment and Urbanization* 21/1: 185–201.

Dooling, S. (2009) 'Ecological gentrification: a research agenda exploring justice in the city', *International Journal of Urban and Regional Research* 33/3: 621–39.

Douglas, I., Alam, K., Maghenda, M., Mcdonnell, Y., Mclean, L. and Campbell, J. (2008) 'Unjust waters: climate change, flooding and the urban poor in Africa', *Environment and Urbanization* 20/1: 187–205.

Dovey, K. (2011) 'Uprooting critical urbanism', *City* 15/3–4: 347–54.

Dovey, K. and King, R. (2011) 'Forms of informality: morphology and visibility of informal settlements', *Built Environment* 37/1: 11–29.

Dow, K. (1992) 'Exploring differences in our common future(s): the meaning of vulnerability to global environmental change', *Geoforum* 23/3: 417–36.

Eidlin, E. (2010) 'What density doesn't tell us about sprawl', *Access* 37/Fall: 2–9.

Ewing, R. (1997) 'Is Los Angeles-style sprawl desirable?' *Journal of the American Planning Association* 63/1: 107–26.

Ewing, R. and Cervero, R. (2010) 'Travel and the built environment: a meta-analysis', *Journal of the American Planning Association* 76/3: 265–94.

Fainstein, S. (2005) 'Cities and diversity: Should we want it? Can we plan for it?' *Urban Affairs Review* 41/1: 3–19.

Fawaz, M. (2009) 'Neoliberal urbanity and the right to the city: a view from Beirut's periphery', *Development and Change* 40/5: 827–52.

Fischer, M.J. and Massey, D.S. (2000) 'How segregation concentrates poverty', *Ethnic and Racial Studies* 23/4: 670–91.

Florida, R. (2002) 'The economic geography of talent', *Annals of the Association of American Geographers* 92/4: 743–55.

Florida, R. (2003) 'Cities and the creative class', *City & Community* 2/1: 3–19.

Florida, R. (2004) *Cities and the Creative Class*. New York: Routledge.

Florida, R. (2005) *The Flight of the Creative Class: The Global Competition for Talent*. New York: Collins.

Florida, R. (2008) *Who's Your City? How the Creative Economy is Making Where to Live the Most Important Decision of Your Life*. New York: Basic Books.

Florida, R., Mellander, C., Stolarick, K. and Ross, A. (2012) 'Cities, skills and wages', *Journal of Economic Geography* 12/2: 355–77.

Foord, J. (2010) 'Mixed-use trade-offs: how to live and work in a "compact city" neighbourhood', *Built Environment* 36/1: 47–62.

Forsyth, A., Oakes, J.M., Schmitz, K.H. and Hearst, M. (2007) 'Does residential density increase walking and other physical activity?' *Urban Studies* 44/4: 679–97.

Franck, K. and Stevens, Q. (eds) (2006) *Loose Space: Possibility and Diversity in Urban Life*. London: Routledge.

Frank, A.G. (1998) *Reorient: Global Economy in the Asian Age*. Berkeley: University of California Press.

Frey, H. (1999) *Designing the City: Toward a More Sustainable Urban Form*. London: E & FN Spon.

Frey, W.H. (2011a) 'Melting pot cities and suburbs: racial and ethnic change in metro America in the 2000s', May. Report. Washington, DC: Brookings Institution. http://www.brookings.edu/~/media/research/files/papers/2011/5/04%20census%20ethnicity%20frey/0504_census_ethnicity_frey.pdf (accessed 6 June 2013).

Frey, W.H. (2011b) 'The new metro minority map: regional shifts in Hispanics, Asian and blacks from Census 2010', August. Report. Washington, DC: Brookings Institution. http://www.brookings.edu/~/media/research/files/papers/2011/8/31%20census%20race%20frey/0831_census_race_frey (accessed 6 June 2013).

Frey, W.H. and Myers, D. (2002) 'Neighborhood segregation in single-race and multirace America: a Census 2000 study of cities and metropolitan areas', July. Working Paper. Washington, DC: Fannie Mae Foundation. http://www.censusscope.org/FreyWPFinal.pdf (accessed 6 June 2013).

Frey, W.H., Brookings Institution and University of Michigan SSDAN (2011) 'Analysis of US Decennial data through 2010'. University of Michigan Population Studies Center. http://censusscope.org/2010Census/ (accessed 6 June 2013).

Frug, G. (2007) 'A "rule of law" for cities', *Urban Age Mumbai Newspaper Essay*, November. London School of Economics. http://lsecities.net/media/objects/articles/a-rule-of-law-for-cities (accessed 6 June 2013).

Gandy, M. (1999) 'The Paris sewers and the rationalization of urban space', *Transactions of the Institute of British Geographers* 24/1: 23–44.

Gandy, M. (2004) 'Rethinking urban metabolism: water, space and the modern city', *City* 8/3 371–87.

Gandy, M. (2005a) 'Learning from Lagos', *New Left Review* 33/March–April: 36–52.

Gandy, M. (2005b) 'Cyborg urbanization: complexity and monstrosity in the contemporary city', *International Journal of Urban and Regional Research* 29/1: 26–49.

Gandy, M. (2006a) 'The bacteriological city and its discontents', *Historical Geography* 34/1: 14–25.

Gandy, M. (2006b) 'Planning, anti-planning and the infrastructure crisis facing metropolitan Lagos', *Urban Studies* 43/2: 371–96.

Gandy, M. (2006c) 'Zones of indistinction: bio-political contestations in the urban arena', *Cultural Geographies* 13: 497–516.

Gandy, M. (2008) 'Landscapes of disaster: water, modernity, and fragmentation in Mumbai', *Environment and Planning A* 40/1: 108–30.

Gans, H.J. (2010) 'Concentrated poverty: a critical analysis', *Challenge* 53/3: 82–96.

Ghertner, D.A. (2010) 'Calculating without numbers: aesthetic governmentality in Delhi's slums', *Economy and Society* 39/2: 185–217.

Ghertner, D.A. (2011) 'Gentrifying the state, gentrifying participation: elite governance programs in Delhi', *International Journal of Urban and Regional Research* 35/3: 504–32.

Ghertner, D.A. (2012) 'Nuisance talk and the propriety of property: middle-class discourses of a slum-free Delhi', *Antipode* 44/4: 1161–87.

Gilbert, A. (1976) 'The arguments for very large cities reconsidered', *Urban Studies* 13/1: 27–34.

Gilbert, A. (2007) 'The return of the slum: does language matter?' *International Journal of Urban and Regional Research* 31/4: 697–713.

Gilmour, T. (2012) *Mixed Communities*. Shelter Brief 48. Sydney: Shelter NWS Incorporated and Eton Consulting.

Gilroy, R. and Booth, C. (1999) 'Building an infrastructure of everyday lives', *European Planning Studies* 7/3: 307–25.

Glaeser, E.L. (1994) 'Economic growth and urban density: a review essay', *Working Papers in Economics* E-94-7. The Hoover Institution, Stanford University.

Glaeser, E.L. (2004) 'Cities and social interactions'. Paper presented to the Leverhulme International Symposium on *The Resurgent City*, London School of Economics, 19–21 April.

Glaeser, E.L. (2011) *Triumph of the City*. New York: Penguin.

Glaeser, E.L. and Gottlieb, J.D. (2009) 'The wealth of cities: agglomeration economies and the spatial equilibrium in the United States', *Journal of Economic Literature* 47/4: 983–1028.

Glaeser, E.L. and Kahn, M.E. (2010) 'The greenness of cities: carbon dioxide emissions and urban development', *Journal of Urban Economics* 67/3: 404–18.

Glaeser, E.L. and Resseger, M.G. (2010) 'The complementarity between cities and skills', *Journal of Regional Science* 50/1: 221–44.

Glaeser, E.L., Kallal, H.D., Scheinkman, J.A. and Shleifer, A. (1992) 'Growth in cities', *Journal of Political Economy* 100/6: 1126–52.

Glaeser, E.L., Resseger, M.G. and Tobio, K. (2008) 'Urban inequality', *NBER Working Paper No. 14419* (October). Cambridge, MA: National Bureau of Economic Research. http://www.hks.harvard.edu/var/ezp_site/storage/fckeditor/file/pdfs/centers-programs/centers/taubman/policybriefs/urban_inequality_final.pdf (accessed 6 June 2013).

Glass, R. (1989) *Clichés of Urban Doom and Other Essays*. Oxford: Basil Blackwell.

Glennerster, H., Lupton, R., Noden, P. and Power, A. (1999) 'Poverty, social exclusion and neighbourhood: studying the area basis of social exclusion', *CASEPaper:CASE/22* (March). London School of Economics Centre for the Analysis of Social Exclusion. http://eprints.lse.ac.uk/3981/1/

Poverty_social_exclusion_and_neighbourhood.pdf (accessed 6 June 2013).

Gordon, I. (2008) 'Density and the built environment', *Energy Policy* 36/12: 4652–6.

Gordon, P. (2012) 'Spontaneous cities', in D.E. Andersson (ed.) *The Spatial Market Process (Advances in Austrian Economics, Volume 16)*. Bingley, W. Yorks: Emerald Group Publishing Limited, 181–209.

Gordon, P. and Richardson, H.W. (1997) 'Are compact cities a desirable planning goal?' *Journal of the American Planning Association* 63/1: 95–106.

Graham, S. (2007) 'War and the city', *New Left Review* 44/March–April: 121–32.

Graham, S. (2010) *Cities under Siege: The New Military Urbanism*. London: Verso.

Graham, S. and Marvin, S. (2001) *Splintering Urbanism: Networked Infrastructures, Technological Mobilities and the Urban Condition*. London: Routledge.

Graham, S. and Thrift, N. (2007) 'Out of order: understanding repair and maintenance', *Theory, Culture and Society* 24/1: 1–25.

Graham, S., Desai, R. and McFarlane, C. (2013) 'Water wars in Mumbai', *Public Culture* 25/1: 115–41.

Grant, J. and Mittelsteadt, L. (2004) 'Types of gated communities', *Environment and Planning B* 31/6: 913–30.

Greenberg, S. (ed.) (1998) *Invisible New York: The Hidden Infrastructure of the City*. Baltimore, MD: Johns Hopkins University Press.

Grimm, N.B., Faeth, S.H., Golubiewski, N.E., Redman, C.L., Wu, J., Bai, X. and Briggs, J.M. (2008) 'Global change and the ecology of cities', *Science* 319/February: 756–60.

Grove, J.M. and Burch, W.R. (1997) 'A social ecology approach and applications of urban ecosystem and landscape analyses: a case study of Baltimore, Maryland', *Urban Ecosystems* 1/4: 259–75.

Guerra, E. and Cervero, R. (2012) 'Transit and the "D" word', *Access* 40/Spring: 2–8.

Hall, M. and Lee, M. (2010) 'How diverse are US suburbs?' *Urban Studies* 47/1: 3–28.

Hall, S. (2012) *City, Street and Citizen: The Measure of the Ordinary*. Abingdon, Oxon: Routledge.

Hamnett, C. and Butler, T. (2011) '"Geography matters": the role distance plays in reproducing educational inequality in East London', *Transactions of the Institute of British Geographers* 36/4: 479–500.

Hardin, G. (1968) 'The tragedy of the commons', *Science* 162/December: 1243–8.

Hardoy, J. and Pandiella, G. (2009) 'Urban poverty and vulnerability to climate change in Latin America', *Environment and Urbanization* 21/1: 203–24.

Harris, A. (2008) 'From London to Mumbai and back again: gentrification and public policy in comparative perspective', *Urban Studies* 45/12: 2407–28.

Harvey, D. (1996) *Justice, Nature and the Geography of Difference*. Cambridge, MA: Blackwell.

Harvey, D. (2008) 'The right to the city', *New Left Review* 53/September–October: 23–40.

Haughton, G. and McGranahan, G. (2006) 'Editorial: urban ecologies', *Environment and Urbanization* 18/1: 3–7.

He, S. (2007) 'State-sponsored gentrification under market transition: the case of Shanghai', *Urban Affairs Review* 43/2: 171–98.

He, S. (2010) 'New-build gentrification in central Shanghai: demographic changes and socioeconomic implications', *Population, Space and Place* 16/5: 345–61.

Henderson, V. (2003) 'The urbanization process and economic growth: the so-what question', *Journal of Economic Growth* 8/1: 47–71.

Heynen, N.C., Kaika, M. and Swyngedouw, E. (2006) *In the Nature of Cities: Urban Political Ecology and the Politics of Urban Metabolism*. New York: Routledge.

Hoch, I. (1972) 'Income and city size', *Urban Studies* 9/3: 299–328.

Hodkinson, S. (2012) 'The new urban enclosures', *City* 16/5: 500–18.

Holmes, C. (2006) *Mixed Communities: Success and Sustainability*. York: Joseph Rowntree Foundation.

Holston, J. and Appadurai, A. (1996) 'Cities and citizenship', *Public Culture* 8/2: 187–204.

ISDR (2009) *Global Assessment Report on Disaster Risk Reduction: Risk and Poverty in a Changing Climate*. Geneva: United Nations. http://www.preven tionweb.net/english/hyogo/gar/report/index.php?id=1130&pid:34&pih:2 (accessed 6 June 2013).

Isin, E. (2007) 'City-state: critique of scalar thought', *Citizenship Studies* 11/2: 211–28.

Jabareen, Y.R. (2006) 'Sustainable urban forms: their typologies, models, and concepts', *Journal of Planning Education and Research* 26/1: 28–52.

Jacobs, A.B. and Appleyard, D. (1987) 'Toward an urban design manifesto', *Journal of the American Planning Association* 53/1: 112–20.

Jacobs, J. (1961) *The Death and Life of Great American Cities*. New York: Random House.

Jacobs, J. (1969) *The Economy of Cities*. New York: Random House.

Jaffe, R., Klaufus, C. and Colombijn, F. (2012) 'Mobilities and mobilizations of the urban poor', *International Journal of Urban and Regional Research* 36/4: 643–54.

Jeffrey, A., McFarlane, C. and Vasudevan, A. (2012) 'Rethinking enclosure: space, subjectivity and the commons', *Antipode* 44/4: 1247–67.

Jenks, M. and Burgess, R. (eds) (2000) *Compact Cities: Sustainable Urban Forms for Developing Countries*. London: E & FN Spon.

Jenks, M. and Dempsey, N. (2005) *Future Forms and Design for Sustainable Cities*. Oxford: Architectural Press.

Jenks, M., Burton, E. and Williams, K. (eds) (1996) *The Compact City: A Sustainable Urban Form?* London: E & FN Spon.

Johnston, B.R. (2003) 'The political ecology of water: an introduction', *Capitalism Nature Socialism* 14/3:73–90.

Jones, G.A. (2011) 'Slumming about', *City* 15/6: 696–708.

Jones, G.A. and Corbridge, S. (2010) 'The continuing debate about urban bias: the thesis, its critics, its influence and its implications for poverty-reduction strategies', *Progress in Development Studies* 10/1: 1–18.

Jorgenson, A.K., Rice, J. and Clark, B. (2010) 'Cities, slums, and energy consumption in less developed countries, 1990 to 2005', *Organization & Environment* 23/2: 189–204.

Jürgens, U. and Gnad, M. (2002) 'Gated communities in South Africa: experiences from Johannesburg', *Environment and Planning B* 29/3: 337–53.

Kaika, M. and Swyngedouw, E. (2010) 'The urbanization of nature: great promises, impasse, and new beginnings', in G. Bridge and S. Watson (eds) *A New Companion to the City*. Oxford: Blackwell, 97–107.

Keil, R. (2003) 'Urban political ecology', *Urban Geography* 24/8: 723–38.

Kenworthy, J.R. (2006) 'The eco-city: ten key transport and planning dimensions for sustainable city development', *Environment and Urbanization* 18/1: 67–85.

Kessides, C. (2006) *Urban Transition in Sub-Saharan Africa: Implications for Economic Growth and Poverty Reduction*. Washington, DC: Cities Alliance.

Kleit, R.G. (2005) 'HOPE VI new communities: neighborhood relationships in mixed-income housing', *Environment and Planning A* 37/8: 1413–41.

Klinenburg, E. (2002) *Heat Wave: A Social Autopsy of Disaster in Chicago*. Chicago: University of Chicago Press.

Knowles, C. (2011) 'Cities on the move: navigating urban life', *City* 15/2: 135–53.

Knudsen, B., Florida, R., Stolarick, K. and Gates, G. (2008) 'Density and creativity in US regions', *Annals of the Association of American Geographers* 98/2: 461–78.

Koolhaas, R. (1995) 'Whatever happened to urbanism?' in R. Koolhaas and B. Mau, *S, M, L,XL*. New York: The Monicelli Press, 959–71.

Kousky, C. and Schneider, S.H. (2003) 'Global climate policy: will cities lead the way?' *Climate Policy* 3/4: 359–72.

Kutzbach, M. (2009) 'Motorization in developing countries: causes, consequences, and effectiveness of policy options', *Journal of Urban Economics* 65/2: 154–66.

Kutzbach, M. (2010) 'Megacities and megatraffic', *Access* 37/Fall: 31–5.

Landman, K. (2004) *Gated Communities in South Africa: A Review of the*

Relevant Policies and Their Implications. CSIR Building and Construction Technology. http://www.csir.co.za/Built_environment/Planning_support_systems/gatedcomsa/docs/review_policies.pdf (accessed 6 June 2013).

Latour, B. (2008) 'A cautious Prometheus? A few steps towards a philosophy of design (with special attention to Peter Sloterdijk)'. Keynote lecture for 'Networks of Design', Design History Society, Falmouth, Cornwall, 3 September. http://www.bruno-latour.fr/sites/default/files/112-DESIGN-CORNWALL-GB.pdf (accessed 6 June 2013).

Latour, B. and Hermant, É. (1998). *Paris: Ville invisible*. Paris: La Decouverte.

Lee, K.M. (2006) 'Urban sustainability and the limits of classic environmentalism', *Environment and Urbanization* 18/1: 9–22.

Lees, L. (2008) 'Gentrification and social mixing: towards an inclusive Urban Renaissance?' *Urban Studies* 45/12: 2449–70.

Lees, L. (2010) 'Planning for urbanity', *Environment and Planning A* 42/10: 2302–8.

Lees, L. (2012) 'The geography of gentrification: thinking through comparative urbanism', *Progress in Human Geography* 36/2: 155–71.

Lefebvre, H. (1996) [1968] 'The right to the city', in E. Kofman and E. Lebas (eds) *Henri Lefebvre: Writing on Cities*. Oxford: Blackwell, 147–59.

Lefebvre, H. (2003) [1970] *The Urban Revolution* (trans. R. Bononno). Minneapolis: University of Minnesota Press.

Legg, S. and McFarlane, C. (2008) 'Ordinary urban spaces: between postcolonialism and development', *Environment and Planning A* 40/1: 6–14.

Leigh-Star, S. (1999) 'The ethnography of infrastructure', *American Behavioral Scientist* 43/3: 377–91.

Lemanski, C. (2006a) 'Desegregation and integration as linked or distinct? Evidence from a previously "white" suburb in post-apartheid Cape Town', *International Journal of Urban and Regional Research* 30/3: 564–86.

Lemanski, C. (2006b) 'Spaces of exclusivity or connection? Linkages between a gated community and its poorer neighbour in a Cape Town master plan development', *Urban Studies* 43/2: 397–420.

Lemanski, C. (2009) 'Augmented informality: South Africa's backyard dwellings as a by-product of formal housing policies', *Habitat International* 33/4: 472–484.

Lemanski, C. (forthcoming) 'Urban theory as empirically embedded: hybrid gentrification and downward raiding in a South African slum', *Urban Studies*.

Lemanski, C. and Oldfield, S. (2009) 'The parallel claims of gated communities and land invasions in a Southern city: polarized state responses', *Environment and Planning A* 41/3: 634–48.

Lemanski, C., Durington, M. and Landman, K. (2008) 'Divergent and similar experiences of "gating" in South Africa: Johannesburg, Durban and Cape Town', *Urban Forum* 19/2: 133–58.

Lindsay, M., Williams, K. and Dair, C. (2010) 'Is there room for privacy in the compact city?' *Built Environment* 36/1: 28–46.

Lipman, A. and Harris, H. (1999) 'Fortress Johannesburg', *Environment and Planning B* 26/5: 727–40.

Liu, X., Park, A. and Zhao, Y. (2010) 'Explaining rising returns to education in urban China in the 1990s', *IZA Discussion Paper No. 4872*. Bonn: Institute for the Study of Labour. http://ftp.iza.org/dp4872.pdf (accessed 6 June 2013).

Lomborg, B. (2001) *The Skeptical Environmentalist: Measuring the Real State of the World*. Cambridge: Cambridge University Press.

Lopez-Morales, E.J. (2011) 'Gentrification by ground rent dispossession: the shadows cast by large scale urban renewal in Santiago de Chile', *International Journal of Urban and Regional Research* 35/2: 330–57.

Low, N.P. and Gleeson, B.J. (1997) 'Justice in and to the environment: ethical uncertainties and political practices', *Environment and Planning A* 29/1: 21–42.

Low, S.M. (2001) 'The edge and the center: gated communities and the discourse of urban fear', *American Anthropologist* 103/1: 45–58.

Low, S.M. (2003) *Behind the Gates: Life, Security and the Pursuit of Happiness in Fortress America*. London and New York: Routledge.

Low, S.M. (2011) 'Claiming space for an engaged anthropology: spatial inequality and social exclusion', *American Anthropologist* 113/3: 389–407.

LSE London (2006) *Density: A Debate about the Best Way to House a Growing Population*. London School of Economics and Political Science.

Lustig, N., Lopez-Calva, L.F. and Ortiz-Juarez, E. (2011) 'The decline in inequality in Latin America: how much, since when and why?' *ECINEQ Society for the Study of Economic Inequality Working Paper Series*. ECINEQ WP 2011-211. http://econ.tulane.edu/RePEc/pdf/tul1118.pdf (accessed 6 June 2013).

Luttmer, E.F.P. (2005) 'Neighbors as negatives: relative earnings and well-being', *Quarterly Journal of Economics* 120/3: 963–1002.

Lynch, K. (1962) *Site Planning*. Cambridge, MA: MIT Press.

Lynch, K. (1965) 'The city as environment', *Scientific American* 21/3: 209–14.

Lynch, K. (1981) *A Theory of Good City Form*. Cambridge, MA: MIT Press.

Lynch, K. (1984) 'The immature arts of city design', *Places* 1/3: 10–21.

Lynch, K. (1995a) [1968] 'The urban landscape of San Salvador: environmental quality in an urbanizing region', in T. Banerjee and M. Southworth (eds) *City Sense and City Design: Writings and Projects of Kevin Lynch*. Cambridge, MA: MIT Press, 205–25.

Lynch, K. (1995b) [1968] 'The possible city', in T. Banerjee and M. Southworth (eds) *City Sense and City Design: Writings and Projects of Kevin Lynch*. Cambridge, MA: MIT Press, 771–88.

Lynch, K. (1995c) [1975] 'Grounds for Utopia', in T. Banerjee and M. Southworth (eds) *City Sense and City Design: Writings and Projects of Kevin Lynch*. Cambridge, MA: MIT Press, 789–810.

Lynch, K. and Rodwin, L. (1958) 'A theory of urban form', *Journal of the American Planning Association* 24/4: 201–14.

McCann, E.J. and Ward, K. (2010) 'Relationality/territoriality: toward a conceptualization of cities in the world', *Geoforum* 41/2: 175–84.

McFarlane, C. (2008) 'Sanitation in Mumbai's informal settlements: state, "slum", and infrastructure', *Environment and Planning A* 40/1: 88–107.

McFarlane, C. (2011) 'Assemblage and critical urbanism', *City* 15/2: 204–24.

McFarlane, C. (2012) 'The entrepreneurial slum: civil society, mobility and the co-production of urban development', *Urban Studies* 49/13: 2795–816.

McFarlane, C. and Rutherford, J. (2008) 'Political infrastructures: governing and experiencing the fabric of the city', *International Journal of Urban and Regional Research* 32/2: 363–74.

McGranahan, G., Balk, D. and Anderson, A. (2007) 'The rising tide: assessing the risks of climate change and human settlements in low elevation coastal zones', *Environment & Urbanization* 19/1: 17–37.

Madanipour, A. (1997) 'Ambiguities in urban design', *Town Planning Review* 68/3: 363–83.

Madanipour, A. (2010) 'Connectivity and contingency in planning', *Planning Theory* 9/4: 351–68.

Maddison, A. (2001) *The World Economy: A Millennial Perspective*. Paris: OECD.

Marcuse, P. (1997) 'The ghetto of exclusion and the fortified enclave', *American Behavioral Scientist* 41/3: 311–26.

Marcuse, P. (1998) 'Sustainability is not enough', *Environment and Urbanization* 10/2: 103–12.

Massey, D.S. (1996) 'The age of extremes: concentrated affluence and poverty in the twenty-first century', *Demography* 33/4: 395–412.

Massey, D.S. and Denton, N.A. (1988) 'The dimensions of residential segregation', *Social Forces* 67/2: 281–315.

Massey, D.S. and Fischer, M.J. (2003) 'The geography of inequality in the United States, 1950–2000', *Brookings-Wharton Papers on Urban Affairs*: 1–40.

Massey, D.S., Rothwell, J. and Domina, T. (2009) 'The changing bases of segregation in the United States', *The ANNALS of the American Academy of Political and Social Science* 626/1: 74–90.

Mayer, M. (2013) 'First world urban activism: beyond austerity urbanism and creative city politics', *City* 17/1: 5–19.

Mbembe, A. and Nuttall, S. (2004) 'Writing the world from an African metropolis', *Public Culture* 16/3: 347–72.

Meng, X., Gregory, R. and Wang, Y. (2005) 'Poverty, inequality, and growth in urban China, 1986–2000', *Journal of Comparative Economics* 33/4: 710–29.

Mera, K. (1973) 'On the urban agglomeration and economic efficiency', *Economic Development and Cultural Change* 21/2: 309–24.

Mills, E.S. (1972) 'Welfare aspects of national policy towards city sizes', *Urban Studies* 9/1: 117–24.

Molotch, H. (2011) 'Objects in the city', in S. Bridge and S. Watson (eds) *The New Blackwell Companion to the City*. Oxford: Wiley-Blackwell, 66–78.

Montgomery, M.R. (2008) 'The urban transformation of the developing world', *Science* 319/February: 761–4.

Morello-Frosch, R.A. (2002) 'Discrimination and the political economy of environmental inequality', *Environment and Plannng C* 20/4: 477–96.

Moser, C. and Satterthwaite, D. (2008) 'Towards pro-poor adaptation to climate change in the urban centres of low- and middle-income countries', *Human Settlements Working Paper Series Climate Change and Cities* 3. IIED, London. http://pubs.iied.org/pdfs/10564IIED.pdf (accessed 6 June 2013).

Mu, R. and de Jong, M. (2012) 'Introduction to the issue: the state of transport infrastructure in China', *Policy and Society* 31/1: 1–12.

Mukhija, V. (2003) *Squatters as Developers? Slum Redevelopment in Mumbai*. Aldershot: Ashgate.

Mumford, L. (1938) *The Culture of Cities*. New York: Harcourt Brace & Co.

Mumford, L. (1956) 'The natural history of urbanization', in W.L. Thomas (ed.) *Man's Role in Changing the Face of the Earth*. Chicago: University of Chicago Press, 382–98.

Murray, M.J. (2009) 'Fire and ice: unnatural disasters and the disposable urban poor in post-apartheid Johannesburg', *International Journal of Urban and Regional Research* 33/1: 165–92.

Murray, M.J. (2013) 'Afterword: re-engaging with transnational urbanism', in T.R. Samara, S. He and G. Chen (eds) *Locating Right to the City in the Global South*. Abingdon: Routledge, 285–310.

Neuman, M. (2005) 'The compact city fallacy', *Journal of Planning Education and Research* 25/1: 11–26.

Neumayer, E. and Plümper, T. (2007) 'The gendered nature of natural disasters: the impact of catastrophic events on the gender gap in life expectancy, 1981–2002', *Annals of the Assocation of American Geographers* 97/3: 551–66.

Neuwirth, R. (2007) 'Squatters and the cities of tomorrow', *City* 11/1: 71–80.

Newman, P. (2010) 'Sustainable cities of the future: the behavior change driver', *Sustainable Developmnent Law and Policy* 11/1: 7–10.

Newman, P. and Kenworthy, J. (1989) 'Gasoline consumption and cities: a comparison of US cities with a global survey', *Journal of the American Planning Association* 55/1: 23–37.

Newman, P. and Kenworthy, J. (1999) *Sustainability and Cities: Overcoming Automobile Dependence*. Washington, DC: Island Press.

Newman, P. and Kenworthy, J. (2000) 'The ten myths of automobile dependence', *World Transport Policy & Practice* 6/1: 15–25.

Newman, P. and Kenworthy, J. (2006) 'Urban design to reduce automobile dependence', *Opolis* 2/1: 35–52.

Newton, P. (2000) 'Urban form and environmental performance', in E. Williams, M. Burton and K. Jenks (eds) *Achieving Sustainable Urban Form*. London: E & FN Spon, 46–53.

Ng, E. (ed.) (2010) *Designing High-density Cities for Social and Environmental Sustainability*. London: Earthscan.

Nijman, J. (2008) 'Against the odds: slum rehabilitation in neoliberal Mumbai', *Cities* 25/2: 73–85.

O'Connor, D. (1996) 'Grow now/clean later, or the pursuit of sustainable development?', *OECD Development Centre Working Papers* 111 (March). Paris: OECD Publishing.

OECD (2011) *Divided We Stand: Why Inequality Keeps Rising*. Paris: OECD Publishing.

Osborne, T. (1996) 'Security and vitality: drains, liberalism and power in the nineteenth century', in A. Barry, T. Osborne and N. Rose (eds) *Foucault and Political Reason: Liberalism, Neoliberalism and Rationalities of Government*. London: UCL Press, 99–121.

Ostrom, E. (1990) *Governing the Commons: The Evolution of Institutions for Collective Action*. New York: Cambridge University Press.

Oswalt, P., Overmayer, K. and Misselwitz, P. (eds) (2009) *Urban Catalyst: Strategies for Temporary Use*. Barcelona: Actar.

Ouroussoff, N. (2008) 'Learning from Tijuana: Hudson, NY, considers different housing mode', *The New York Times*, 19 February. http://www.nytimes.com/2008/02/19/arts/design/19hous.html (accessed 18 June 2013).

Owens, L. (2008) 'From tourists to anti-tourists to tourist attractions: the transformation of the Amsterdam squatters' movement', *Social Movement Studies* 7/1: 43–59.

Park, A. and Wang, D. (2010) 'Migration and urban poverty and inequality in China', *IZA Discussion Paper* 4877. Bonn: Institute for the Study of Labour.

Park, R.E. (1936) 'Human ecology', *American Journal of Sociology* 42/1: 1–15.

Peach, C. (1996) 'Good segregation, bad segregation', *Planning Perspectives* 11/4: 379–98.

Peck, J. (2012) 'Austerity urbanism', *City* 16/6: 626–55.

Peñalosa, E. (2007) 'Politics, power, cities: private interest and public good', in R. Burdett and D. Sudjic (eds) *The Endless City*. London: Phaidon, 307–19.

Perlman, J. (1976) *The Myth of Marginality: Urban Poverty and Politics in Rio de Janeiro*. Berkeley: University of California Press.

Perlman, J.E. with O'Meara Sheehan, M. (2007) 'Fighting poverty and environmental injustice', in *State of the World 2007: Our Urban Future*. Washington, DC: Worldwatch Institute, 172–239. http://www.

megacitiesproject.org/pdf/SOW_07_chapter_9.pdf (accessed 6 June 2013).

Pieterse, E. (2011) 'Grasping the unknowable: coming to grips with African urbanisms', *Social Dynamics* 37/1: 5–23.

Popkin, S., Katz, B., Cunningham, M., Brown, K., Gustafson, J. and Turner, M. (2004) *A Decade of HOPE VI: Research Findings and Policy Challenges*, Washington, DC: The Urban Institute/The Brookings Institution.

Portes, A., Castells, M. and Benton, L.A. (eds) (1989) *The Informal Economy: Studies in Advanced and Less Developed Economies*. Baltimore, MD: Johns Hopkins University Press.

Pucher, J., Korattyswaroopam, N., Mittal, N. and Ittyerah, N. (2005) 'Urban transport crisis in India', *Transport Policy* 12/3 185–98.

Pucher, J., Peng, Z.-R., Mittal, N., Zhu, Y. and Korattyswaroopam, N. (2007) 'Urban transport trends and policies in China and India: impacts of rapid economic growth', *Transport Reviews* 27/4: 379–410.

Raman, S. (2010) 'Designing a liveable compact city: physical forms of city and social life in urban neighbourhoods', *Built Environment* 36/1: 63–80.

Rapoport, A. (1975) 'Toward a redefinition of density', *Environment and Behavior* 7/2: 133–57.

Rauch, J.E. (1993) 'Productivity gains from geographic concentration of human capital: evidence from cities', *Journal of Urban Economics* 34/3: 380–400.

Rérat, P. and Lees, L. (2011) 'Spatial capital, gentrification and mobility: evidence from Swiss core cities', *Transactions of the Institute of British Geographers* 36/1: 126–42.

Revel, J. and Negri, A. (2007) 'Inventer le commun des hommes', *Multitudes* 31/4: 5–10.

Revi, A. (2008) 'Climate change risk: an adaptation and mitigation agenda for Indian cities', *Environment and Urbanization* 20/1: 207–29.

Richardson, H.W. (1972) 'Optimality in city size, systems of cities and urban policy: a sceptic's view', *Urban Studies* 9/1: 24–48.

Richardson, H.W. (1976) 'The argument for very large cities reconsidered: a comment', *Urban Studies* 13/3: 307–10.

Roberts, M. (2007) 'Sharing space: urban design and social mixing in mixed income new communities', *Planning Theory & Practice* 8/2: 183–204.

Robinson, J. (2002) 'Global and world cities: a view from off the map', *International Journal of Urban and Regional Research* 26/3: 531–54.

Robinson, J. (2006) *Ordinary Cities: Between Modernity and Development*. Abingdon, Oxon, and New York: Routledge.

Rose, C. (1994) *Property and Persuasion: Essays on the History, Theory and Rhetoric of Ownership*. Boulder, CO: Westview Press.

Rose, C. (1998) 'The several futures of property: of cyberspace and folk tales, emission trades and ecosystems', *Minnesota Law Review* 83/129: 129–82.

Roy, A. (2004a) 'The Gentleman's City: urban informality in the Calcutta of the New Communism', in A. Roy and N. AlSayyad (eds) *Urban Informality: Transnational Perspectives from the Middle East, Latin America, and South Asia*. Lanham, MD: Lexington Books, 147–70.

Roy, A. (2004b) 'Transnational trespassing: the geopolitics of urban informality', in A. Roy and N. AlSayyad (eds) *Urban Informality: Transnational Perspectives from the Middle East, Latin America, and South Asia*. Lanham, MD: Lexington Books, 289–312.

Roy, A. (2009) 'Strangely familiar: planning and the worlds of insurgence and informality', *Planning Theory* 8/1: 7–11.

Roy, A. (2011) 'Slumdog cities: rethinking subaltern urbanism', *International Journal of Urban and Regional Research* 35/2: 223–38.

Roy, A. and Ong, A. (eds) (2011) *Worlding Cities: Asian Experiments and the Art of Being Global*. Oxford: Wiley-Blackwell.

Salcedo, R. and Torres, A. (2004) 'Gated communities in Santiago: wall or frontier?' *International Journal of Urban and Regional Research* 28/1: 27–41.

Sandercock, L. (2003) *Cosmopolis II: Mongrel Cities in the 21st Century*. London: Continuum.

Sanyal, R. (2011) 'Squatting in camps: building and insurgency in spaces of refuge', *Urban Studies* 48/5: 877–90.

Sarkis, H. (1997) 'Space for recognition: on the design of public space in a multi-cultural society', *New Political Science* 19/1: 133–70.

Sarkissian, W. (1976) 'The idea of social mix in town planning: a historical review', *Urban Studies* 13/3: 231–46.

Sartre, J.-P. (2004) [1960] *Critique of Dialectical Reason: Theory of Practical Ensembles* (trans. A. Sheridan). London: Verso.

Sassen, S. (2005a) 'Fragmented urban topographies and their underlying urban connections', in A. Brillembourg, K. Feiress and H. Klumper (eds) *Informal City: Caracas Case*. Munich: Prestel Verlag, 83–7.

Sassen, S. (2005b) 'Cityness in the Urban Age', *Urban Age Bulletin* 2: 1–3. http://neture.org/wp-content/uploads/Saskia_Sassen_2005-Cityness_In_The_Urban_Age-Bulletin2.pdf (accessed 6 June 2013).

Satterthwaite, D. (2007) 'The transition to a predominantly urban world and its underpinnings', *Human Settlements Discussion Paper Series: Theme – Urban Change 4*. London: IEED. http://pubs.iied.org/pdfs/10550IIED.pdf (accessed 6 June 2013).

Satterthwaite, D. (2008) 'Cities' contribution to global warming: notes on the allocation of greenhouse gas emissions', *Environment and Urbanization* 20/2: 539–49.

Scott, J.C. (1998) *Seeing Like a State: How Certain Schemes to Improve the Human Condition Have Failed*. New Haven, CT: Yale University Press.

Segal, D. (1976) 'Are there returns to scale in city size?' *The Review of Economics and Statistics* 58/3: 339–50.

Sennett, R. (1970) *The Uses of Disorder: Personal Identity and City Life*. New York: Knopf.

Sennett, R. (2007) 'The open city', in R. Burdett and D. Sudjic (eds) *The Endless City*. London: Phaidon, 290–7.

Sennett, R. (2011) 'Boundaries and borders', in R. Burdett and D. Sudjic (eds) *Living in the Endless City*. London: Phaidon, 324–31.

Shiva, V. (2002) *Water Wars: Privatization, Pollution and Profit*. London: Pluto Press.

Simon, D. (2011) 'Situating slums', *City* 15/6: 674–85.

Simone, A. (2001) 'Straddling the divides: remaking associational life in the informal African city', *International Journal of Urban and Regional Research* 25/1: 102–17.

Simone, A. (2004a) *For the City Yet to Come: Changing African Life in Four Cities*. Durham, NC: Duke University Press.

Simone, A. (2004b) 'People as infrastructure', *Public Culture* 16/3: 407–29.

Simone, A. (2011) 'The surfacing of urban life', *City* 15/3–4: 355–64.

Smets, P. and Salman, T. (2008) 'Countering urban segregation: theoretical and policy innovations from around the globe', *Urban Studies* 45/7: 1307–32.

Soja, E.W. (2010) *Seeking Spatial Justice*. Minneapolis: University of Minnesota Press.

Soja, E.W. and Kanai, M. (2007) 'The urbanization of the world', in R. Burdett and D. Sudjic (eds) *The Endless City*. London: Phaidon, 54–69.

Solinger, D.J. (2006) 'The creation of a new underclass in China and its implications', *Environment and Urbanization* 18/1: 177–93.

Sternberg, E. (2000) 'An integrative theory of urban design', *Journal of the American Planning Association* 66/3: 265–78.

Stoll, M.A. and Covington, K. (2012) 'Explaining racial/ethnic gaps in spatial mismatch in the US: the primacy of racial segregation', *Urban Studies* 49/11: 2501–21.

Storper, M. and Venables, A. (2004) 'Buzz: face-to-face contact and the urban economy', *Journal of Economic Geography* 4/4: 351–70.

Suttles, G.D. (1968) *The Social Order of the Slum*. Chicago: University of Chicago Press.

Sveikauskas, L. (1975) 'The productivity of cities', *Quarterly Journal of Economics* 89/3: 393–413.

Swyngedouw, E. (2006) 'Circulations and metabolisms: (hybrid) natures and (cyborg) cities', *Science as Culture* 15/2: 105–21.

Swyngedouw, E. (2009) 'The antinomies of the postpolitical city: in search of a democratic politics of environmental production', *International Journal of Urban and Regional Research* 33/3: 601–20.

Swyngedouw, E. and Kaika, M. (2000) 'The environment of the city or . . . the urbanization of nature', in G. Bridge and S. Watson (eds) *A Companion to the City*. Oxford: Blackwell, 567–80.

Talen, E. (2006) 'Design that enables diversity: the complications of a planning ideal', *Journal of Planning Literature* 20/3: 233–49.

Talen, E. and Ellis, C. (2002) 'Beyond relativism: reclaiming the search for good city form', *Journal of Planning Education and Research* 22/1: 36–49.

Tilly, C.F. (1999) *Durable Inequality*. Berkeley and Los Angeles: University of California Press.

Tonkiss, F. (2013) 'Austerity urbanism and the makeshift city', *City* 17/3: 312–24.

Torrance, M. (2008) 'Forging global governance? Urban infrastructures as networked financial products', *International Journal of Urban and Regional Research* 32/1: 1–21.

Trentmann, F. (2009) 'Disruption is normal: blackouts, breakdowns and the elasticity of everyday life', in E. Shove, F. Trentmann and R. Wilk (eds) *Time, Consumption and Everyday Life: Practice, Materiality and Culture*. Oxford: Berg, 67–84.

Tunstall, R. (2003) '"Mixed tenure" policy in the UK: privatization, pluralism or euphemism?' *Housing, Theory and Society* 20/3: 153–9.

Turner, J. (1976) *Housing by People: Towards Autonomy in Building Environments*. London: Marion Boyars.

Turok, I. (2001) 'Persistent polarization post-*apartheid*? Progress towards urban integration in Cape Town', *Urban Studies* 38/13: 2349–77.

Uitermark, J. (2003) 'Social mixing and the management of disadvantaged neighbourhoods: the Dutch policy of urban restructuring revisited', *Urban Studies* 40/3: 531–49.

UN-Habitat (2008) *State of the World's Cities 2008/9: Harmonious Cities*. London: Earthscan.

UN-Habitat (2009) *Global Urban Indicators – Selected Statistics*. UN Habitat Global Urban Observatory. http://www.unhabitat.org/downloads/docs/global_urban_indicators.pdf (accessed 6 June 2013).

UN-Habitat (2010) *State of the World's Cities 2010/11: Bridging the Urban Divide*. Nairobi: United Nations Human Settlements Programme (UN-Habitat).

UN-Habitat (2012a) *State of the World's Cities 2012/3: Prosperity of Cities*. Nairobi: United Nations Human Settlements Programme (UN-Habitat).

UN-Habitat (2012b) *Urban Patterns for a Green Economy: Leveraging Density*. Nairobi: United Nations Human Settlements Programme (UN-Habitat).

United Nations (2007) 'City planning will determine pace of global warming', General Assembly GA/EF/3190. http://www.un.org/News/Press/docs/2007/gaef3190.doc.htm (accessed 6 June 2013).

United Nations (2012) *World Urbanization Prospects: The 2011 Revision*. United Nations Population Division, Department of Economic and Social Affairs. New York: United Nations Secretariat.

United Nations Population Division (2008) 'An overview of urbanization, internal migration, population distribution and development in the world', UN/POP/EGM-URB/2008/01. New York: United Nations Secretariat. http://www.un.org/esa/population/meetings/EGM_PopDist/P01_UNPopDiv.pdf (accessed 6 June 2013).

Unruh, J. D. (2007) 'Debates: urbanization in the developing world and the acutely tenure insecure', *City* 11/1: 115–20.

Urban Task Force (1999) *Towards an Urban Renaissance*. London: HMSO.

Vale, L.J. (2013) *Purging the Poorest: Public Housing and the Design Politics of Twice-Cleared Communities*. Chicago: University of Chicago Press.

Varady, D.P. (ed.) (2005) *Desegregating the City: Ghettos, Enclaves and Inequality*. Albany, NY: SUNY Press.

Vertovec, S. (2007) 'Super-diversity and its implications', *Ethnic and Racial Studies* 30/6: 1024–54.

Visser, G. and Kotze, N. (2008) 'The state and new-build gentrification in central Cape Town, Africa', *Urban Studies* 45/12: 2565–93.

Wacquant, L. (2008) 'The militarization of urban marginality: lessons from the Brazilian metropolis', *International Political Sociology* 2/1: 56–74.

Walker, R.A. and Bulkeley, H. (2006) 'Editorial: geographies of environmental justice', *Geoforum* 37/5: 655–9.

Wang, W. (2003) 'Sustainability is a cultural problem', *Harvard Design Magazine* 18/Spring–Summer: 1–3.

Webster, C., Gasze, G. and Frantz, K. (2002) 'The global spread of gated communities', *Environment and Planning B* 29/3: 315–20.

Wheeler, C. (2004) 'Wage inequality and urban density', *Journal of Economic Geography* 4/4: 421–37.

Wheeler, C. (2006) 'Urban decentralization and income inequality: is sprawl associated with rising income segregation across neighborhoods?' *Federal Reserve Bank of St Louis Working Paper* 2006-037A. http://research.stlouisfed.org/wp/2006/2006-037.pdf (accessed 6 June 2013).

Whitehead, C. (2008) *The Density Debate: A Personal View*. London: East Thames Housing Group.

Williams, E., Burton, M. and Jenks, K. (eds) (2000) *Achieving Sustainable Urban Form*. London: E & FN Spon.

Williams, K. (2000) 'Does intensifying cities make them more sustainable?' in E. Williams, M. Burton and K. Jenks (eds) *Achieving Sustainable Urban Form*. London: E & FN Spon, 30–45.

Williams, K. (2009) 'Space per person in the UK: a review of densities, trends, experiences and optimum levels', *Land Use Policy* 26S: S82–3.

Wirth, L. (1938) 'Urbanism as a way of life', *American Journal of Sociology* 44/1: 1–24.

Wirth, L. (1940) 'The urban society and civilization', *American Journal of Sociology* 45/5: 743–55.

Wirth, L. (1945) 'Human ecology', *American Journal of Sociology* 50/6: 483–8.

Wolman, A. (1965) 'The metabolism of cities', *Scientific American* 213/3:179–90.

Wood, M. (2003) 'A balancing act? Tenure diversification in Australia and the UK', *Urban Policy and Research* 21/1: 45–56.

Woodcock, J., Banister, D., Edwards, P., Prentice, A.M. and Roberts, I. (2007) 'Energy and transport', *The Lancet* 370/9592: 1078–88.

World Bank (2009) *World Development Report 2009: Reshaping Economic Geography.* Washington, DC: IBRD/World Bank.

World Bank (2011) *Climate Change, Disaster Risk, and the Urban Poor: Cities Building Resilience for a Changing World.* Washington, DC: IBRD/World Bank.

World Commission on Environment and Development (1987) *Our Common Future.* Oxford: Oxford University Press.

Wright, A. (2008) 'What is the relationship between built form and energy use in buildings?' *Energy Policy* 36/12: 4544–7.

WWF (2000) *Social Platform through Social Innovations: A Coalition with Women in the Informal Sector.* Chennai: Working Women's Forum.

Yiftachel, O. (2009) 'Theoretical notes on "gray cities": the coming of urban apartheid?' *Planning Theory* 8/1: 88–100.

Young, I.M. (1999) 'Residential segregation and differentiated citizenship', *Citizenship Studies* 3/2: 237–52.

Zacharias, J. (2012) 'Resisting motorization in Guangzhou', *Habitat International* 36/1: 93–100.

Zhang, J., Zhao, Y., Park, A. and Song, X. (2005) 'Economic returns to schooling in urban China, 1988–2001', *Journal of Comparative Economics* 33/4: 730–52.

Zhao, P. (2010) 'Sustainable urban expansion and transportation in a growing megacity: consequences of urban sprawl for mobility on the urban fringe of Beijing', *Habitat International* 34/2: 236–43.

Zukin, S. (1991) *Landscapes of Power: From Detroit to Disneyworld.* Los Angeles: University of California Press.

Zukin, S. (2009) 'Changing landscapes of power: opulence and the desire for authenticity', *International Journal of Urban and Regional Research* 33/2: 543–53.

Index